ROUGH T..P THROUGH YELLOWSTONE

THE EPIC 1894 WINTER EXPEDITION OF EMERSON HOUGH, F. JAY HAYNES, AND BILLY HOFER

Including the Capture of Notorious
Buffalo Poacher Ed Howell

An Eyewitness Account by
Emerson Hough

With photographs by
F. Jay Haynes

Edited with an Introduction by
Scott Herring, University of California

RIVERBEND
PUBLISHING

Rough Trip Through Yellowstone: The Epic 1894 Winter Expedition of Emerson Hough, F. Jay Haynes, and Billy Hofer

Introduction and annotations © 2013 Scott Herring
Published by Riverbend Publishing, Helena, Montana

ISBN 13: 978-1-60639-066-5
Printed in the United States of America.

5 6 7 8 9 VP 26 25 24 23 22

Text design by Barbara Fifer
Cover design by Sarah Cauble, sarahegrant.com

CONTENTS

Acknowledgments	4
A Note on the Text	5
Introduction	7
The Account of Howell's Capture.	23
No. 2. Actual Interviews on Segregation.	41
No. 3. [More Interviews on Segregation.]	53
No. 4. The Story of the Trip.	67
No. 5. [The Story of the Trip. Part 2.]	77
No. 6. In the Heart of the Mountains.	95
No. 7. Midwinter in the Mountains.	113
No. 8. The Headquarters on Hayden Valley.	125
No. 9. Still More Buffalo.	141
No. 10. The Effects of Solitude.	159
No. 11. A Night March on the Skis.	171
No. 12. The Counting of the Elk.	185
No. 13. Game in the Segregation Strip.	199
No. 14. The End and Some Conclusions.	215
Notes	225

Acknowledgments

This book benefited greatly from the help of the National Park Service, especially the Yellowstone National Park Heritage and Research Center staff. The park's official historian, Lee Whittlesey, and curator Colleen Curry were especially helpful. I could also not have put this volume together without the assistance of the Montana Historical Society, specifically Lory Morrow and Becca Kohl. who were able to locate the precise photographs by F. Jay Haynes that appeared in the original *Forest and Stream* series.

A Note on the Text

The text of this book reproduces the 1894 series exactly. Throughout, when a word appears to be misspelled, I have merely kept the spelling from the original. In these cases, almost always, Hough's spelling simply follows variants common in the 19th century, and I have not bothered to add a [sic]. Spelling problems with proper nouns are explained in the numbered endnotes. In places, the problem is clearly an error by a compositor, a slip by an editor, or some technical glitch with the lead type or the printing press. Most often, a single piece of type has simply gone missing. In all such cases, the original intent is clear, and I have added the characters needed to repair the error inside brackets.

Two chapters were published in *Forest and Stream* without main titles; substitute titles in the current edition are enclosed in brackets.

INTRODUCTION

WHEN THE journalist Emerson Hough swung off a railroad coach at Cinnabar, Montana, in March, 1894, it was hardly an earth-shattering occasion. Cinnabar was the end of the line for a spur of the Northern Pacific. The town itself was so marginal that when, not quite a decade later, the railroad moved end-of-track a few miles east, Cinnabar disappeared so completely that not even a ghost town remained, just some lines on the ground that only a handful of locals could read.

Hough (rhymes with "rough") was a working journalist, not particularly well-known at the time. He met his prearranged contacts and rode in an army wagon, packed in with a load of commissary supplies—eggs, cabbages, and the like—up the hill to the remote little two-troop U.S. Cavalry outpost on the plateau above and to the south, at Mammoth Hot Springs.

Once at the top, however, Hough would enter into a personal adventure that also involved a cast of characters so extraordinary that for them all to have come together in one time and place is outright marvelous—and especially in *that* time and place, one of the most inhospitable, impenetrable spots in the West. He, and the people he met, would together be instrumental in changing the course of conservation history.

Hough, born in Iowa in 1857, would later become famous as an author of books about the Wild West. The place he was going to, in that army wagon, was already famous: Yellowstone National Park, then under the protection of the cavalry because the National Park Service did not yet exist. He came as the representative of some very influential people indeed. He wrote for *Forest and Stream*, a popular outdoor-sports journal edited by George Bird Grinnell, one of the most prominent conservationists in the country (he had, for instance, helped found the Boone and Crockett Club with, among others, Theodore Roosevelt). Yellowstone was the home to the last wild herd of American bison—what everyone then called buffalo—large enough that it might survive, but disturbing news about the well-being of the herd had its friends concerned.

Forest and Stream sent Hough to investigate, and to look into any other threats to the integrity of the park he could find. He found plenty, enough that it took him fourteen individual articles, run as weekly installments in the journal, to explain what he had seen. This book collects those fourteen parts together to form a continuous story.

And it is a story, because Hough was not just delivering the facts. He was telling the tale of his grand adventure. He arrived in the middle of March, when, in most of the country, the weather was making its lion-to-lamb transition. In Yellowstone National Park, perched atop the high Northern Rockies, it was still the dead of winter. That was a good time to count animals, since the snow concentrated them into a limited number of livable areas, known to long-time park residents. The problem was getting there. Today, thousands of people visit Yellowstone in the winter, carried by snowmobiles, tracked snowcoaches, or sophisticated modern cross-country skis. Across the northern part of the park, one lengthy stretch of road, kept open by plows, can even be driven in a car.

In the 1890s, during the long, long winter, no one visited at all—no one, that is, except criminals. Hough had only two, and really only one, option. What we today call snowshoes, Hough mentioned only briefly as "web shoes," considered for his trip and instantly dismissed as too slow. What Hough called "snowshoes" were, throughout, what we call cross-country skis, although we would hardly recognize them as such. Propelled by a single pole, the heavy wooden ski of the era resembled a surfboard more than a ski. Throughout the series, *Forest and Stream* italicized the word *ski*, as befitted a foreign word. Borrowed from Norwegian, the word was then so alien that Hough even had to explain how to pronounce it.

He would have been lost but for that extraordinary cast of characters he met in the park. The most important of these by far was Elwood Hofer, known universally as Billy and, as he became the grand old man of the park, Uncle Billy. He arrived when the park itself was five years old, in 1877, and stayed for a half-century. He worked primarily as a guide, but although Hough made him look like a typical Western man of action, he was quite literate, and worked for newspapers on occasion, including *Forest and Stream*. He guided presidents and countless VIPs, and by the time Hough arrived, Hofer had come to know the park about as well as anyone who had ever lived. He served Hough as a ski instructor, wildlife expert, geographer, local historian, and general guardian angel. He saved Hough's life more than once during their trip.

While he was undergoing his quick-and-dirty introduction to the ski, Hough was the guest of George Anderson, the U.S. Army captain who was the park superintendent. Probably the most effective of the army superintendents, before the National Park Service took over in 1916, Anderson was always deeply conscious of the responsibility he bore for this extraordinary piece of land he had been given to guard and zealous to protect it from insult. He would probably have cultivated the *Forest and Stream* man and representative of George Bird Grinnell in any case, but Anderson and Hough clearly hit it off. Both were outdoorsmen, both deeply worried about the fate of the remaining big game in North America, so Anderson surely stopped preaching to the choir early in his conversations with the *Forest and Stream* man.

Then one evening, the telephone rang, and history pivoted. When he returned from taking the call, according to Hough,

Anderson was literally quivering with excitement. The man who would become the most famous poacher in Yellowstone history, Ed Howell, had just been taken into custody. An army patrol had found Howell's path where he had skied into the park, and discovered their prey when they heard Howell's rifle. He had just felled five bison, and was in the process of skinning one when the army scout stuck a pistol into what must have been an extraordinarily surprised face. Bison had become so rare that mounted heads, sold by taxidermists, went for obscene sums. Just wholesaling the raw product, Howell himself estimated that he would have made $2,000, had he not been caught. He had the salable remains of the bison he had killed earlier in the winter stashed in gunnysacks and hung in trees to keep off the wolves, dangling there like obscene parodies of Christmas ornaments.

But now came the crushing disappointment, for both Anderson and Hough. Howell would spend time in the guardhouse, and he would lose all the possessions he had brought with him on his expedition. Howell himself valued his wretched possessions at $26.75. His stay in the guardhouse would be brief, however, because no law spelled out a more adequate retribution for poaching in the national park. Perhaps most laughably, part of the punishment involved escorting Howell out of the park. To make that punishment effective, the soldiers would have had to escort him out of the park and then deliver him to Tierra del Fuego.

But, while travel in Yellowstone was primitive, the park had entered the era of modern communication. The scout had, after all, reported the arrest by the park telephone network. Hough himself immediately sent the story to *Forest and Stream* in New York City by wire. A number of other newspapers picked up the report. George Bird Grinnell understood quickly that Hough had delivered the ammunition he needed. He traveled to Washington, where he enlisted influential friends to put pressure on Congress. Representative John Lacey introduced a bill that soon found itself on the fast track. By early May, it was law. The Lacey Act, as it has been known ever since, provided serious penalties for poaching in Yellowstone. Even in its less-harsh clauses, it called for devastating fines, the kind no mountain vagabond could pay. It had options for such cases. If Howell repeated his performance and got caught, he would spend a long time in a penitentiary.

The bison herd had been optimistically estimated at 500, a number that would probably have been sufficient to ensure the survival of the herd—assuming that the number was accurate. Hough was only partly aware of the true scale of events in the nation's capital that he and Anderson, and that remarkable scout up in the frozen park, had set in motion. He assumed that the bison counts had been overly optimistic, and that heavy poaching would continue. He continued with his primary mission: to actually count the herd, and the numbers of elk, as well, and more. His mission morphed and expanded as he went along.

Billy Hofer gave him a—literal—crash course in skiing, and the two set off to fulfill Hough's mission, off into what Hough called the "big snow country." It is crucial, at this point, to understand the local topography. When Hough arrived at the train station, he had been at the bottom of the Yellowstone River valley, close to the point where the river left the park. At about 5300 feet, this location sat deep within a rain shadow created by the high mountains to the south, inside the national park. Even counting snow, this location got only about ten inches of precipitation a year. Rattlesnakes and cactus were common.

During his visit with Anderson, Hough had stayed at what he always called "the Post," the park headquarters at Fort Yellowstone. At 6200 feet, the area provided enough snow for Billy to run Hough through his paces on the new Norwegian skis, with which Hough had no experience. Even here, however, the weather was temperate, by Yellowstone standards. Once they started on their journey, Hofer and Hough passed through the Golden Gate and onto Swan Lake Flats, 7000 feet and more above sea level. The two would not pass back down, through 7000 feet, until they returned to the Post.

As they penetrated the great plateaus that make up the core of the park, they would climb higher and higher. It was, furthermore, a wet and cold March. When Hough spoke of the severe conditions, the deep snow and the danger of storm, or of a fall into open water, he was not bluffing.

Yet even though this was his first visit to Yellowstone National Park, Hough kept up his end. His rewards were great. True, they were not always happy. The bison survey revealed far fewer animals than expected; at the time, the herd looked doomed. The survey was perhaps the best made of a wild herd before the era of aircraft, because Hough's time on the plateau was characterized by more of that outright marvelous quality I referred to earlier. Deep inside the big snow country, Hough and Uncle Billy met, and joined forces with, Frank Jay Haynes.

F. Jay Haynes, as he was invariably known—except when people called him "the Professor"—had been associated with the park about as long, and almost as intimately, as Billy had. Haynes began photographing Yellowstone in 1881, building both a massive portfolio and a small business empire inside the park that his son would take over when the Professor died in 1921. He would have been drawn to the place eventually by his job as official photographer of the Northern Pacific Railway. In an era when the railroad delivered nearly every visitor to the park, the Northern Pacific, Yellowstone, and Haynes would have been intimately involved no matter what, but Haynes was personally drawn to the place. He would later be called "Official Photographer of Yellowstone National Park." No such position existed, but no one denied him the honor either.

He even had that rarest of assets, experience of the winter park. He had been the "official photographer" of the 1887 attempt by Frederick Schwatka to explore the high plateaus of the inner park in January. Schwatka had proven himself a tough and resourceful explorer of the Arctic, but his "exploration" of

Yellowstone was ill-conceived, overburdened, and very much over-hyped. In his *Forest and Stream* articles, Hough had a great deal of fun at Schwatka's expense, his "exploration" having blown to bits almost immediately. While the rest retreated, Haynes and two others, joined by an army scout, continued. Despite nearly being killed by a three-day blizzard, Haynes completed the trip, and also produced the very first photographs of the wintertime park. Now, in 1894, he was going back for more.

He, too, had been in the right place at the right time for the Howell arrest. He was even able to photograph Howell on the way to the guardhouse. Hough knew Haynes was up there, and managed to intercept both the photographer and the soldiers who had accompanied him near the Grand Canyon of the Yellowstone (Hough, like most 19th century authors, used the older spelling that revealed the word's Spanish root: Cañon). The groups joined forces and were together able to execute the best bison survey possible at that time. Haynes photographed both the animals and the humans. The Haynes images that illustrated the *Forest and Stream* 1894 series will appear later in this book.

Given how that survey went, this would be the point that always arrives in a book of this sort in which your editor is supposed to scold the subjects of the book for engaging in activities that "are no longer approved." They engaged in two that are no longer approved for maximally good reasons. Both activities, however, emphasize the special nature of their mission. Just before they met Haynes, Hough and Hofer wandered among the thermal features of the Norris Geyser Basin, and would, before they were done, visit most of the major thermal areas in the park. They used the hottest ground as routes around the snow drifts, ironically enough. Hough was no fool, and Hofer even less so, but they were blithely unaware of the danger. Hot ground was just the sort of place where the crust was thin, because a new thermal feature was, perhaps, getting ready to burst into view. A fall through the crust or into a hot spring can be fatal, although perhaps not so instantly fatal as a victim might prefer.

Second, when they joined forces with Haynes and executed their survey of the bison, the men chased the animals around in a manner that, to the modern skier, is cringe-inducing. It was close to the end of winter, but not quite there yet, and so the animals were as stressed as they would get. They needed every calorie they had managed to accumulate—and here their supposed friends were, chasing them around and even, as Hough states repeatedly, observing their terror. This particular activity is no longer approved because it pushes the weaker animals over the brink, really the last thing Hough wanted to do.

I cringe, but I can forgive them, because it was a different time with different regulations, and because of the special nature of their mission. Visitors to the thermal areas are today told to stay on the boardwalks to keep from falling in. Hough and Billy had no boardwalks to stay on. Furthermore, the intrusion of the Haynes and the *Forest and Stream* parties was unique, and their half-comic, half-brutal pursuit of the bison would not recur for a long, long time. It was partly the limitations of their technology that had them ambushing the "game," as Hough always called the larger animals. If a photographer wanted a shot of a bison with a mid-1890s camera, he had to get close. Furthermore, the uniqueness of the trip required a visual record. It can be argued that these were the 1890s equivalent of Apollo astronauts. Their public wanted to see what their privileged eyes had seen, and the audience of *Forest and Stream* could not get enough photographs of animals, even if the photos did perhaps lead to fantasies about shooting those animals someday. Among other things, *Forest and Stream* was, after all, a hunting magazine.

That day has long since arrived, because Hough was successful in his most important goals. He wanted the public to see the animals that he was beseeching them to protect. The protection arrived, and was to a significant extent his doing, even though he was filled with foreboding as he and his comrades scared up far fewer bison than they expected. Pressed for fuel to make a fire, at one point in their exploration, Hough used the old standby of American Indians and pioneers: "on digging away the snow for a place to make a fire, I found quantities of buffalo chips. Of these I made my fire, and I imagine this was the last camp-fire in America ever built of the old-time *bois des vaches.*" He was wrong. I built one myself when I was new to the region, in 1990. The smell takes some getting used to— like burning hair, or rags—but they do burn, guttering rather like coal. Many who live in Yellowstone have occasion to try this experiment eventually, because the stuff is lying around all over the place.

Yellowstone thus became a nursery for big game. Teddy Roosevelt later wrote that "What has been actually accomplished in the Yellowstone Park affords the best possible object-lesson as to the desirability and practicability of establishing such wilderness reserves. This reserve is a natural breeding-ground and nursery for those stately and beautiful haunters of the wilds which have now vanished from so many of the great forests, the vast lonely plains, and the high mountain ranges, where they once abounded." Roosevelt used this aspect of the place as an argument against the claim that wildlife and wild-land sanctuaries were "elitist," intended as pleasure-spots only for the wealthy tourist. On the contrary, Roosevelt said. A place like Yellowstone ensured that the national forests around it would be filled with game that could be hunted by anyone, unlike the Old World aristocratic game parks, available exclusively to the aristocrats. He was right. Today, we have so many bison and elk we do not know what to do with them. Among other things, we hunt them.

Americans have famously short historical memories. Stop a few hundred on the street and ask them when "environmentalism" began, and apart from the majority of shrugs, people will vaguely remember hippies and the 1960s. A few more interested respondents might recall back through Rachel Carson, or Aldo Leopold, or Gifford Pinchot and John Muir duking it out over the Hetch Hetchy dam. But environmentalism in the United States, as a movement to halt the destruction of natural habitat and its fauna, is older still. It began with the hunters and anglers who beheld the destruction of North America's wildlife and decided to call a halt. During the later 19th century, "sportsman" did not mean "frivolous killer." It was the opposite of "market hunter." It designated a hunter who was not in it for money, and so could be expected to follow ethical rules. An analogy could be made with the modern Olympic Games, which would begin two years after Hough emerged from the Yellowstone wilderness. In the new Games, the rule that athletes had to be pure amateurs had the effect of keeping Irish bar fighters out, and seems to have been designed to do just that. It's not "inclusive," but you get a more family-friendly Olympiad that way. Similarly, amateur sportsmen could be expected to leave a few animals alive when the day's shooting was done. Ed Howell could not.

So we have to forgive Hough and the rest as they chased those exhausted bison around. He was helping in a long campaign that was beginning to achieve decisive success.

Not just with the bison—and *again*, with the marvelous quality of the trip. After finishing their count of the bison and touring the largest geyser basins, Hough and Hofer stopped briefly at the Post before carrying out one last mission, to count the elk in the country that is today traversed by the Mammoth-to-Tower road, then the Northeast Entrance Road, leading out of Yellowstone National Park toward Billings, Montana. They stopped at Yancey's, where they were the guests of Uncle John Yancey, grizzliest of the old men of the mountains: "My impression," Hough admitted, "is that he was there before the Cañon was finished." One of the park's few individual concessionaires, Yancey had long run an inn in remote Pleasant Valley. The modern visitor, upon reaching Tower Junction, is at one end of the valley. Yancey's was at the other, and his foundations are still faintly visible where the park hotel-and-restaurant concession company has its summertime cookouts, specifically on the exact spot where the wranglers park their horses.

Even more important than Yancey was the about-as-grizzled guide who was at the inn when Hough and Hofer arrived. "I have mentioned John Folsom, winter keeper of the Cañon Hotel, as the most silent man I ever knew," Hough comments. "The second silent man is Taswill Woody." Although he never brought it up, Hough was obviously carrying a sizable notebook along with everything else in his pack. He did not have a smart phone, however, and so had no way of checking on unusual or obscure proper nouns associated with Greater Yellowstone. His companions could not always help; a mountain man was not necessarily a good speller. Hough had to spell by sound, often enough with the wind howling and the snow swirling around him. He got the names of these two silent men wrong: Folsom was actually "Fossum," and Woody's first name was "Tazewell." It was an unusual name for an unusual man.

So unusual, in fact, that he almost offhandedly accomplished what Hough's entire tour of the park, complete with its astonishing train of adventures, had so far failed to do: move him to the outermost extremes of emotion. In his quiet way, Woody promised to take them to a place where a thousand elk were visible at a time. He led them to a spot we can easily identify, a point on high ground on the south side of the Yellowstone River from which they could survey a broad swath of the north side, "between the Cottonwood and the Roaring Fork and beyond them." The "Roaring Fork" is today Hellroaring Creek, easily visible from the modern highway, although a long hike away. It lay unvisited in winter, 1894.

It lay unvisited by humans at least, and capable of lifting Hough to the highest peak of emotion. The river valley,

> here laid open before us as though by special plan, was alive with elk. In all my life I had never seen so much game at one sight. For the first time in the Park I felt an absolute thrill of amazement and delight at seeing the

great animals in such numbers, in such content, in such apparent security and freedom from suspicion. After a long look at these and other crowds of elk, he ended with a partly speculative census of 25,000. That number could look optimistic or even outlandish, both to us and to plenty of Hough's contemporaries. It was neither. Given the brevity of his visit, the limitations of scientific knowledge in 1894, and the depth of the snow, Hough could only partly understand the extent to which, during his ski journey, he had covered two radically different landscapes. To the south, when he was among the geysers, and the bison near the canyon, he had been inside what has come lately to be called the Yellowstone Supervolcano, in truth a multitude of calderas that overlap each other and are all of relatively recent birth. At the Post, and at Yancey's, he was on what we today call the northern range. It was a much older landscape, more promising in places for winter feeding by grazing animals in large numbers, and in many places not so impossibly elevated as the terrain to the south.

Hough's count of 25,000 was also in line with various counts and estimates of elk numbers on the northern range until quite recently. In fact, park authorities would, not too far in the future, decide there were too many elk, and would begin a long, controversial effort to cull the herd. In more recent years, for good or ill, a long drought combined with the reintroduction of wolves to Yellowstone in 1995 has dropped the northern range elk population well below ten thousand. Few observers today are concerned, except local hunters and professional guides. Elk today live in vast numbers elsewhere, their populations restored from their late-19th–century low in part by the Yellowstone herd.

At that time, and ironically, the low number of bison and the high number of elk served Hough equally well, as data for his side in the fight to conserve the park. The bison poaching set off the Lacey Act, already moving through Congress while Hough was counting the animals. He trumpeted the high number of elk because it served yet another of his causes: that of finally slipping a dagger into the dying hulk of the segregation scheme. As Hough will explain, the segregation scheme was a long-running plan, floated over and over by Montana businessmen and their friends in Washington, to give the mining town of Cooke City a railroad by carving a right-of-way from the national park. Cooke City was not a city, and never would be. It was a small mountain village, although there was gold in the hills above town. Even with the gold, Cooke City never rated the expensive construction that the more ambitious versions of segregation envisioned, nor the loss of park land. The railroad was always a long shot.

Yet this was and remains the sort of challenge park managers and their friends have faced since the national parks have existed. Someone always has a design on the park—every park, eventually. Lever this little tiny piece off—just this little piece, with no animals or scenic wonders on it—and great rivers of money will flow.

In this matter, and in others, Hough's journey had qualities that made it eternal. At first glance, his experience of a wintertime Yellowstone that was so nearly deserted appears as a stark contrast with today, when Old Faithful is a noisy and crowded place on some winter days. There exist, however, plenty of other places where even a modestly adventurous skier will cross vast distances and never see a soul.

As I noted, I have a long-running relationship with Greater Yellowstone, but, having been raised in a desert, I was frankly frightened of its winters. It was only in recent years that I decided to confront them, and it was just as I was finally mastering the art of cross-country skiing that I accidentally came upon Hough's series in *Forest and Stream*. Its original title was "Forest and Stream's Yellowstone Park Game Exploration, 1894." My university library owned a complete, long-undisturbed set.

How could I fail to be charmed, when his baffled and precarious introduction to the ski was identical to my own? Part of the charm lay in the surprise. My skis are an uncomplicated pair of Rossignols, barely six feet long, requiring no wax and, made out of some kind of mutant plastic, weighing next to nothing. The bindings—what skiers call New Nordic Norm bindings—combine a rotating toe pin with a clip that together make a pair that is both simple and, to judge from the effects of my own inept abuse, indestructible.

Compare the skis of Hough's era, which could be twelve feet long, and always of wood (what alternative material was there? Granite?). They required constant, careful, expert attention with wax, heated over a fire that had to somehow be kindled in deep snow. The "bindings" were a pair of fore-and-aft leather straps so crude that even so expert a skier as Billy Hofer suffered injured feet, during the long journey.

Yet my experience has been so similar to his as to be identical. He and I both have noted that bizarre capacity of the ski to do as it pleases. The skier can stand perfectly, obediently still, and the ski shoots off in a direction of its own choosing. The fall that ensues exactly matches what happens to Charlie Brown when Lucy pulls the football away. Furthermore, the following experience has not changed in the slightest:

> It would seem easy to get up after falling in the snow,
> but let one try this in deep, soft snow, and he will find
> that his hand and arm sink deep down, but afford him no
> support when he tries to raise himself. He can get no bear-
> ing until he gets above his *skis*, which do not sink in the
> snow. He must therefore get his *skis* under him, somehow.
> That somehow is best understood after a wrestle or two in
> trying to get one's feet untangled and located once more
> intelligibly. Getting up from a fall in soft snow or a steep
> side hill is a very delicate operation.

It can also be a lengthy operation. A friend—who, it is true, crashed into a deep drift in a record snowfall year—once spent nearly an hour at it.

Hough described another and even more familiar disaster that occurred when he reached higher elevations, late on the first day of the trip:

I was taken desperately faint and sick, so that at length I fairly toppled over off my *skis*. I don't know what it was, unless the unusual exertion, combined with the unusual altitude, caused the stomach to resent the unusual dose of bitter tea I had given it. Anyhow, I got desperately weak, and pretty soon I didn't care a copper whether I went anywhere or not.

The feeling persisted until he reached shelter, ate, and got some sleep, after which it vanished for good. He was wrong about the tea, and right about the altitude: he experienced a textbook case of altitude sickness. Today, the medical term for the disorder is hypobaropathy. This is not the high-altitude pulmonary or cerebral edema of the Himalayan climber. Those conditions may cause you to die. Altitude sickness only makes you feel like you want to.

Nor has the place changed that much since Hough's day. On the calendar, the last week of Hough's adventure happens to coincide with my university's spring break, which also, happily, begins at about the time the National Park Service normally locks the gates and ends the snowmobile season. During a recent trip, I parked the car and skied on a route close to that used by Hofer and Hough to reach Yancey's. I covered fifteen miles. I did not see another human. I did see bison, over a hundred, with evidence of hundreds more in the tossed and smashed snow, which was covered also by countless frozen chips.

Here were the marks of passage not just of the bison, but of Billy Hofer and Emerson Hough. Obviously, the Lacey Act was not the work of a single person, or a pair, no matter how adventurous and competent that pair. However, what the animals of Yellowstone National Park needed more than anything, in 1894, was an eloquent and well-connected advocate. Hough was certainly eloquent, and the only connection he needed was that with his publisher, George Bird Grinnell. Hough's on-the-spot description of what was really happening in Yellowstone was one of the essentials required to help push the Lacey Act all the way through to the President's desk. More would be required to keep the bison herd from dwindling. The park's managers would eventually decide that the herd required not only protection, but also active breeding to keep it from declining to extinction. The law was a crucial step in attacking the menace represented by outlaws like Ed Howell. With multiple revisions, it remains a tool that is perhaps most useful as a weapon to deter today's versions of Howell. It stands also as a historical benchmark. The most important force preventing misuse of a place like Yellowstone is a broad national consensus that such misuse—including poaching, theft, and vandalism—is just plain wrong, in purely moral terms. That attitude was not especially common among rural folk in the 1890s, but gradually, haltingly, they came to agree with Hough, Grinnell, and other conservationists that the indiscriminate slaughter of wildlife had to end. Poaching—along with its more-common close relations, vandalism and theft—of course all remain a problem in the national parks. The Lacey Act is not all-powerful; neither does it change minds on its own, except to the extent that its penalties scare the potential offender off. That effect is not trivial, however, and the law also marks a moment when influential people began to listen more closely to conservation advocates like Hough, Hofer, Grinnell, and Theodore Roosevelt, leading the way for the rest of us.

The effects can be seen in Yellowstone today, where my ski trip was halted over and over by bison crossing my path. They seemed to be everywhere.

THE ACCOUNT OF HOWELL'S CAPTURE.

THE FIRST NEWS.

CHICAGO, Ills., April 27.—The FOREST AND STREAM Winter Exploration of the National Park, now just concluded, was a venture singularly fortunate in every respect. Not devoid of certain hardships, and not free from possible dangers of more sorts than one, it was nevertheless brought to a close without illness or accident to any of the party other than of the most trifling sort, and from start till close progressed with the smoothness and merriness, if not the ease and indolence, of a summer picnic. Fortune was kind and raised no obstacle too hard to be overcome. Thus the FOREST AND STREAM may truthfully say that it is the first and only paper ever to send a staff man through the Park during the winter time. Schwatka[1] once made 20 miles of this 200 miles winter journey in the interests of the New York World. Overcome by his failing, and perhaps discouraged or disgusted by the amount of unavoidable hard work ahead (for the only possible method of locomotion in those high, rough and snowy regions, is by one's own snowshoes), he allowed his undertaking to come to failure, and returned to his starting point with no results to show. Since him one or two other men have gone to the gates of the Park, looked at the big snow land, and resolved that it was easier to write about the winter scenery of the Park from imagination than from fact. The only man ever successful enough to go through the Park in winter, and intelligent enough to make a newspaper account of it, was Mr. Elwood Hofer,[2] whose stories of his two trips, simply and clearly written, appeared in FOREST AND STREAM. Mr. F. Jay Haynes,[3] the able St. Paul photographer who has done so much to make public the beauties of this wonderful region, went through the Park after the collapse of the Schwatka expedition, but never wrote of it, so far as I know. His party was lost on Mount Washburn for three days, and they all came near perishing.

The effort to learn of the winter life of this tremendous and fateful region had hitherto been, let us then say, severely frowned upon by Fortune. When FOREST AND STREAM, always rather a favorite of the fickle dame, made the attempt, Fortune relented, and all became possible and plain. To this end, FOREST AND STREAM was in the first place highly fortunate in having Mr. Hofer as a member of the party. His guidance, counsel and assistance constituted the difference between success and failure. Without him the trip could not have been what it was, and it is to him, very much more than to its staff representative, that this journal is indebted for the success of the undertaking just completed. What were the obstacles to be overcome before success could be reached, and what were the trials, the pleasures and the incidents of the winter journey through the mountains of the Great Divide, it will be a pleasure to recount later, but the first duty is to tell at first hand, and exclusively, the story of the capture of the man Howell,[4] who was caught in the act of butchering the Park buffalo. This story, taken from FOREST AND STREAM's first and exclusive report,[5] has appeared in various forms and in some inaccurate shapes, in the press all over the country, and such is the importance of the occurrence that it has driven Congress to an action delayed years too long.[6] This is undoubtedly the most dramatic and sensational, as well as the most notable and important piece of sporting news which has come up in recent years. It is news which will be historic. The Howell buffalo slaughter marks an epoch, the turning point, let us hope, in the long course of a cruelly wasteful indifference on the part of the United States Government in the matter of one of the most valuable possessions of the American people—a possession growing yearly less and less through this indifference, and which as it has grown less has increased in value, since when once destroyed, it can never by any human power be replaced. Had not FOREST AND STREAM been born under a lucky as well as an energetic star, it could not have enjoyed the journalistic good fortune of having a man right on the spot—and a most remote and improbable spot, too—to obtain exclusively for its service this most important piece of news. Now that we are out of the mountains, the first opportunity offers to give the story in accurate detail.

THE TELEPHONE CARRIES IT.

Capt. Anderson,[7] the best superintendent the Park ever had, and one good enough to be retained there for an indefinite term, is a thoroughly fearless and energetic man, and disposed to do all that lies in his power, with the limited means at his disposal, to protect the vast tract of land which lies within the bounds of this peerless reserve of wilderness. How difficult a task this would be with many times the troops and many times the money no one can understand perfectly who does not know the Park, and who does not know what winter in the mountains means. A part of the system of the winter patrol consists of little details, usually a sergeant and two privates, stationed at remote parts of the Park. Thus there is a sub-station of this sort on the east part of the Park, on Soda Butte Creek; one on the west side, known as Riverside Station; one twenty miles from the Post, at Norris Basin; one forty miles from the Post, and near the center of the Park, at the Lower Geyser or Firehole Basin; and one at the extreme south end of the Park, known as Shoshone Station. Communication with these stations can only be made by snowshoe parties. The winter's supplies are carried into the stations by pack trains early in the fall, before the impassable snows have covered all the trails. Under such conditions news would naturally travel slowly. Yet we knew of Howell's capture, some seventy miles from the Post, the very day he was caught in the act of his crime, the news coming by telephone from the Lake Hotel. The Park Association[8] keeps attendants at three hotels within the upper Park, not counting the one at the Mammoth Hot Springs (Fort Yellowstone), on the entrance side of the Park. There is one attendant, or winter keeper, at the Cañon Hotel, one at the Lower Basin Hotel, and a man and his wife at the Lake Hotel. All these hotels are connected by telephone with the Post, elsewise the loneliness and danger of the life of the solitary men thus cut off from the world through the long months of an almost Arctic winter would deter even such hardy spirits from undertaking a service worse than that on a lighthouse tower at sea. When the telephone line fails to work, as naturally in such a wintry country of mountain and forest it often does, old Snowshoe Pete,[9] the lineman, is sent over the line to locate and repair the damage. He is the only man allowed to go alone through the Park in winter, and he has had some rough and dangerous experiences. When the soldiers of the out-stations wish to report to the Post they go to the nearest hotel, perhaps fifteen, perhaps forty miles, and telephone in, if the telephone happens to be running. Burgess, the only scout whom the munificent U.S. Government provides for the protection of this peerless domain—a domain which any other power on earth would guard jealously as a treasure vault—makes scouts from time to time in all directions through the Park, traveling of course on snowshoes. He may sleep and get supplies at some one of the out-stations, or of one of the three winter keepers of the hotels, or it may be that he will hole up for the night in one of the several shacks built at certain secluded portions of the mountains for this purpose; still again, he may have to lie out in the snow, perhaps without a blanket, perhaps with nothing to eat. This all depends on circumstances. A poacher's trail has to be followed hard and sharp, with no let-up and no returning. It was fortunate for Burgess that he caught his man within a day's march of the Lake Hotel. He brought him in to the Lake Hotel that day and at once telephoned to Capt. Anderson, commanding officer at the Post, Mammoth Hot Springs. The message was received at the Post about 9:30 in the evening, Monday, March 12. This was just before Hofer and I started into the Park from the Post, and as I was the guest of Capt. Anderson at the Post, of course I learned the news at once, and at once put it on the wire for FOREST AND STREAM, which had the information within twelve hours of the capture, which latter had occurred 2,000 miles away in the roughest part of the Rocky Mountains, and four days' journey from the nearest telegraph station, by the only possible means of travel. The next day FOREST AND STREAM was represented in Washington. Within thirty days the Lacey bill had passed the House. To FOREST AND STREAM, born under a lucky, as well as an energetic, star, will be due more than to any other one agency the thanks of the public for the ultimate preservation of one of the public's most valuable heritages. No other paper has made the fight for the Park that this one has, and it deserves the utmost success which now seems certain to attend it. When the people finally come to look upon an un-divided National Park, and one tenanted once more with some specimens at least of its grand though vanishing animals, they may thank all the men who nobly and fearlessly worked for that and so carried out the actual will of the people—they may thank all these friends of intelligence and justice and public honor and decency; but they will have only one newspaper on earth to thank, and that one will be FOREST AND STREAM.

CAPT. ANDERSON'S STORY.

When Capt. Anderson came in after hearing the news of this capture, he was positively jubilant through every inch of his 6ft. 2in. of muscular and military humanity. He couldn't sit still, he was so glad.

It was some time before I could get from him the story of the plans leading up to the capture.

"I knew that Howell had been in the Park," said he, "and had an idea that he was over on Pelican Valley somewhere. I sent Burgess[10] in after sign once before this winter, but Burgess broke his axe and had to come back. I told Burgess this time that I wanted him to come back this time with a whole axe and a whole prisoner, if possible. I knew that Howell had come out of the Park for supplies, not long ago. He came out from Cooke City, where he hails from. He brought out his toboggan, and took back a load of supplies with him. I knew he must leave a broad trail, and knew that if Burgess could strike his trail and follow it into the Park, not out of it, he could catch him sure. Burgess has been scouting on Pelican, as directed. He says, by telephone, that he found the trail early in the morning, and followed it till he found a cache of six buffalo heads, hung up in the trees. Then he followed the trail a good distance till he found Howell's tepee. While he was there he heard shots. Approaching carefully, he saw Howell skinning out the head of one of five buffalo he had just killed. Making a careful run over the 400yds. of open ground between Howell and the timber he got the drop on Howell . Burgess had with him no one whatever but one private, Troike,[11] who was not armed and who stayed back in the timber. Capt. Scott, Lieut. Forsyth and party were at the Lake Hotel not engaged in this scout at all. I must say that Burgess's action has been in every way highly courageous and commendable, and I shall be glad to commend him publicly. He made his arrest alone and brought his man into the Lake Hotel to report for orders. I have ordered him to bring his prisoner on in to the Post as quickly as he can. To-morrow I start out a party on snowshoes from here to bring in all the heads and hides of the buffalo killed. I have ordered Howell's tepee and supplies burned. His arms and outfit will be confiscated, and I will sock him just as far and as deep into the guard-house as I know how when I get him, and he won't get fat there, either. That is all I can do under the regulations. I shall report to the Secretary of the Interior and in due course the Secretary of the Interior will order me to set the prisoner free. There is no law governing this Park except the military regulations. There is no punishment that can be inflicted on this low-down fellow. I only wish I had the making of the law and the devising of the penalty. I'll bet you this man wouldn't soon go at large if I did have."

SCOUT BURGESS'S STORY.

This was Capt. Anderson's story of the plan that led to the capture, a plan evidently wise and well laid. But how wide a difference there remained between this plan and the actual arrest I never knew until I had seen the Park itself in all its immensity, its impenetrableness, its forbidding and awful regions of forest, precipice and crag, until I had traversed with weary feet some of those endless miles of bottomless snow; until I learned how utterly small, lonely and insignificant a man looks and feels in the midst of solitude so vast, so boundless, so tremendous and so appalling. Then I knew that the man Howell was in his brutal and misguided way a hero in self-reliance, and that Scout Burgess was also in courage and self-reliance a hero, nothing less. Howell, or any like him, I hate instinctively, but I salute him. To Burgess the salute will come more easily from any man who knows the facts and knows what a winter trail in the Rockies means.

Burgess's story of the capture, as told by himself, simply and modestly, would make it out no great thing. This story I heard from Burgess himself at Norris Station, which point he had reached, coming out with his prisoner at the same time the FOREST AND STREAM party made it, going in. We spent the night there together.

"I expect probably I was pretty lucky," said he. "Everything seemed to work in my favor. I got out early and hit the trail not long after daybreak. After I had found the cache of heads and the tepee, over on Astringent Creek, in the Pelican Valley, I heard the shooting, six shots. The six shots killed five buffalo. Howell made his killing out in a little valley, and when I saw him he was about 400yds. away from the cover of the timber. I knew I had to cross that open space before I could get him sure. I had no rifle, but only an army revolver, .38cal., the new model. You know a revolver isn't lawfully able to hold the drop on a man as far as a rifle. I wouldn't have needed to get so close with a rifle before ordering him to throw up his hands. Howell's rifle was leaning against a dead buffalo, about 15ft. away from him. His hat was sort of flapped down over his eyes, and his head was toward me. He was leaning over, skinning on the head of one of the buffalo. His dog, though I didn't know it at first, was curled up under the hindleg of the dead buffalo. The wind was so the dog didn't smell me, or that would have settled it. That was lucky, wasn't it? Howell was going to kill the dog, after I took him, because the dog didn't bark at me and warn him. I wouldn't let him kill it. That's the dog outside—a bob-tailed, curly, sort of half-shepherd. It can get along on a snowshoe trail the best of any dog I ever saw, and it had followed Howell all through the journey, and was his only companion.

"I thought I could maybe get across without Howell seeing or hearing me, for the wind was blowing very hard. So I started over from cover, going as fast as I could travel. Right square across the way I found a ditch about 10ft. wide, and you know how hard it is to make a jump with snowshoes on level ground. I had to try it, anyhow, and some way I got over. I ran up to within 15ft. of Howell, between him and his gun, before I called to him to throw up his hands, and that was the first he knew of any one but him being anywhere in that country. He kind of stopped and stood stupid like, and I told him to drop his knife. He did that and then I called Troike, and we got ready to come on over to the hotel. It was so late by the time I found Howell—you see he was a long way from his cache or his camp—that we didn't stop to open up any of the dead buffalo. We tried to bring in some heads, but we found we couldn't, so we left them.

"Howell had been in camp over there for a long time. I only found 6 heads cached. He wrapped them up in gunny sacks and then hoisted them up in trees so the wolves couldn't get at them. He had a block and tackle, so that he could run a heavy head up into a tree without much trouble. He was fixed for business. "Howell said to me that if he had seen me first, I 'would never have taken him.' I asked him why, and he said, 'Oh, I'd have got on my shoes and run away, of course.' I don't know what he meant by that, but he'd have been in bad shape if he had, unless he had taken his rifle along, for I had already found his camp."

HOWELL'S STORY.

Howell was, we found, a most picturesquely ragged, dirty and unkempt looking citizen. His beard had been scissored off. His hair hung low on his neck, curling up like a drake's tail. His eye was blue, his complexion florid. In height he seemed about 5ft. 10in. His shoulders were broad, but sloping. His neck stooped forward. His carriage was slouchy, loose-jointed and stooping, but he seemed a powerful fellow. Thick, protruding lips and large teeth completed the unfavorable cast of an exterior by no means prepossessing. He was dressed in outer covering of dirty, greasy overalls and jumper. He had no shoes, and he had only a thin and worthless pair of socks. He wrapped his feet and legs up in gunny sacking, and put his feet when snowshoeing into a pair of meal sacks he had nailed on to the middle of his snowshoes. The whole bundle he tied with thongs. His snowshoes (*skis*) were a curiosity. They were 12ft. long, narrow, made of pine (or spruce), Howell himself being the builder of them. The front of one had its curve supplemented by a bit of board, wired on. All sorts of curves existed in the bottoms of the shoes. He had them heavily covered with resin to keep the snow from sticking to them. To cap the climax he had broken one shoe while in the Park—a mishap often very serious indeed, as one must have two shoes to walk with, and

elsewise cannot walk at all. With the ready resources of a perfect woodsman, Howell took his axe, went to a fir tree, hewed
out a three-cornered splice about 5ft. long, nailed it fast to the
bottom of his broken shoe, picked out some pieces of resin,
coated the shoe well with it, and went on his way as well as
ever. He said he could travel as far in a day on those shoes as
any man in the party could with any other pair, and I presume
that is true. Moreover, Howell pulled a toboggan behind him
all the way from Cooke City with a load of 180lbs. None of
us could pull a toboggan behind *skis,* and we would not wear
web shoes. Howell's toboggan was 10ft. long, and had wide
runners, like *skis.* He said a flat-bottomed Canadian model toboggan was no good, as it pulled too heavy.

At the Cañon Hotel Howell ate twenty-four pancakes for
breakfast. He seemed to enjoy the square meals of captivity.
At Norris he was always last at table. He was very chipper and
gay, and willing to talk to the officers, Capt. Scott and Lieut.
Forsyth, on about any subject that came up, though the officers
mostly looked over his head while he was talking. He was apparently little concerned about his capture, saying, as have already mentioned, that he stood to make $2,000, and could only
lose $26.75. He knew he could not be punished, and was only
anxious lest he should be detained until after the spring sheep
shearing in Arizona. He is an expert sheep shearer, sometimes
making $10 and $15 a day. He has money always, and was not
driven to poaching by want or hunger.

"Yes," Howell said, in reply to our questions, "I'm going
to take a little walk up to the Post, but I don't think I'll be there
long. About my plans? Well, haven't arranged any plans yet
for the future. I may go back into the Park again, later on, and
I may not. No, I will not say who it was contracted to buy the
heads of me. I had been camped over on Pelican since September. It was pretty rough, of course. If you don't think it's a hard
trail from Cooke City to Pelican Valley, you just try pulling a
toboggan over Specimen Ridge.[12]

"If I'd seen Burgess first, he'd never had arrested me. I'd have got away from him. It was so windy and stormy, I never heard him till he got right up against me and hollered for me to put up my hands. He was sort of blowin', and was nervous like. I see I was subjec' to the drop, so I let go my knife and came along."

PRIVATE LARSEN'S STORY.

Larsen, one of the men Capt. Anderson sent in with our party, talked with Howell later in the day, when most of us were away, and Howell was freer with him. Larsen says that Howell told him he had been camped in the Park since September and that at first he had a partner, a man by name of Noble, but that they had a falling out and he run Noble out of the camp. Noble went out at the south end of the Park, not going back to Cooke City. Howell said there was nothing in being arrested, they couldn't do anything to him. Howell also said he "supposed them —— fellers would want to get a photograph of him in the morning, but he wasn't going to let them." (Nevertheless, one had already been made of him and in the morning I got a shot at him without his consent, while he was stooping over and fastening his shoes. He tried to spoil the picture by rising and coming toward me. He had told me previously that he would not have any pictures taken and I was sorry to be so impolite about it. Capt. Scott, who had at that time gone on down the trail with Lieut. Forsyth, had said to me that if I preferred it he would give me the privilege of photographing Howell standing on his head. On the whole I believe that would have been nicer, if Howell could have been induced to look pleasant. The negative is not yet developed, but my impression is that he wasn't looking so very pleasant over the surreptitious FOREST AND STREAM shot at him.)

THE BUTCHER'S WORK.

The party sent out by Capt. Anderson to bring in the heads and hides of the slaughtered buffalo consisted of Sergt. Kell-

The poacher and captors, Yellowstone National Park, 1894. Poacher Ed Howell is probably at far right, his dog lying near his skis.

MONTANA HISTORICAL SOCIETY RESEARCH CENTER, PHOTOGRAPH ARCHIVES, HAYNES FOUNDATION COLLECTION ner and two privates. They passed the in-coming party between Norris and the Cañon, and pushed on down at a hot pace to the remote corner of the Park where the butchery took place. The second day out from Norris found them near the spot, but it was two days later before the animals were found, a fall of snow having covered them up, and Troike, the private who was with Burgess at the capture, having lost his head entirely about the localities. If it was so hard a spot to locate among the interminable mountains, even after a man had been there but a few days before, how much harder must it be to locate a poacher whose whereabouts is not known at all, but who has the whole great winter wilderness of the Park to surround him and his doings? The only wonder is that arrests can be made at all, where the country is so great and so difficult, and the special police of the Park limited to just one scout. The need of more scouts is too apparent to require comment.

When finally the butcher's work had been found again, it was learned that most of the robes and some of the heads were ruined for lack of proper care, Howell having been stopped too early in his work for this. The scene of the butchery was a sad sight enough for any one who has the least thoughtfulness in his make-up. The great animals lay slaughtered in the deep snow in which they had wallowed and plunged in their efforts to escape. To run up to them on the *skis* and to shoot them down one by one—only six shots to kill the five buffalo outright—was the work of the clumsiest butcher. In the snow these animals are absolutely defenseless. Howell could have killed more of the band, if there had been more, and he would not have stopped had there been more to kill. As I shall show later, I think he had killed far more than the eleven head discovered. I think his partner, Noble, left the camp of his own free will, and took out a load of heads at the lower end of the Park. I do not consider it impossible, from news I had after I left the Park, that Howell took out some heads with him when he went out to Cooke City after supplies. As FOREST AND STREAM has said, he was killing cows and calves in this last killing. He had been in camp since September, and he was killing cows and calves. I cannot evade the belief that he would kill any buffalo he could get to. He could prepare and hang up a good many in five months. The heads and the available robes were brought first into the Lake Hotel. Capt Anderson sent another party over the long trail from the Post, and the spoils were finally received at the Post the first week of April. The capture of Howell had required two trips by Burgess, aggregating 250 to 300 miles, one trip by the first detail of three men, nearly 150 miles, and a final trip of a little less than the latter distance by the detail who carried in the plunder. The heavy heads and hides all had to he packed in on the backs of the men. Every foot of the way had to be traveled on snowshoes. No men but just these hardy ones could do this work. For a time the Park had more men in it than it ever had in winter time before. The stir was all over this miserable specimen of humanity who was heartless enough to kill all he could of the few remaining buffalo left alive on earth to-day. These bare words convey no idea whatever of the hardships and dangers incurred in the winter patrolling of the Park. To criticize the military, or to say that Capt. Anderson should have caught the fellow sooner, is to display a total ignorance of the conditions, and to be absurdly unjust as well as ignorant. For such ignorance and injustice we must look first in just the quarters where it should not exist. Nowhere can we find an ignorance and indifference on this subject equal to that which has so long existed in the halls of Congress. It is time the change should come.

No Penalty.

Let us remember, then, first, that Howell was killing cows and yearlings; second, that the few buffalo left are helpless when pursued in the snow; third, that for a crime of this sort Congress *provides no penalty!* As this is written the word comes that the Secretary of the Interior has ordered the release of Howell from custody. On this old basis he can now go into the Park again and kill more buffalo, and have another hunt made after him by the U. S. Army. Let us hope that by the time this shall be in print there will have been a new basis established by Congress, so that such villainy as this shall obtain a punishment, prompt, adequate and just. Kill a Government mule and try what the U. S. Government will do to you. Yet a mule can be replaced. A buffalo cannot be replaced. This is the end. But kill a Government buffalo, and what does the U. S. Government do? Nothing! Absolutely nothing! This is the old basis. Let us sincerely hope that the new basis will come soon and that it will be widely different. Gentlemen of Congress can surely only need to have the matter called to their attention, and this has been done in the various measures this year submitted by the members who know the facts.

In a later article I shall advance the facts on which I base the firm belief that half the buffalo of the Park have been killed, and that not over 200 now remain alive. The Howell killing above described has been only a part of the total. Nineteen head were killed by Indians southeast of the Park last fall. Seven heads were offered to a Bozeman taxidermist for sale (not of these 19 heads) from Idaho this winter. We found what we supposed to be 6 or 8 dead buffalo in the Hayden Valley. I have track of several other heads that have this year appeared in Montana towns. No one knows how many heads have been quietly bought by Sheard[13] or another Livingston taxidermist. Certain it is, that the traceable total of buffalo killed this year in the Park is alarmingly, appallingly large. There are not very many more now left to kill.

THE SNOWSHOE TRAIL.

The method of work in scouting for a poacher is simple if arduous. The scout must know the country and the course likely to be taken in the Park. He circles to cut the trail of the man he wants. The snowshoes leave a deep, plain trail on any ordinary snow (except crust), and this will remain for weeks.

Even if covered by later snow, the trail will eventually become evident again. The trail packs the snow under the line of the shoes. In the spring when the snow begins to melt, a snowshoe trail will not melt and sink, but will show up in the form of a little ridge above the level of the snow, the other snow melting and sinking below it. The poacher can get in in no possible way but on snowshoes, and he cannot travel without leaving a trail which for the rest of the season will endure, though part of the time it may be invisible under new snow.

A Plucky Scout.

I can not leave this description of the Howell capture without mentioning one fact showing the indomitable grit of the scout Burgess who brought Howell in. We were all looking out over the trail when Burgess and his prisoner came in sight. Howell, of course, was ahead, but we noticed that Burgess was limping very badly. How he was able to travel at all was a wonder. When he got in by the fire he said nothing, but took off his heavy socks, showing a foot on which the great toe was inflamed and swollen to four times its natural size. The whole limb above was swollen and sore, with red streaks of inflammation extending up to the thigh. How the man ever walked I can not see. I noticed that Burgess had lost the two toes next to the great toe, and that the scar of the cut ran half way through the great toe. He told me, quietly, that the Crow Indians did that for him. They made him put his foot on a log, and amused themselves by cutting off his toes, taking two off clean and nearly cutting off the great toe. Since then the circulation had been bad in that member, and he had frozen it more than once. It had been frozen again on this trip, and was now in bad shape. Yet in spite of this injury, which would have disabled most men, Burgess passed the evening calmly playing whist, and the following morning again took the trail, making the twenty miles to the Post before evening, and delivering his prisoner safely. The post surgeon, Dr. Gandy, after making examination of Burgess's foot, at once amputated the great toe, thus finishing what the Indians had less skillfully begun some years before.

Actual Interviews on Segregation.

All About Calmness.

CHICAGO, Ill., May 5.—In many past issues of FOREST AND STREAM there have appeared editorial articles handling the question of the proposed division of the Park by a railroad from Cinnabar to Cooke City.[14] FOREST AND STREAM has opposed that railroad and all other railroads through the Park, and has made the one consistent and unfaltering newspaper fight to keep the Park as it is—unhurt, untouched, as the people of America have by their representatives declared it should be kept. In doing this FOREST AND STREAM has acted in the name of honor, of sportsmanship and of public decency. It has kept faith with its constituency and its principles. In doing this it must needs have given the subject of the proposed segregation the most thorough and careful attention, and have acquired a most intimate knowledge of the matter in all its bearings, not only from extended reading, but from a various familiarity with the entire region in question.

I recall that a Chicago paper, which claims to be published in the interest of sportsmanship but is really open to the use of any man or men with an axe or axes to grind, once published an article by W. S. Brackett, who held forth that the occupant of a "far-off Eastern sanctum" could not possibly be so well posted on Park matters as those living near the Park. This is a trifle amusing, when one comes to it. "Col." Brackett has lately bought a little ranch on the Yellowstone, between Livingston and Cinnabar, where he and his family pass a part of the summer. I don't know where he spends the rest of the year, but it is my opinion that he is not very closely identified with property interests about the Park. (If he is, then he is taking an unfair advantage of the so-called Sportsman's Journal and Miner's Friend[15] which he favors with his stories on segregation.) Yet I happen to know—what no one else would ever know through the editorial page of FOREST AND STREAM—that the gentleman who has written the FOREST AND STREAM editorials is a ranchman owning property in Wyoming, who is in cattle and horses for revenue and not for summer resort purposes; that he has spent years in all the phases of Western life, and that he knows not only all of the Park and its environs but most of the Montana mountains as well, no doubt a good deal better, if I could commit the impoliteness of so direct a comparison, than Mr. Brackett or many of his neighbors do. I do not doubt that Mr. Brackett feels himself a Montana citizen when he is in Montana, and that he says he has "come to stay," and that moreover he catches a warm flush of generous sympathy from the talk of the interested men about him; but he is unjust to himself when in ignorance he accuses a courteous opponent of an ignorance that does not exist. One must not accuse Mr. Brackett of demagoguery in this, but only of bad general-ship in not learning the enemy's forces. This lack of forethought leaves FOREST AND STREAM quite in position to say, suavely and calmly—if it ever could be so impolite as to do such a thing—that probably it is Mr. Brackett who doesn't know such a frightful lot more about this subject than be ought to, himself.

It all comes of not being calm. With calmness, I should think Mr. Brackett would make a very good advocate of just the doctrine FOREST AND STREAM maintains, and not the fire and sword tenets under which the local Cooke City and Livingston contingent propose to wipe the Park and the military off from the face of the earth, to mutilate Capt. Anderson and even burn up the geysers, the falls and the Yellowstone Lake. I wish Mr. Brackett would be calm, because I saw him on the Cinnabar train one day, going up to visit his ranch (he didn't know any FOREST AND STREAM man was there) and he is a mighty nice looking man and appeared intelligent looking, too. I should think a great deal could be made out of him with care. If he will only be calm and think this thing over as a man and as a sportsman he will come out of this epoch of fire and blood pretty near to the FOREST AND STREAM position in belief. He will be welcome. FOREST AND STREAM will be in just about the same position, or maybe a little further ahead. It is a great deal nicer to be on the side of good judgment, good sportsmanship and good citizenship than to be a left-handed Marco Bozzaris or Toussaint L'Ouverture, or One-eyed Riley,[16] or any of those martyr fellows. I wouldn't be any martyr if I were Mr. Brackett. I wouldn't burn up the geysers or disfigure Capt. Anderson if I were Mr. Brackett, as in his article he suggests will be done. I wouldn't do that. I would be calm.

FOREST AND STREAM being therefore in full possession of the facts in this case, as it is in most cases which it under-takes to handle, it would ill become me to attempt to add any weight to what has already been better said, and I should not touch on this matter at all did I not hope that some of the actual little interviews I had with segregationists and others might prove at least amusing if not instructive.

J. G. SAX, OF LIVINGSTON.

Mr. Sax keeps a fruit store and newstand. He does not keep FOREST AND STREAM for sale. I asked him why not.

"I've got no use for that paper," he said.

"Why not?" said I.

"It's all the time fighting us," he replied. "If it hadn't been for that dash-binged paper we'd have had a railroad to Cooke before this through the Park. The fellows here are all down on

Forest and Stream, and won't have it. I see you are at it again this fall."

"How do they know we are fighting you if they don't read the paper?" I asked him.

"I carry what there is a demand for," said Mr. Sax, stiffly, ignoring the conundrum.

W. F. Sheard, of Livingston.

Mr. Sheard is a taxidermist, and no doubt buys more furs and trophies at all sorts of seasons than any other man in that part of the country. He is the man who wrote to one of the winter keepers in the Park, asking him to poison animals in the Park and send out the small skins by mail to him. This letter, which was written on Mr. Sheard's own letterhead, was, I believe, published by Forest and Stream, which has often spoken very frankly and understandingly about Mr. Sheard and his practices.[17] Of course, I was innocent and ignorant of all that when called on Mr. Sheard, and Mr. Sheard, thinking, no doubt, that I had never been west of the River before, gradually thawed out and after a while became positively entertaining. He introduced me to several friends, showed me around, and took me through his really magnificent collection of furs and trophies. He showed me a little bit of timber up on the mountain side above town, and said he never had to go further than that to kill deer. "I killed six up there one day," said he, "I got the whole band." (I think he said he killed them all at one shot, but a little thing like that should not matter.)

Mr. Sheard disclaimed that he had ever bought a Park buffalo head. He thought, perhaps, some of the other taxidermists had done such a thing. They were wicked men. He wouldn't buy such a head. Dear me, no.

Mr. Sheard told me confidentially that "the military up at the Park was all a fake—didn't amount to anything; that it didn't protect the Park and was no good; that the Park would have to be opened some day." Mr. Sheard also assured me that the road to Cooke City should be built through the Park; that all it could cut off would be a little bit of rocky hills of no value whatever and a region where the game never came at all. He said that if this road were built Livingston would blossom like the rose and every citizen would have a smelter running on the Cooke City ores. I told him I thought it more likely that Livingston would get up in the night and go to Cooke, or that the smelters would go up near Cinnabar, or at Horr, where plenty of coal was at hand. Mr. Sheard couldn't think so. He pictured to me the wrong done by Congress to the Cooke City mine owners, who had waited twenty years without having the way to fortune opened to them by act of Congress. I told him that I had been waiting twenty years to get rich too, but Congress hadn't done anything for me and I didn't believe it was going to. Mr. Sheard couldn't see the parallel. No man in Livingston or Cooke City can see the parallel. Yet it is a perfectly just and fair one. The disappointed Cooke City men are just the same as those disappointed in any other line of life and the world is open for them to go into something else if they are not satisfied where they are.

Mr. Sheard took me to a map, and explained to me that only by one route under the shining canopy of heaven could a road be built to Cooke City, and that was through the Park. "But all we want," said he, drawing a nice mark with his pencil, "is to go into the Park for about a half mile south of the Yellowstone, for just a little way, then right out along the hills just above the north line. There is no game in there, not a geyser and not a single object of natural interest." Yet later I found that even this statement would cut off forever the entire band of antelope in the Park, which has only a little winter range right along the Yellowstone Valley. I knew the statement was inaccurate by about fifty miles in length and by some thousands of feet of rocky, vertical walls in height, and later I learned by my own eyes that there are more elk in winter time in just the part of the Park proposed to be cut off than in any one section of it whatever.

I don't remember any specific statement to that effect by Mr. Sheard, but I gathered the impression that he was going to burn the Park up next week, and I presume that he has done it. I don't see why he did it, because the Park must have been a source of revenue to him especially.

THE PRESS OF LIVINGSTON.

I met the editors of the leading Livingston paper, a prominent and radical advocate of segregation and the Cooke City road, and as members of the "perfesh" we had a pleasant talk.[18] Mr. Wright unrolled a map, and I must say that I listened to a very fair statement of the local side of the case. I am able to see how personal interest can blind a man to national interests, though unconsciously, and I told my newspaper friends that had my lot fallen in Livingston, and had I never known the doctrines of FOREST AND STREAM, I would no doubt have done as they did. On the other hand, I asked them to be equally fair, and to realize the folly of FOREST AND STREAM, by profession devoted to the preservation of the forests and the game, leaving its own field to go into a field of an absolutely foreign interest. I told them that FOREST AND STREAM did not claim to be a mining journal, but a sportsman's journal, and that as such the only course was to do what it thought was right, and so try to preserve the Park and the Park game. Mr. Wright thought perhaps FOREST AND STREAM did not know all the facts—that it did not know how little the Park would be damaged, etc., and that really there was little game in the country proposed to be cut off. In this I personally learned later that Mr. Wright was misinformed, and that Capt. Anderson's report (which the Livingston *Herald* ridiculed), was correct when it stated that large herds of game wintered in that very part of the Park. Nevertheless, I am obliged to my friends of the Livingston newspaper fraternity for a statement of the case, which I think was meant to be fair, and we are all obliged for the later editorial in the *Enterprise*, on the poacher, Howell, in which it was said that "Howell's act will find few apologists in this section."

MR. WITTICH, OF LIVINGSTON.

The Wittichs are taxidermists, two sons and their father. Only one of the sons was in the business when I was there, and I think the firm was Wittich & Son. Here I received very nice attention. Young Wittich has Cooke City property, and is a very ardent segregationist. He has often had occasion to go through the Park on the trail to Cooke City, and rebelled against the regulations. He told me how he compelled Capt. Anderson and the Secretary of the Interior to yield to his imperious demands for the privilege of bearing arms in the Park and going where he pleased. (Capt. Anderson's account of this is a shade different. I haven't heard from the Secretary of the Interior.) Young Wittich was hotter-headed than his father, who held the same beliefs, but was temperate in them. Young Wittich said the soldiers ought to be abolished and was of the belief that the Cooke City road must be built through the Park peaceably if it could, by force if it must. He pitied the poor Cooke City miners, who had been developing their propositions for twenty years and were still broke because they couldn't get their ore out of the camp. He couldn't see the sense of my renewed remark to the effect that I also was mostly broke in Chicago, and that Congress wasn't going to build any railroad for me.

"The men of this country will burn the whole Park up, if something isn't done," said young Mr. Wittich, impressively.

"Oh, no they won't," I said, "you don't really mean that, now do you?"

"Well," said he, cooling down a trifle, "it ought to be burned."

Old Mr. Wittich was not so radical. We all three chatted pleasantly for a while, and the old gentleman invited me to go fishing with him when I came out from the Park. I am sorry time was too short for me to do so, for I know we should have had a good time.

Young Mr. Wittich said that everybody knew that heads of Park buffalo, thirty or forty of them, had been offered at the taxidermist shops around the Park, at Livingston and elsewhere, "within the last two or three years." Other taxidermists of Livingston had maybe taken some of these heads. He wouldn't dream of doing such a thing.

F. B. TOLHURST, OF LIVINGSTON.

Mr. Tolhurst is another Livingston taxidermist, and is an honest workman in my belief. Mr. Tolhurst was busy and I could not talk with him much. Mr. Tolhurst thought maybe the other Livingston taxidermists might buy a Park buffalo head once in a while, but as for him, he wouldn't dream of it.

MATT. BLACK, OF BOZEMAN.

Mr. Black is a newsdealer at Bozeman. He doesn't handle FOREST AND STREAM. Says he hasn't any use for it. (The other Bozeman dealer doesn't have any Cooke City mining property, so he handles FOREST AND STREAM). Mr. Black was the most rabid segregationist I met in my entire trip, and was more violent in his expressions of hatred for FOREST AND STREAM than any one I talked with. He allowed the FOREST AND STREAM man was a tenderfoot. We will let it go at that. Evidently I got myself disliked by Mr. Black by venturing to work for a paper which doesn't run a mining department or a free-for-all editorial page. "It's a blanked noble mission FOREST AND STREAM has in life, ain't it!" said Mr. Black, "trying to stop the development of the resources of this country! Here's men who have been holding valuable claims over at Cooke for 20 years, before the Park was ever heard of, and you fellows want them to waste their entire lives!"

"No, we don't," I ventured to say, "but if they don't like it at Cooke, why didn't they go somewhere else?"

This made Mr. Black jump up and down, and this was where he allowed I was a tenderfoot. (I lived in a mining camp before I ever saw a copy of FOREST AND STREAM and we wanted a railroad in our camp and never got it. Congress never did anything for me.)

"There'll be some killing done up around that Park some day," said Mr. Black with an awful impressive air, which should probably have curdled my blood, "and if it happens, FOREST AND STREAM can just blame itself for it. What business is it of yours, meddling in the affairs of this country and trying to stop the growth of one of the richest camps on the range?"

(This, however, FOREST AND STREAM has not done, but has editorially shown that a road could much better be built in from the east. I cited the letter of Mr. P. M. Gallaher).

"There's only one way to get into Cooke," said Mr. Black, in a tone as of one who intended to settle the question forever, "and that's through the Park. That's the only route we can raise capital for. We could once have got capital for that, but I don't believe we could get capital to build the road now if we had the right of way. You fellows in the East are a blanked nice set of men, ain't you. You've raised such a hurrah over this that I don't believe we'll ever be able to do anything now."

In this latter statement I believe Mr. Black is practically correct, but I can not avoid the belief that the now dead segregation scheme had no enemies more deadly than its own friends, who too often have indulged in just such wild talk as the above. Such talk displeases the American people, which after all is practical and fair.

Mr. Black claimed that the poacher Howell did not belong at Cooke City. He disapproved of Howell's action in killing the Park buffalo, and said Howell ought to be hung, and that he would like to help hang him, as he had injured the spotless record of Cooke City. I recommend this to Mr. Howell's attention.

THEY SHOULD ALL BE CAREFUL.

They should all be more careful how they talk, all these rabid segregationists who have been making utterances like the above. I have quoted them all fairly and without garbling, to the best of my knowledge and belief, and have given the statements because I believe the cause of segregation is most hurt by telling the truth about it, and by making public the ill-tempered and unreasonable methods by which these men seek to gain their purely personal ends.

There is no call for a road through the Park to Cooke City but a personal call. There is no public demand for it. There is on the contrary a public demand for this great national preserve, a heritage to be kept unchanged and inalienable. The Government can not give each child what it wants, but it can give all its children a great gift that will be good for all of them.

By no means should it be understood that the above utterances represent the feeling of the great State of Montana. On the other hand, they come from but a very small section and from only a few men in that section. To build this road through the Park would be the death blow to Livingston. It would benefit Cooke City alone. It would be also a death blow to the Park. Is the benefit to the few greater than the benefit to the many? Therefore, is the position of FOREST AND STREAM on this matter selfish, illiberal or unfair? Who is there who can think so?

It will be a great pleasure in a later article to give the reverse of this sordid and distempered view, and to show the other side of the picture, and I shall then quote engineers and railroad men of authority in support of the FOREST AND STREAM belief that the Cooke City men are subserving their own best interests in insisting on this road through the Park. If FOREST AND STREAM held it in its hand to forever seal the fate of a prosperous community, to kill its future, to prevent the happiness and success of many families, I do not think it would do so. But it is not determined that the matter amounts to this. If FOREST AND

STREAM can keep the Park intact, and yet by calm and temperate counsel show to these few inconsiderate and hard-talking men that Cooke City can still be opened to the world, it has done a wise and good work. This latter it has already shown, more ably than can be done here, although further interviews may be interesting as additional proof and will therefore be submitted.

ADDITIONAL NEWS OF THE PARK BUFFALO.

Later.—Since the above was written I have received a letter from Mr. E. Hofer, at Gardiner, Mont., dated April 30, which is given below. The additional news that Howell admits having been in the Park on the Pelican Valley for three winters, and that he says there are only a few buffalo there, can only point to one conclusion, namely, that the total number left alive in the Park are even less than the FOREST AND STREAM expedition of this winter would make out. Capt. Anderson has always thought it likely that a good number of buffalo had moved over to winter in the Pelican hot countr[y], but no report has been made of buffalo in that little-visited portion of the Park, and no expedition has gone in there to investigate. Howell has been investigating for three years in a locality where it was next to impossible to find him, and his statements made to Mr. Hofer, no doubt made in candor, constitute the best available report of facts as to the buffalo supply in the Pelican country. Outside of this there remains practically only the Hayden Valley herd, the largest count of which is 103 head. Congress has done well to act speedily in passing the protection act. It was time if any of the buffalo are to be left. These facts, and the facts which I picked up after I left the Park lead to only one possible belief—the Park buffalo can not be counted for even 200 head this winter. There may not be 150, perhaps not 125. This is not mere alarmist talk. We may hope and may even believe that there are 250 buffalo somewhere in the Park, but how shall we prove it? The Park has been better scouted this winter than it ever was before, but by whose report shall we place the number of buffalo actually seen at more than 125?

On the heels of this sickening conclusion note the statement that Howell is again at large, free to go in again and complete a fourth year in the Park, free to kill the remainder of the herd now left so sadly cut down in numbers, free to finish up the rest of the great animals which we found panic-stricken, timorous, running till exhausted in the deep snow, in terror for their lives.

Mr. Hofer's letter follows:

"Howell is out of the guard house as per order from Washington. Capt. Anderson was away when the order came. Howell was held about two weeks longer.

"Howell called at my cabin to see me and the papers that had an account of his arrest. He is pleased to know he made such a stir. He says they can thank him if they get laws passed to protect the game and the Park. He says, too, that he had seven buffalo, not five, killed when they found him, one was over a ridge, the boys did not see or find it at all.

"Howell has been in there three winters, and knows all about the buffalo on the east side of the river, says there are only a few there. I suppose you know the reason. He spoke about the picture you made, and said he supposed he ought to have let you take it, but you was so fresh he did not like to. [Thanks, but the picture I got anyhow will do very well.]

"The snow is getting off the first hills and higher table-lands, one can see a bit of green here and there. The antelope are scattered over more ground now. They can go to the top of the hills and get grass, until they get on the eastern side of the hills, where they find snow. I have been out and had another whirl at the antelope with the camera."

Mr. Hofer's letter is the last word obtainable on the grave question of the numbers of the Park buffalo. FOREST AND STREAM can well claim the credit of an exclusive presentation of these important facts, unwelcome as they are to the people of the United States and their representatives in Congress.

[MORE INTERVIEWS ON SEGREGATION.]

CHICAGO, Ill., May 12.—Last week I gave some expressions of opinion heard among the friends of the Cooke City Railroad through the Park, commonly known as the "segregation road" or the "segregation scheme." The latter is the better term. The project was never at any stage more than a scheme, and is now a good scheme because it is a dead scheme, thanks much to FOREST AND STREAM's repeated expositions of the facts. Facts are the deadliest medicine on earth for schemes. In the candid belief of many of the best Montana merchants and business men in general, there never was at any time any money behind the Cooke City Railway scheme except the fund raised by its adherents for the purpose of enlarging the disgraceful record of American lobbying. Actual capital to build the road is not now in evidence. Friends of the scheme say it once "could have been raised." Opponents to the scheme allege the opposite, and declare that all the pushers of the Cooke City scheme expected or wanted was to get the right of way. The right of way would of course be valuable even for the purpose of locating mineral claims, and as a salable franchise of course it would have a certain speculative value. The arguments used to back it were very plausible, very specious, very well-appearing, and especially strong in the two points most brought into play—sympathy for the industrious miners and the practical industrial development of a valuable portion of a great State. There are many Montana men who believe that behind these two masks of apparent sincerity there hides actually the visage of a selfishness and unscrupulousness which is either narrow or absolutely insincere. It would be arrogating a very swift quality of wisdom to myself to claim that I knew all, or even much, about either aide of this question, in regard to which there is so wide a local divergence of opinion, and I do not so claim. But I do claim that FOREST AND STREAM knows more about, and has gone to the bottom of it more fully, and has set forth the exact truths in regard to it more fairly and justly, than any other journal on earth, of any class whatever, and whether of Montana or elsewhere. To accuse FOREST AND STREAM of an Eastern prejudice when it is working for a Western benefit is unjust enough, but to accuse it of ignorance of the theme in hand is to show a local folly and ignorance hardly worth a good healthy contempt. It is my privilege and duty to add to the FOREST AND STREAM fund of information by telling, fairly and fully, what the men in Montana say about this segregation scheme. Last week I told what the friends of the scheme say. This time I want to quote a few men who do not believe in segregation. I think both the one and the other are going to be a little rough on the scheme itself, which is doubtlessly blessed by friends whose hot-headedness leads them to wild and injurious statements. Such intemperance of statement, I am bound in justice to add, I did not find among the opponents of this scheme, although I do not doubt they are just as much in earnest and just as apt to be in the fight at the end of the issue—if, indeed, the end is not already reached to-day.

CAPT. ANDERSON, SUPERINTENDENT OF THE PARK.[19]

The representative of FOREST AND STREAM was entertained by Capt. Anderson at Fort Yellowstone, and one could hardly quote the unreserved statements of a host. This, however, is not necessary, for the position Capt. Anderson has alway[s] maintained as to the integrity of the Park is something too well known throughout Montana to require reiteration. The organs of the Cooke City faction have abused him continuously in the hot-headed, ill-advised fashion to which I have called attention, but in this abuse he takes a placid pride and satisfaction, regarding it as the highest possible tribute to his efforts at keeping the Park as it is, the property of the whole people and not of a few of the people. "The more they hate me, the better I shall like it," said he, "but just abusing the Park superintendent isn't going to scare the U. S. Army, and it isn't going to throw open this Park to poachers and land-grabbers. As to this road proposed, you just go over the route yourself and you will see the reasons why I or any other thinking man must oppose the idea. In the first place, any road in means all roads can come; in the second place, this road would ruin the Park and leave it without a boundary on the north, where now it has a very practical boundary; in the next place, this road is impracticable even if it were right to undertake it; and in the last place, and especially, to have that road built would be to kill all the antelope, and to practically cut off forever the thousands of elk which winter in the northeastern part of the Park. Moreover, and besides all that, this Park is too grand an affair to be touched. It is here, and let us keep it as it is. For my part, I love it, and I hope never to see it spoiled."

I suppose now I should add that I did go over the route of the proposed segregation railway, but the fact is, I didn't. Nobody ever has or ever will, in all probability. But our party kept away to the right of the white mountains that line the deep-sunken Yellowstone, along which the Cooke City road must go if it goes through the Park. We climbed the Gardiner Hill, about four miles straight up in the air, crossed the succession of hills and streams which cover that upper region, and ten miles further on ran down five miles more, steep as a house roof, into the valley at Yancey's. When it came to going back, some one jokingly proposed we return down the Yellowstone

Bison near Alum Creek. MONTANA HISTORICAL SOCIETY RESEARCH CENTER, PHOTOGRAPH ARCHIVES, HAYNES FOUNDATION COLLECTION

cañons, along the "railway" route. "My boy," said Uncle John Yancey, "you couldn't get down there in ten years."[20] From this I infer that a railroad couldn't get up in ten years, also that it will not, even in a thousand years. If it ever does, it will have a good solid roadbed, sure, and plenty of snowsheds. As to the game which winters in the valleys making down the big river, I have already hinted and shall speak fully later. Capt. Anderson's reasons against the Yellowstone Valley road are patent to any one who knows that country as it actually is. Years of residence at the Park, and continuous exploration of it, would seem to give that knowledge to the superintendent of the Park.

Mr. J. D. Losekamp, of Billings.

Mr. Losekamp is a typical Western business man, shrewd, practical and quiet. To him more than to almost any other one man in his State belongs the credit of the exposé of the Cooke City Park railroad scheme. Contrary to local sentiment and local timidity, Mr. Losekamp stood out first alone and uttered the first word against the scheme to open the Park to the railroads. He wrote the first newspaper article against the Cooke City road that was ever written, and has since then seen local sentiment change and local papers adopt the side of reason all over the State. He has always been foremost in the fight against the Cooke City project in all its phases, and he has put out more information in regard to the true inwardness of the proposed deal than any other ten men together. It was he who obtained for FOREST AND STREAM the valuable letter from Civil Engineer P. M. Gallaher, published last fall, which showed the practicability of a road into Cooke City from the east, along the Clark's Fork.

"I notice that railroads are not doing things for fun," said Mr. Losekamp, "and they don't do things backward, either. Now, if there is mineral or coal to be had in that New World district,[21] the bulk of it will have to go east for its main market. Does a railroad want to pull that stuff west over the divide through the Park, around by Cinnabar and Livingston, and then east again over the same mountains to get back toward the market it wants to reach? I don't think so. Mr. Oakes, of the Northern Pacific, didn't think so, either. He was over that western line, and saw Cooke City, and he reported that the Northern Pacific didn't want any of it. I can't see why a railroad should want to spend two or three million dollars making a road across a landscape, just for the sake of pulling its freight three times as far over grades three times as hard. Maybe they will, but I doubt it.

"On the other hand, we have the B. & M. assured for Billings.[22] [A telegram announcing this was received by Mr. Losekamp during my stay at Billings.] This road, if once built into Cooke City, would be as good as any for that town, if it was only after an outlet, as it claims. But do they want any outlet from the west? Oh, no. Nothing but the Park route will do them. Why? Well, you just let the segregation scheme go through and you'll see why. Cooke City 'll have something to sell then, and it won't be ore, either. There isn't a dollar actually put up to build that road, though I don't doubt that the majority of the boys who have claims there are sincere in their belief that the road would be built if the bill once passed Congress. They are simply ignorant, though sincere. If the bill did pass, there would be a lot of money made before a shovel ever hit the dirt. Besides, long before that road was begun, the best of the Park would be handed out to other parties by way of other franchises.[23] I can see no use for this. It's hard to get any road up to Cooke, and any engineer knows this, but the route from the east, up the Clark's Fork,[24] has had the survey of a good engineer, and it can be built. No one claims so much for the Park route. If the Cooke City men have nothing up their sleeve, and are only anxious for an outlet, why should they oppose a cheaper and more practical route from the east side?

"Another thing is, strange as you may think it, after all you have heard of Chinooks,[25] and that is, there is four times as much snow on the west side of the mountains around Cooke City as on the east side. I will leave that to your own observation. You see, the country the Cooke City road would have to cross is not west of the Continental Divide, but east, just as this is." [It was two weeks later than my Yancey's trip that I was at Billings, but the truth of Mr. Losekamp's remark was no less obvious than surprising. The snow was not there and it never is there in such quantity as in the Park. We drove far up the gentle Stillwater Valley and away up the Rosebud, but the ground was dry. On the opposite side of the range the snow was 8ft. on an average, in drifts 40ft. or more on the Bl[ack]tail, when we left.[26] It never averages so deep on the east slope at the same altitudes.]

P. M. GALLAHER, C. E., BILLINGS.

Mr. Gallaher has already favored FOREST AND STREAM with the most conclusive document ever published on this subject, and it is needless to repeat his statement as to the feasibility of the Clark's Fork route to Cooke City. Mr. Gallaher is the best known engineer in Montana. He had charge of the survey that ran the lines of the Timber Reserve of the Park for the Government,[27] and has been all over that entire region, as probably no other one man has been except the old-time trappers and hunters. Mr. Gallaher I knew in this country twelve years ago, before he went to Montana, and even then he had a reputation. I can find no reason extant to-day for believing him anything but a conservative and accurate man, with the pride in his profession which is so singularly deep among civil engineers as a class. Mr. Gallaher said:

"So far as I know, no actual survey has ever been run over the Park route to Cooke City, nor do I think it will ever come to that, as any engineer can see the difficulties of the route proposed. Of course, you co[u]ld build a road there, and you could build one anywhere, but it would cost more money than any road could pay interest on. The grades would be very severe, and the tremendous snows of that region would tie the road up half the year unless it were under shed. There must be a great incentive before such a vast outlay of money is begun, and the only incentive alleged is the mining camp of Cooke City. Certainly it has good mineral, but is that enough to show a corporation asked to put a road through such a country?

"On the other hand, on the Clark's Fork route you have distance in which to climb. Of course you know what that means. You can go any height, if you only have room to do it in. Now, you have been up the Stillwater and Rosebud valleys, and know the long grades of the streams coming down this side of the slope. The Clark's Fork is even more gentle, because it is much longer. You see the long horseshoe it makes. That gives us distance for our climb. Instead of heavy rock work all the way, we have a water grade for the greater part of the way. At the cañon of our stream we have unquestionably got a lot of expensive rock work to do; but we've saved enough money to have some left to do it with, and after you get over the cañon, you are in easier sailing again.

"Now, I'll draw you a little map.[28] You know, there's a road already built up to Red Lodge. Suppose we call the point where this road makes its bend to the west of the Clark's Fork 'point E.' Now we will call the Bear Creek coal fields D. From E to D is 30 miles. Call the box cañon of the Fork C, and from D to C is 20 miles more. From C to A, which latter we will call Cooke City, is 55 miles further. As I have said, there would be plenty of rock work on a limited part of this line, but it could be built—and most of it could be built on a water grade—below the heavy cuttings of the cañon. This is the natural route out from Cooke City, and the natural way for a railroad to haul out mineral—down hill, not up over the same hill a couple of times.

"A very hard part of this road would be the getting to Cooke over the last three or four miles, but while I presume this could be accomplished, the problem of an outlet is practically solved if you get steam in so near as that.

"You will observe that the road from the east slope has a double purpose to urge it to build. It has the Bear Creek coal fields—almost as useful and valuable as gold, for you must have good fuel at a practical distance in mining or railroading, or in any branch of commercial activity. You have on the east Cooke City plus the coal, plus the natural grade; on the west you have only Cooke City and an unnatural railroad proposition.

"But I have not yet spoken of the very greatest inducement for a road to go up at Clark's Fork, and this is something which the Cooke City people do not seem to think. They are sure of the wealth of their mines, but the whole world, especially the railroad world, is not sure of that. I do not say it is not true, doubtless it is true, but railroads take no chances. They must see a certain field, a country to be developed, lasting industries to be created, before they spend millions of dollars building roads across mountain ranges.

"Nothing appeals to railroad companies like an agricultural proposition. There is their certain and big money.

"Now, if you will look at this part of the country south and east of the Park and west of the Big Horn Mountains—all this section lying along the Stinking Water, Grey Bull and Big Horn rivers and their tributaries, you will be seeing what is known as the Big Horn Basin. There are millions of acres of land there lying untouched, and you can get water all over the whole of it. There is no better watered part of the West than this basin. The first railroad in there has an empire for itself. This is the largest and best body of land owned by the United States left undeveloped by the railroads, and it is the greatest railroad proposition now left open, unless we later find something to do in Alaska. All this region can be put under ditch at unusually low expense, on account of the many strong watercourses which cover it. The railroad which goes in here, builds ditches and so makes possible the settlement of this big district by an agricultural population, is going to have the best opening now left. Capital has no such chance left in America. I am not saying this from hearsay or from personal reasons, for I know that district thoroughly, although I own nothing there. There is nothing worth owning until a railroad is built.

"Now, let us call this point on the Grey Bull River, say at Otto, B, and you know we called the cañon of the Clark's Fork C. From C to B is only 75 miles. That is, the road which goes up the Clark's Fork has the Bear Creek coal and the Cooke City mineral, and for 75 miles more of road built to the south, it has also this Big Horn basin for territory, worth unspeakably more than all the rest. Perhaps this road will not be built, but it seems to me more likely than that a road will ever be put through over the rocky range from the west, with not one-twentieth the railroad reasons for existence, with ten times the railroad difficulties to overcome, and against the wish of the people of the United States, who have said they wanted the wonders of the Park preserved, and who always will want them to stay preserved as they are, so long as they have a fair and truthful showing of the actual facts put before them. Such a statement of facts these Cooke City men have not offered. In their selfishness they have been willing to offer anything, to promise anything, to do anything, to threaten anything, in order to attain their own ends. The general sentiment of Montana is that that isn't right. The case should have a just and fair and truthful showing to the public. Certainly FOREST AND STREAM deserves the utmost credit, for it is the only paper on earth that has been accurate, just and painstaking in getting all the facts on this question, and broad-minded enough to hear both sides of the case calmly and impartially."

I shall make no comment on Mr. Gallaher's clear statement of the above interesting facts. They do not need comment.

CHAS. S. FEE,
G. P. A. OF THE NORTHERN PACIFIC.

Mr. Chas. S. Fee is the general passenger agent of the Northern Pacific road, and no man in the world is better posted on the Park situation in every respect. To him things must have a practical and not a theoretical value or excellence. Mr. Fee's remarks had the brevity and clearness usual with men of his calling, and their meaning was unmistakable.

"The Northern Pacific road does not want to build into Cooke City," said he, "and the Northern Pacific road and all its men emphatically do not want to see the Park divided or touched in any respect. We make our money by carrying people out to see the wonders of the greatest wonderland on the face of the earth. Throw that wonderland open to the rapacity of the few or of the many, and you have no wonders left to see. The Park would then be no better than any beaten road. I hear there is a proposition made to Congress to grant a right of way to a road down Soda Butte Creek, in the northeast corner of the Park, and to run along a part of the Grand Cañon of the Yellowstone, thence across to the Firehole Basin. I am a railroad man, but the thought of a thing like that fills me with shame. A railroad in the Grand Cañon of the Yellowstone! The idea is monstrous! No, sir, if you ask whether we want to go through the Park or any corner of it, for any purpose, my reply is, 'No, emphatically no, not for any purpose whatever.' That Park belongs just as it is, unchanged forever.

"The Northern Pacific Railway," continued Mr. Fee, "has done more for the National Park than the nation itself ever did. If we did not stand behind the hotels and the transportation, these services to the public would no longer exist.[29] This railway has shown a spirit which the United States Congress never has. We have always stood for the integrity of the Park, and have helped protect its lines and to promote its attractiveness. What has the Government ever done? It won't pay even the cost of one additional special officer to protect the game. It shows no interest in the Park, apparently knows and cares nothing about it, while all the time people come from all over the earth to look at this most wonderful part of the earth. It takes people from Europe to go into ecstacies over the Park. If this Park were in Europe I rather think it would be protected! The way Congress has treated the Park is an outrage and a shame. To run this road to Cooke through the Park may or may not be possible. I am told by an engineer that it would be a very difficult problem to build to Cooke from the east. But be that as it may, this road doesn't want to go through any portion of the Park, and doesn't want any other road to do so. The Park is the Park, and belongs as it is."

The above hearty doctrine may be unpleasant to some of the friends of the Cooke City scheme.

E. Hofer, Park Guide, Gardiner.

Lastly, I shall quote "Billy" Hofer, the Park guide, who was my companion in the Forest and Stream winter expedition. This I do because he knows personally more about the game supply of the Park, where the game is to be found, where it is at certain seasons, and how to get to it, than does any other living man. In our trip over the Yancey trail, Billy pointed out to me the line of the proposed segregation road, as nearly as we could get to it. We did not go over it, because that cannot very well be done without a balloon, and we had no balloon. When I saw a band of elk, I would ask Billy, "Are they across the segregation line?" and he only too often replied that they were. We probably saw 3,000 to 4,000 elk on country which would b[e] cut off if the road were built. We could not claim that we saw all there were, for our search could not be thorough on so great and wild a region; but we saw these and perhaps 1,000 more, for all I can say, the latter south of the proposed line. They all might as well be called outside of the line, for a road along the valley of the East Fork, where we saw so many bands of elk, would mean no boundary at all, and the killing would go on on both sides the same as if it all were open, because that is a region far from any patrol, and could only be patrolled by the use of a large body of men. The north line of the Park, nearest the settlements, now patrols itself, because it crosses a range too hard to get into, so rough, indeed, that no railroad could be built over it by any means on earth.

"You can see," said Billy, "just what this road would mean for the game. The antelope would all be killed or driven from the Gardiner Flats back into the higher mountains, where they could not live in winter, because they can't paw snow to any depth. The elk that now winter in the rough country along the Yellowstone, on Hell Roaring or Slough creeks, and along the East Fork and the streams coming in on the northeast, would all be killed or run out. The elk have to come in here to winter, because the country is bare. It is not 'hot country' to any extent, but it is struck by the wind along the ridges, and so has bare places where the elk can get to the feed. There is a good deal of snow on it, but the snow doesn't lie all over like a deep blanket, the way it does in the upper Park. As it is the elk are dying all through the mountains in hundreds this winter. If you drove all these elk out of this country where they are wintering, they would have to go out of the Park or out of the game, for if they had to go back into the big snow country, they would starve to death.

"They can say all they please about the Cooke City road not hurting the game of the Park, and that there is nothing in that part of the Park, but that is all nonsense to anyone who knows anything about the facts. There is no one thing that could be done to hurt the antelope and elk of the Park so much as to build that road. The worst of it is, too, that the slice taken off would be practically twice or three times as big as it measured, for there would practically be no north line any more."

ARE MORE FACTS NEEDED?

If the above facts, as stated in offset to the intemperate utterances of the Cooke City factionists quoted last week, are not enough to convince any one of the inadvisability and the uselessness, if not the impracticability of the proposed segregation road, then FOREST AND STREAM will give more facts and more reasons. Forest and Stream will not "change its policy" on this matter, and it never will quit the fight until it has won an unquestioned victory there as it has in its other measures for the betterment or the preservation of the National Park for the people of the world. In this fight it has been alone in the newspaper world. It has spent money and taken chances to get at its facts, but it got them and has them, and can use them and will use them. The Park police bill just signed by the President of the United States and so made a law is, as one must verily believe, the result of no one cause so much as the unfaltering work of this one newspaper. The segregation scheme is the next thing. It is probably dead to-day. If it isn't will it kindly wiggle its head?

The Dead Buffalo Find.

Later.—Under date of May 8 Capt. Anderson writes:

"Burgess very carefully investigated your eight dead buffalo in Hayden Valley, and found four of them were really carcasses, while the other four were pieces of the former that had been dragged off to some distance by wild animals."

This is twice as good as we feared. We had no means of digging down to the carcasses. The strangest part of it, however, is brought up by Billy Hofer's letter to me of May 9, in which he writes: "Burgess says none of the scalps or hides had been taken, and thinks the buffalo died there, but that's too thin, for four buffalo would not have died a natural death at that time of the year and all so close together and at the same time."

Either the poacher was scared away too soon or else the buffalo were killed in wantonness. The new Park police bill will prove useful.

THE STORY OF THE TRIP.

CHICAGO, Ill., May 24.—When the FOREST AND STREAM man stepped off from the train at Cinnabar there was an eager and a nipping air coming down off Electric Peak,[30] a slick-looking young U. S. lieutenant coming up the platform, an ambulance with four gray and woolly Army mules coming up the street, and Billy Hofer coming up into the car. All of which made a good environment. In about two minutes, after I had become well acquainted with Lieut. Lindsley, we all went over and got something to eat, and then started for the Post, the ambulance being filled with eggs, cabbage, oranges, side meat and other *delicatessen* beside Billy and myself, who were both good things: Lieut. Lindsley, upon whom devolves the commissary work of Ft. Yellowstone, followed later in a buckboard and a buffalo coat.

The first thing curious I noticed was the belt worn by the driver who negotiated the four woolly mules. He wore one of the U. S. blanket-and-canvas storm coats, better than a buffalo coat, which was girt close about him by this most formidable belt—an affair made of sole leather, over a foot wide, and fastened with three or four smaller straps and buckles at the ends. In place, this belt covered the whole body closely from the hips more than half way to the shoulders, and kept all air from flowing up under the clothing, as well as protecting the vitals by an impervious shield. When the driver threw this belt on the platform in front of the post office at Gardiner it sounded as if he had dropped a keg of nails. He took off his belt there so that be could drink something, I believe, it being too tight for that purpose when in place. The driver told me that the stage coach drivers and others exposed to the severe winter weather of the mountains could hardly endure the exposure without these big belts, which made them warmer than anything else they could wear—"a heap warmer than any overcoat," he said.

WILD GAME.

An army ambulance is built for utility and not for fun. The windows are cut so low at the top that you can't get much good out of the landscape, if the latter stands on edge, as it does in this country. I nearly broke my neck trying to see the top of the mountains, and had to sit flat down on the floor while I was trying to see the antelope Billy was pointing out to me as we crossed the Gardiner Flats and went fairly into the great National Park. There the antelope were,[31] sure enough, with their white harness hard to make out against the white background, though Billy's more practiced eye picked out group after group, while my big game eyes were getting their first practice after a long rest.

Beyond the flats, we began the steady climb up the Gardiner[32] to the Post, the wheels crunching through snow in places apparently four feet deep. The river on our right came tearing and boiling down, a lovely stream. We saw some mallards contentedly swimming in a quiet part of the stream and they did not fly, though we passed within 20yds. of them. The little purple water ousels were flying up and down the roughest parts of the water, at home in the turmoil, and singing sweetly and shrilly, apparently content in their wintry and forbidding home. We also saw a bluebird, away up there in the snow, and it did not seem unhappy or alarmed by the mountains and the snows. In fact, even so early, one could see that in this enchanted land summer and winter go hand in hand the year round. The ice and snow are in spots parted by warm streams or broken up by large areas of warm ground. Nowhere in the great snow country can game winter as it can here, and for this reason the wonderful region should be forever preserved. Thus presently we came to the "Boiling River," pouring its hot flood out of the rocks into the Gardiner River, and near here we saw still more of the waterfowl and birds which winter in this part of the Park. If our cameras had been ready we could have photographed wild mallards.

The driver had that morning seen three mountain sheep (bighorns) on the rocks near the Eagle's Nest,[33] the big ledge overhanging the road which will be remembered by all Park tourists, and we hoped that we should be fortunate enough to get sight of them, but it seems that they had taken fright at a dog which accompanied one of the teams. They are very often seen near the road, and are very fearless and tame. This is within three miles of the Park line, I believe. So much for summer-in-winter, and for protection of the game. The game knows the country and it takes it but a very short time to learn of the protection. There is no known place on earth now, outside of the Park, where one may approach within 80yds. of wild bighorns without their taking fright on seeing one.

THE VESTIBULE OF WONDERLAND.

A bruising pull through the deep snow of the last hill, and we came out on the parade ground of the Post, the little flat valley nature has arranged as the vestibule for her house of wonders. The big Mammoth Hot Springs hotel, untenanted except by Manager Deane and his wife, stood opposite, and at the right were the "new quarters" of the Post. Beyond, Liberty Cap and the Minerva Terrace, the latter steaming in the cold air that circled every wondrous cauldron. Around, the mountains shouldered in closely, all white and shivery looking. Still beyond, valley and cañon and crag crowded together, unwilling to give entrance even to an eye, and apparently grudging even the scantiest knowledge of the treasures they had in keeping from the hand that made it all. Mount Everts's gray unshapely front, the hills back of the Terrace, the cañon of the Gardiner winding beyond the Post meadows, the peaks that flank the upper flats and edge the Golden Gate, all these many have seen brown and gray and black and green in the summer, but who has seen them white and solemn in the depth of the mountain winter time? Only a few. This and the sights beyond—the winter landscape of this wild tremendous region—the panorama of the Wonderland when wrapped in its robes of snow—to see that, to intrude upon the brooding mountains when they rest and plan their mysteries—where is a greater privilege accorded any traveler? It is the journey of a lifetime. What wonder that one thrilled even at the anticipation!

And now Capt. Anderson, commanding officer of the Post and superintendent of the Park, met us as we topped the hill where the "old quarters" lie, hauled us forth from the ambulance and took possession of the FOREST AND STREAM man forthwith as being a suspicious character. As I had supposed the programme was to sleep out in the snow every night after crossing the Park line, I was able to stand this for a few days. The Captain's cook is notoriously the best in the Army. As for the Captain himself, you would better get acquainted with him yourself.

At Capt. Anderson's pleasant quarters I remained from Saturday, March 10, till Wednesday, March 14, preparing for the trip into the mountains, and learning about the Park, its game, its system of patrol, the pleasant and the harassing nature of some of the duties connected with its supervision. I could learn something of this, something of the difficulties of the work, something of the inadequacies of the equipment to the task, but never until I was actually into the wilderness and had seen the terrors of that winter reign, could I realize the magnitude of the task asked at the hands of this handful of devoted and hard-working troopers. Under the old regime this was a task almost too hard and too thankless to ask of any men; yet from officer to private I can say I never heard a murmur of complaint, and among privates as well as officers there seemed to exist a singular enthusiasm for the arduous and sometimes almost unmilitary labors asked of them in their duty of protecting the Park. Now, thank Providence, there is a better law, and the "snowshoe cavalry," as some of the *ski*-running troopers call themselves, will not have only their labor for their pains.

The Yellowstone is a two-company post, and is probably one of the busiest of the mountain posts in the winter. It has an unusually large number of good snowshoers in its force, due to the scouting trips of earlier years and the *ski* practice which officers encourage as so useful in this mountain work. Even the children wear *skis* at Ft. Yellowstone, and it is no rare sight to see four or five little pairs of *skis* on the front stoop of a house. Most of the officers know a bit about *ski* running, and at the time I arrived at the Post two of them, Capt. Scott and Lieut. Forsythe, were absent with the Haynes photographic expedition, of which I shall write later.

PHOTOGRAPHING ANTELOPE.

Capt. Anderson has a most pleasant family of young officers with him—besides those above named, Post Surgeon Gandy, and Lieutenants Daniels, Nance and Lindsley. The terms army officer and sportsman are synonymous, and in the case of Dr. Gandy we found that a love for amateur photography was also included.[34] The result of this was that Dr. Gandy, Billy Hofer and I went out on a photographic still-hunt for antelope on the Gardiner Flats the first clear day we got. We found the antelope abundantly enough and obligingly tame, but the wind was so high we had trouble to get good pictures. Dr. Gandy often set up his tripod deliberately within good range of the beautiful creatures, and took shot after shot while I lay on the ground and tried to hold steady the vibrating legs of the machine, but we got only one picture of any value. Billy had a long range special outfit, and had some beautiful shots at antelope standing, marching, trotting and running, but the Smithsonian Institution, to whom he sent the negatives for development, has calmly absorbed them and made no sign so far as I know.

We saw, probably, the entire band of the Park herd of antelope, about 400. Often they crossed in little bunches not 75yds. in front of us, and we had a unique and valuable opportunity of studying them. There was one old leader, a buck, which was a distinct trotter and rarely broke his long-reaching trotting stride, although the entire band behind him were on the run. I will back this trotting antelope against any other trotting antelope on earth, and it's a "moral" for the Gardiner Flats beast.

This was the beginning of the spectacle of the great game in the Park, a fraction of what we were to see. Every day we heard of the sheep down by Eagle Nest, and every day that I was at the Post, without exception, we saw a band of elk on the high bare ridge back of Minerva Terrace. These Capt. Anderson calls his "pets," and daily he watches them from his window as he sits and reads.[35] Often they come lower down, and once he saw forty elk just back of Lieut. Lindsley's quarters. Sometime, too, a herd of blacktail deer will come down the hill almost into the Post limits. The Post is located at a comparatively low altitude, and the snow does not lie so deep there as in the upper Park. Once we had a Chinook, and under the breath of that mysterious wind the snow settled and fled in the most surprising manner. This was in early March. We had purposely postponed our trip till March, as by that time the snow has become less fluffy and more solid, therefore better for snowshoeing. Let no one suppose that March means spring in the Park. The snow envelops everything there till June. While we lay at the Post it snowed almost every day. A drift 12ft. high lay along the walk in front of the officers' quarters. Around the great springs of the Minerva Terrace the white garment of winter was apparently 6 to 10ft. high, and in drifts we could only guess how deep.

WARNINGS.

Or course it is hard for the summer tourist to realize the difference between the Park in summer and the Park in winter. In the summer one rides through the Park in comparative ease. In the winter one cannot even walk. No friendly pack horse can lighten one's load, and if he is tired he cannot swing into the saddle or loll upon a wagon scat. Every inch of the way must be traveled on the snowshoes, and when a man's own muscles cease to work he ceases to advance. There is no way of lightening or evading the labor, and emphatically it is every man for himself. These things were pointed out to me by friends. Before I left Chicago one friend almost besought me never to go into the Park in the winter, as he had once been caught by a snowstorm there and hardly got out alive. As I approached the Park these warnings became more frequent and more ominous. At Livingston guides and old-timers shook their heads, and civil engineers advised me not to go in. At Gardiner, as I learned later, bets were freely offered that our party would get no further in than the Swan Lake flats, beyond the Golden Gate. Even at the Post there were not wanting those who said quietly, "I do not envy you the trip." Here, then, one was placed against the first edge of the enterprise, and began to realize something of the quality of the work ahead.

THE OUTFIT.

Billy and I had brought in both the Canadian web shoes and the Norwegian *skis*, also a toboggan. We thought at first of using the web shoes and pulling the toboggan, but Billy later decided very wisely that it was better to stick to the *skis*, almost universally used in the Rockies, and to leave the toboggan behind, carrying everything on our backs in packs. The wisdom of this arrangement was most obvious later on. The Haynes photographing party started with a toboggan, but abandoned it at the Cañon. They learned that it took the whole party to get the flat-bottomed thing along. It is next to impossible to pull any weight behind the *ski*, and if one wears webs, and so gets traction power, he can not take the long runs down hill by which so much of the time is made in *ski* running. All the mountain men seem to unite in condemning the web or Indian shoe for this mountain work. They say the *ski* is far easier and faster.

For clothing, Billy's advice was followed implicitly. We wore heavy wool underwear, wool trousers, canvas overalls and canvas leggings. The underwear was supplemented by a lighter wool undershirt, over which a blue flannel shirt was worn. A canvas vest came on top of that, but no coat or overcoat was worn. Of course the latter would have been an impossibility, and the coat was replaced by a light canvas "jumper."

"You've got to have canvas to break off the wind," said Billy, "and to shed the snow, and you've got to have plenty of wool underneath to keep you warm. You'll find that you won't want much on while you're traveling, but when you stop you get cold mighty quick."

This I found to be true. Indeed, I discarded my fine heavy wool overshirt, made like a fireman's shirt, on which I had rather prided myself. I found it too warm to wear while shoeing, even in the coldest weather. When I came out from the trip, indeed, I was wearing only one suit of underwear and a light cotton drilling shirt, under my canvas waistcoat and jumper. While on the trail, even these upper garments would be worn open, though often the thermometer was below zero. In shoeing over the mountains one uses every muscle of his body at such intense pitch that he gets all in a glow of heat. To avoid the chilling out when we stopped, I carried in my pocket my elegant fireman's shirt and a heavy sweater, which I slipped on at once when we paused even for a little while.

By Billy's wise advice, we wore wide felt hats of the Western type. These were better than caps, as they kept the snow from getting down the neck. In extremely cold weather we tied up the ears with a large silk handkerchief.

Of course we wore belts, for a belt is warm as a coat. We carried no weapons except a straight-bladed butcher knife apiece, for we were not hunting and needed to trim down every ounce possible in order to succeed in our mission. On our hands we wore soft castor gloves,[36] unless the weather was very sharp, when we slipped on over the gloves heavy calf mittens, fleece lined. In travel, the gloves, mittens and handkerchief, with maybe a strip of burlaps for strings, would be often tucked into the belt when not in use elsewhere, and Billy always wore his tin cup at his belt. When Billy got into full regalia, big camera and all, he made a wild sight, and I often teased him to stop and let me photograph him, though he always objected, and I fairly had to do that by stealth.

The Importance of Feet.

The feet are the main thing to be cared for in snowshoeing, for they are ground deep in the snow all day long, and in a climate where the thermometer sometimes drops to 45° below zero it is not hard to freeze the feet. The snowshoer keeps his feet carefully clean, washing them in cold water sometimes. He may wear wool socks, common broad shoes, and overshoes, surmounting the whole with canvas leggins[37]—Billy always preferred the buckled leggins, as easier to handle when full of ice and snow—or he may use the heavy "German sock" (a felted wool sock nearly half an inch thick), which is drawn on over the light sock, and then surmounted by an […] Arctic overshoes. If the German sock is warm, no leggins are required, the trousers being tucked into the sock, which is drawn tight about the calf of the leg by a string. The sock sheds snow very well, and is soft and easy to the foot. Nearly all the shoers about the Post prefer the sock overshoes. Billy insists that the leggin keeps the foot in better order. It is almost impossible to keep the feet dry anywhere, for the snow water will grind through the best Artic overshoe in a few days. Lieut. Forsythe found that if he wore a light pair of calf shoes inside his German sock he was more comfortable and had better control of his shoes. For myself, I disobeyed Billy's orders, threw away the shoes which had begun to give me a sore heel, and from that time on used the following outfit for my feet, which I found warm and comfortable: First I wore natural wool socks, light, then a pair of Indian moccasins, then a pair of heavy gray army socks, then the Arctic overshoes and leggins, the latter of the army cut, and very good as I found. A sportive dog carried off my buckled leggings at the Post, and lost them in the snow.

Two pairs of colored glasses were taken along by each man, the bows being carefully wound with silk to prevent freezing the face where the steel touched. Without these glasses the glare of the snow would soon render one snow-blind.

A last item in our equipment was a wide canvas patch cemented on the front of our overshoes, where the toe strap of the *ski* passed over, used to prevent the chafing of the strap on the shoe, which is quite severe. A pair of Arctic shoes lasts only a few days in active shoeing.

We each took along an extra pair. We used heavy, double-buckled, high overshoes, not so heavy as the cavalry shoe, but heavier than the ordinary street overshoe.

This was our outfit as to dress, the result of experience and not of theory. I mention it in detail because, though we found it amply comfortable and excellently adapted for the needs of the trip, it seems ridiculously light for work almost Arctic in its nature at times. It should be borne in mind that ours was a walking and not a riding trip. Furs and heavy wools we could not use, because we could not carry them. Schwatka's outfit fell to pieces because it was too heavy. Every ounce was figured on by our party. Yet light as we started we came back lighter yet at the end of the 200 miles, and at the close of our most eventful and most delightful trip.

What we carried and how we carried it, and how we engaged in combat with the fiery untamed *ski* in the early stages of the trip, will do to speak about the next time.

[THE STORY OF THE TRIP. PART 2.]

CHICAGO, May 30.—In the first article of this series I made the statement that no one except Mr. Hofer had ever made the winter trip through the Park and written a newspaper account of it. Mr. F. Jay Haynes, the well-known St. Paul photographer, who has long been official artist for the Northern Pacific Road, and who has done so much to set forth the beauties of the Park in a pictorial way, calls my attention to the fact that the story of his winter trip, mentioned in my first article, was written by himself and printed in a Chicago paper, *Harper's Weekly* also running full illustrations of it. This I did not know. Mr. Haynes adds that he took with him four men of the unfortunate Schwatka party, and made the circuit of the Park, regardless of trails, and passing over Mount Washburn, as I stated. It was on Mount Washburn that this party were caught in a storm and nearly lost their lives. On that trip Mr. Haynes did not try for any game pictures, but this winter, as I stated last week, he went into the Park again after game pictures, and I hope to show the readers of FOREST AND STREAM some of the beautiful results of his skillful camera later on in this story, Mr. Haynes himself being pleased exceedingly with the results in this magnificent and novel field of winter photography—into which I believe the FOREST AND STREAM cameras were the only other ones ever to go. We met the Haynes party at the Cañon very pleasantly as I shall later mention.

Short-Tailed Coats Better.

The Schwatka expedition, as is well known, was sent out by the New York *World,* and it made a magnificent and elaborate failure. Schwatka had along enough baggage to supply an army. He had long-tailed reindeer coats, plenty of furs, sledges, etc., and in short was equipped for an Arctic trip. Unfortunately one cannot sit in a sledge and be hauled by dog team through the Park, because the snow is too soft and it snows too much and too often there, and the hills are too high and steep. The only way to go is by one's own muscle. Schwatka got his big party and all his lumber into the Park just 20 miles, and then he found he had enough of it, and so marched down the hill again. The Forest and Stream outfit, the first and only staff party ever to go through the Park in winter, did not wear long-tailed reindeer coats. They only wore short-tailed canvas jumpers, but they got there just the same.

The Introduction to Ski-Going.

One thing is certain; at the time of which I was writing last week I had never been through the Park in my life. Another thing is certain, and that is that I had never been on *skis** in my life. [Note in the original: * Pronounced *skee*.] Therefore two startling experiences in my life remained ahead of me.

Billy took me out where the snow was about 11 ft. deep and introduced me to a pair of long, low, rakish, piratical-looking things, with a good deal of overhang forward, and—as I learned later—without any centerboard, keel or moral principles anywhere in their composition. You can talk about a vessel being a "thing of life," and "instinct with soul," and all that sort of thing, but she isn't in it with the lowly *ski,* not for a minute. A pair of *skis* make about the liveliest way of locomotion, if you give them a chance, of anything on earth, and if you don't think they are alive and full of soul, you just try them and see. They've got a howling, malignant devil in every inch of their slippery surface, and the combination will give the most blasé and motionless man on earth a thrill a minute for a good many minutes. You don't want to go in for the sport of *ski*-running, not on a hill, anyhow, unless you want to be carried away with it.

Billy started me in on a hill, and I was quite carried away. They dug me out of the snow, somewhere down along the hill, I don't remember just where, and we started back up again, to do it some more. It was then I discovered that a *ski* is like a poor rule, because it won't work both ways. My *skis* had been bright and cheerful when it was suggested that we go down hill, but when we talked about going up hill they became ugly and rebellious. They would slip backward down hill, but wouldn't go up. I began to reflect then that I had 200 miles ahead of me, every inch of it up hill according to accounts, and I was thoughtful.

"Slap your shoe down hard on the snow," said Billy, "and take up all the weight you can with your pole. Lean forward, and don't lift your heel."

Billy is one of the best snowshoers in the mountains, having learned the art while carrying mail for years among the mining camps of Colorado. Moreover, Billy is a philosopher, and disposed to find out the theory of things. Moreover again, he is not disposed to excessive and untimely mirth on serious occasions like this. So, watching Billy, and trying to get close enough to smash him one with the pole if he got too gay, I found I could get up the hill a little by using industry and economy. Pretty soon we came to a steep pitch, which even Billy could not walk up.

"Here we have to 'corduroy,'" said he.[38] "You turn your shoes at right angles to the trail, this way, instead of straight along the way you want to go. That keeps you from slipping down hill. Now you side-step up the hill, lifting the shoe clear from the snow each time. You go right on up sideways, this way, one foot after [...] another, getting up only a foot or so at a step. Keep your shoes at an angle up the hill, just all the angle they will stand till they begin to slide back down hill, and keep on side-stepping up the hill, on the angle, this way, till you get to where the natural bite of the shoe on the snow will allow you to go straight ahead again. That's 'corduroying.' Some folks use clogs, which they buckle around their shoes. With a clog, you slap your foot down and go straight ahead. You can tie a knotted piece of gunny sack under the shoe and get the same result. It's a nuisance, though, to be stopping putting such things on and off all the time, at every little hill. You will find that the best *ski* runners don't use any clogs, but depend on 'corduroying' up the steep places. Some fellows can go straight up steep hills, without 'corduroying,' where other fellows can't. It's a good deal in the way the shoe is planted down on the snow, and left clinging there without breaking the hold till the other foot has been shoved forward. But any fellow has to corduroy sometimes, and his average in speed per hour depends on his ability to do it fast, without slipping, and without losing anything out of his uphill angle. You want to keep your shoes at just all the uphill angle they'll stand, and you want to side-step as high up hill as you can each time, and you don't want to lose any time slipping back, or plunging, or crossing your shoes, or trying to recover yourself. Just take it easy and regular. Time in snow-shoeing is made by keeping at it steadily, not stopping and not taking spurts."

All this was plain enough, and I got up the hill. I found, however, that the awkwardness of using the unskilled muscles required in the work, brought on a profuse perspiration, though it was a cold winter day. It was at the top of this hill that I found out I wasn't going to be able to wear my nice new fireman's shirt, because it was too warm.

"You'll find muscles in you you never dreamed of," said Billy, "and you'll find you don't need much clothing while you're on the trail."

Army Discipline.

Over the hill, I became exalted in spirit, for I had discovered that the way to do was not to lift the whole 10ft. of shoe off the snow, but to slide it along on the snow, letting it carry its own weight, and dragging it forward by the toe strap. I was going at a great gait, like a boy with a new pair of galluses,[39] right along in front of D company barracks, and rather glad a lot of blue-coated gladiators were out watching the tenderfoot learn to *ski*-go, when all at once I learned something more. I got my feet crossed, somehow, and right at the critical moment I went end over end in the snow, with the *skis* fairly braided around my neck in the most extraordinary and inexplicable fashion in the world. The *skis* got away the best of that fall. D company laughed long and hearty, as one man. A company always does that way, I suppose, owing to the army discipline, but I felt like trying to lick D company, while Billy was trying to untackle and unbraid me and get me dug out again.

It would seem easy to get up after falling in the snow, but let one try this in deep, soft snow, and he will find that his hand and arm sink deep down, but afford him no support when he tries to raise himself. He can get no bearing until he gets above his *skis*, which do not sink in the snow. He must therefore get his *skis* under him, somehow. That somehow is best understood after a wrestle or two in trying to get one's feet untangled and located once more intelligibly. Getting up from a fall in soft snow or a steep side hill is a very delicate operation.

National Pork.

Billy and I made our way up the mountain side where lies that marvelous geyser formation known as the Miner[va] Terrace. Earth has no mammoth hot spring to compare with this one, whose giant stairway now lay before us, and the year holds no time like that of midwinter to see it at its best. The graded pools rose one above another like jewels on a cloth of white.

The snow, yards deep, made a setting for each pool. Out of the pools the water sparkled, boiling hot, cut through the snow, melted the ice, bid defiance to winter. Evidently, nature's plans beneath the surface of the earth were at variance with those about it. The paradox was startling. Billy and I crawled on our *skis* close along the edge of the giant pools, crossed some of the rocks on foot where it was too hot for the snow to lie, and at length, bracing ourselves from slipping into the hot bath, we stood over 10ft. of snow on a rock which overlooked the ultimate pool, whose blue, scalding flood pours up eternally through an unfathomable crevice in the mountain side. Around us swept the incomparable panorama of the snow-clad hills. Surely the scene was an impressive one and one such as should win forgiveness for a brief feeling of emotion and of sentiment.

I know a fellow oughtn't to "spill over," and oughtn't to "make a scene," because it isn't good form. Yet I hope I should be forgiven for the thought which came to me as I gazed into that ceaseless fountain of red hot water which flows forever, day and night, summer and winter. What a place for Mr. Armour![40] What a place for scalding hogs!

I commend this thought to those who wish to cut apart the Park, who wish to put railroads through it, who wish to ruin and make common its wonders. It has been suggested that a railroad through the Park would be a useful thing to some few men who wish to carry freight. I believe it has not yet been brought to their minds that the hot springs might be made useful in scalding hogs. By all means let us do away with horses and vehicles in the Park. Let us make the trip in two days. Let us have an electrical railroad, and a grand national pork concern, thus utilizing the hot water nature has evidently provided with the design of scalding hogs. Niagara is harnessed. Why not the Park? National Pork! There is a music in the sound, a similitude in the form, and a close fit in the thought behind the form. It will do for a label. By all means let us have in the railroads at once. And over the gate which lets them in let us have the fitting announcement and the fitting epitaph for the desecrated wonderland—National Pork! Would Congress then know the difference in the sign, and would it then realize what the design of this last instance of national porkism had been from first to last?

BILLY HAS SOME FUN.

"Come," said Billy, "and I will have some fun with you."

He did, he did, and let no man say to the contrary. He took me through the heavy pines up to the top of a steep rise above the terrace, and politely requested me to follow my leader, saying which, he let go and slid off down the hill like a bird, calling back to me to "keep my feet together and put on brakes with the pole." This I did as nearly as I could, and in a moment, with an ease and precision which pleased us both, I also was at the foot of the hill, but upside down, with the *skis* on top.

"We'll try another one." said Billy, who wasn't near as much discouraged as I was. "There's a pretty swift little pitch over here a way, and you can ride your pole down there."

"Riding the pole" I learned to be sitting astride of it, with the rear end of the pole dropping deep in the snow behind and thus serving as a brake. I was rejoiced to see by this means I could regulate the speed a little bit, so that I didn't feel so much as if I was going to get off the earth. Billy was pleased to be flattering when he saw that I was on top of the *skis* at the bottom of the hill, instead of their being on top of me.

"Now we'll take one steeper yet," said he. "I'll show you the way to do where it's too steep to stand up. Come ahead."

Billy stopped at the head of a sharp little pitch, which was so steep that we couldn't see to the bottom of it. All we could see was a rounded curve of white dropping down, apparently off into the blue substance which the poets call æther. Here Billy unbuckled the straps of his shoes, took the shoes off, put them together, pointed them down hill, and sat down on the middle of the two, on top of the shoe-straps. Then he gave a push or so with his hands, started, gathered speed, and whish! he was over into the unknown, apparently sliding on the seat of his overalls.

As I knew of no way of getting out of there except by doing the way Billy did, I also took off my shoes and sat down on them, putting them carefully in the tracks left by Billy's. I was looking thoughtfully at the carved dragon heads on the ends of my *skis,* and wondering how far off the end of that hill was, when all at once the malignant creatures took a slip and a start and away I went. There was an astonishing slipping past of trees stuck on a broad ribbon of snow, then a feeling of keen exhilaration at the smooth, even flight through the air; then came a second of still more winged flight, clear out into the air, and a smother of something white and soft. The dragon-headed *skis* and the eagle-eyed newspaper man had gone clear over a 30ft. bank of snow, and buried themselves in the soft drift at its base. I had taken my first *ski*-jump, and taken it sitting down, at the take-off and the landing.

"It was steeper than I thought," said Billy, when he could undouble himself from laughing, "and the fact is, I did just what you did. I had to hurry to get out of the drift, or you'd have lit right on top of me.

"Now you've seen the gaits," continued he, "and you see how it's done. The rest you'll have to learn from practice. We'll go home now, for you don't want to get too tired at first."

The next day, thanks to a muscular system already in pretty fair order from the training I had gone into preparatory for the trip, I was not so very stiff, though I found the new muscles Billy had prophesied, more especially some north of my knees. The dreadful mal de raquette of which I had read in books, I never felt at all.[41] That day we took a rather slow run down the hill to the Boiling River a mile or so, the snow being sticky. This concluded my entire experience on the *skis* before we started on our journey, less than half a day in all. I remember that I thought it a great feat to get down the Boiling River hill.

When I saw the same hill, on coming out of the Park after the trip, it seemed a very innocent and tame affair.

MAKING UP THE PACKS FOR THE START.

Wednesday morning, that of our start, dawned bright and fair enough. The two privates, Larsen and Holte, detailed by Capt. Anderson to accompany us, reported in due season, and Billy, as chief pack master, was early busy in arranging the packs we were to carry. Larsen and Holte took absolutely no blankets, saying they would rather not carry them. Billy took only one blanket, and generously insisted on my taking his light sleeping bag, made of wildcat skins, and weighing only about 6lbs. We had also a light canvas lodge-lining, about 6ft. by 15ft. Billy's camera, the special long-range outfit made for him by the Smithsonian Institution, weighed 25½lbs. without the plate holders, and made all the load Billy could carry. The holders, plates, rolls of films, ruby lantern, etc., which belonged with this camera, made a goodly part of the other packs. My camera, weighing about 10½lbs, made a good basis for a third pack. We had a light and very excellent camp axe. The men carried their army revolvers. They had in their packs extra socks, and also the warm muskrat skin caps issued by the army, which latter they rarely wore. Billy and I had extra underwear and plenty of socks, of course, and each had a heavy woolen shirt extra, to which I added a sweater. We carried each an extra pair of overshoes, and we were careful to have each an extra pair of colored goggles, an important precaution, for to be without some protection for the eyes in that snowy glare, is to practically go blind. I had along a pair of moccasins in my pack—which I am most thankful I carried in spite of Billy's injunction to cut down weight. Billy had a few screws, in case of a broken *ski,* I had a needle and thread, and we had plenty of wax for the shoes. Of course we had plenty of good matches. We carried lunch enough for two meals, intending to make the soldiers' quarters at Norris Basin, 20 miles out, and to replenish there.

We had some tea, the very best we could buy; Billy said we must not drink coffee, but tea, as tea was "better to work on." In this the miners and lumbermen nearly all agree with him, but I am such a coffee drinker myself that I became mutinous after the first day out, and finished the trip on coffee. We had two of the army quart tin cups, the sole dishes or utensils that we carried. As I have said, Billy and I carried no weapon but our scabbard-knives. Item, the men had their tobacco. I put in my kit some such simple remedies as vaseline, quinine, etc., and we also carried a pint of brandy. This was all the spirits we took along, and we had about half of that when we got back, thus establishing a marked difference between our own and the Schwatka outfit.

The above, with a most scanty allowance of toilet articles, constituted all of our simple baggage, yet one will be surprised to learn that made up into four packs it made each pack weigh between 25 and 30lbs. Billy, one of the most experienced packers in the mountains, soon made up two solid, oblong packs for the soldier boys, adjusting them with soft whang leather carrying-straps.[42] Billy had a carrying harness—and an abominably stiff and awkward one, too—attached to his camera. Sometimes I carried that camera to give Billy a chance for his life, and I always wished the Smithsonian man who invented that harness had it around his neck. For myself, in spite of Billy's entreaties, I stuck to the Lake Superior pack bag, made in Duluth, which I had in long trips through the pine woods previously found so roomy and so easy to carry. This bag was made of heavy canvas, and weighed 3½lbs., but its straps, "tote" strap (the head strap by which alone Indians will carry a pack) and shoulder straps are put on this bag so understandingly that one can carry additional weight and not feel it as he would with ordinary straps. We found this bag handy for the loose small articles. Of course, being not new at packing, we carried our packs lying well down along the spine, so that shoulders and hips shared the weight. We found a breast strap, of leather or gunny sacking, passed across the front and pulling the shoulder straps a trifle together, made the carrying easier. For this I usually engaged my silk handkerchief. We all carried strips of gunny sacking at our belts. Billy had made two sets of snowshoe clogs. We carried these three miles and threw them away.

Off.

At 9 o'clock the last pack had been lashed, the last strap adjusted, the last grunt of protest uttered by the human pack train Billy was cinching up, and we were on our way up the first slopes of the great Golden Gate hill, beyond which lay the wonders and the trials of the wild region of the upper Park. The journey was on. Since I was a boy and used to lie awake all night before the days when my father was going to take me with him on a fishing trip or camp hunt, I can not remember ever to have felt so keen a thrill of curiosity and anticipation as I did then. In anticipation it was the trip of a lifetime, and in the realization it proved all and more than I had hoped.

Trials of the Narrow Pass.

The Golden Gate hill rises about 1,500ft. or so in three and a half miles, and it isn't so awfully particular how it does it, either. It is the terror of the soldiers and scouts who have to snowshoe in the Park, and is considered about the hardest climb in the Park. Certainly it constitutes a delightful place to break in a greenhorn on the *skis* with a 30lbs. pack on his back and a reputation for dignity to sustain.

The worst of it was the snow stuck to our shoes and made it hard going even on the places where we didn't want to slip back any. We paused at the end of the first half hour or so and scraped off our shoes. The day was cold, but we were all perspiring with the work.

"Put on your glasses," said Billy to me. "Your eyes aren't bigger than slits in a blanket already. Do you want to go blind? And stop eating that snow. Whatever you do, and no matter

Camp in Hayden Valley, near Mud Volcano patrol cabin; individuals are unidentified, but include soldiers and possibly Hough and Hofer.

how thirsty you get, you must not eat snow. If you get heated up and take one drink of cold water, that knocks you out worse than four hours of work. It weakens you right away. You must not drink between meals, and you mustn't eat snow."

This struck me as being hard luck, for just then I would rather have eaten snow than do anything, but I obeyed. We pushed on up the sharp grades the best we could, or rather the best I could, for of course the others could leave me as they liked. We let the two privates go ahead, with instructions to build a fire at the top of the hill, opposite the magnificent Cathedral Rock. They were joined further on by the detail sent out by Capt. Anderson to bring in the poacher Howell, who had just been caught—Sergt. Kellner and two privates, all good shoers. At last Billy and I made the last rise—I'm sure I don't know how—and in a moment more we were beside our little fire, melting snow to make tea. I drank about a quart of strong tea—and nearly met a Waterloo by doing it, for it made me sick. We ate also a bite of lunch, and fixed up our shoes, heating them scorching hot and then rubbing them quickly with wax. Billy showed me how, enjoining me by no means ever to allow a drop of water to fall on either surface of the *skis*, as it would freeze and cause the snow to stick to it. The theory of the *ski* is to slip over and through the snow without dragging any along. It is quite an art to learn all the tricks of *ski* work, and keeping the *skis* in order is one of the most important ones.

Travelers through the Park will remember the rock cut, the trestle and the bridge just below the entrance of the Golden Gate proper. Above the wall of rock rises straight up and on the left as one ascends the mountain side drops sheer off into the cañon which makes down below the Cathedral Rock. This is a pretty bit of road in summer. As we saw it there was no road at all, but a drift of snow filling the road 30ft. deep. We had to leave the road at a point above the trestle, take off our *skis* and make our way the best we could along the mountain side, climbing up steps cut in the snow to the point right at the last little bridge, under the rail of which we crawled. Then, after this ticklish piece of business was over, we put on the *skis*, pushed around the corner, ran up the last faint rise and lo! before us lay the wide and storm-swept plain of the Swan Lake Flats.

Big white mountains hemmed in this high plateau—Electric Peak, Sepulcher Peak, Joseph Peak, Quadrant Mountain, Antler Peak, Trilobite Point, Mount Holmes; all these could be seen standing sentry. White Mount Washburn, highest peak of the Park, could be seen far off in the wild central region of the Park.[43] We could even see over to the Yellowstone range toward Cooke City. Certainly it was a most impressive landscape and rendered not the less forbidding by the stalking pillars of snow which went in procession across the wind-swept plateau which made the near foreground.

A Friend in Need is a Friend Indeed.

Billy now told me that we had eight miles more to go before we could make the Crystal Springs "shack," the only practicable stopping place this side of Norris quarters.[44] It was so late, and the shoeing was so bad, that he had given up all hope of making Norris that night. He added that the eight miles was not so hard as the three miles we had just passed, and bade me be of good cheer. Larsen and Holte, whom we found to be excellent *ski* men, as befitted their Scandinavian ancestry, Billy advised to go ahead and turn in at the Crystal Springs, as we did not wish to hold them back. They hit off a swinging gait at this, and were soon mere specks on the other side of the flat. Billy could have kept up with them, of course, but remained with me, who equally of course could not go such a pace my first day on the *skis*.

If Billy had not stayed back with me, it is very probable I should never have gotten into camp that night or any other night. That he did so was only what he would in mountain honor consider himself bound to do, but none the less the fact that he did has always left a soft spot in my heart for Billy, and a feeling that if he were in a tight place I should like to stay with him in turn. Certainly he helped me through a tight enough place—about as bad an afternoon as 1 care to put in.

On the windy flats the snow was hard and made fair shoeing, and I plodded along behind Billy's shoes methodically enough, and did not really feel so very tired. At the Gardiner River,[45] however, four and a half miles still from the shack, I was taken desperately faint and sick, so that at length I fairly toppled over off my *skis*. I don't know what it was, unless the unusual exertion, combined with the unusual altitude, caused the stomach to resent the unusual dose of bitter tea I had given it. Anyhow, I got desperately weak, and pretty soon I didn't care a copper whether I went anywhere or not. Billy would not let me stop for more than a moment, however, knowing the effects of a chilling through. He fished out the brandy bottle and for almost the only time on the trip I drank a little of it—about a thimbleful was Billy's idea of a plenty. This braced me up a little, but for over an hour I was so weak, and moreover so dull and apathetic, that it seems to me I know how it must feel to be left on the trail. In my belief a fellow wouldn't care much about it, one way or another, if he got much further along than I was. Billy was anxious, I know, for the day was waning, and it had come on to snow most dismally. Worse still, the snow began to stick to the shoes when we entered the dense forest, and it was hard plugging for a man even at his best. We worried along over one little hill after another, not daring to stop long enough to build a fire and wax our shoes. Once in a while we would turn from the trail, tramp a hole down in the snow—which was 8ft. deep on the level here—and sit for a moment resting, with our packs leaning on the snow. Then we would cut a pine bough and rub the *skis* hard with the resinous tips and needles. This would help the shoes for a way, when perhaps we would cut off another bough, throw it on the snow and drag the *skis* across that to cut off the adhering snow, and "slick" the shoes a little. Billy would not let me sit down long at a time, but kept me moving; and at length toward evening I began to get stronger.

"It's only three-quarters of a mile further now," said Billy finally. "Can you make it?"

"Betcherlife, Billy," I said, making an awful bluff.

"Come on, then," he said, and so set out at a better pace. But it transpired that he had feared I could not go even that distance, for it was not a quarter of a mile further before he turned out to the left from the trail, into a deep thicket of pines that fringed a little stream.

"Brace up, old man," said he, "we're home now."

Home, Sweet Home.

And home it was, a very blessed one, this little shack of rough boards, buried roof deep in the snow which folded the whole forest in like a great white blanket. There was a blue wisp of smoke rising, and there were voices of welcome as we came in sight, and that is the most of home.

We learned that Kellner's party had been unable to make Norris quarters that day, owing to the stickiness of the shoeing, and it therefore became necessary for all seven of us to pass the night in the little shack, not over 9ft. square. This, however, we found not an unwelcome prospect. Everything in life is relative. For my part I threw myself down on a board somebody had propped up off the floor, and for over half an hour I knew nothing of what was going on. This might have been sleep, or it might have been sheer exhaustion. I heard somebody say, "That feller's purty tired." Then somebody gave me a warm sandwich with corned beef hash in it, and a tin cup of coffee. This combination saved my life, and pretty soon I got quite peart again. The boys cut a lot of boughs and put down on the floor, and brought in plenty of wood for the old cook stove which Uncle Sam had left in there against just such an emergency as this. Not one of the party but Billy and myself had a blanket, for the soldiers declare they would rather sit up by a fire all night than pack a blanket all day. Billy spread down his piece of canvas and his one blanket, insisting on my taking the sleeping bag, and so we all turned in the best we could, the soldier men squatting, lying or crouching about the stove as the taste and fancy of each dictated.

This ended my first day on the *skis*, and it served at least to teach me what a snowshoe trip through the Park meant, how serious a thing it might become and how impossible help would be in case of sickness or accident. When I lay down to sleep that night I had not the slightest idea that I would be able to travel the next day, for I thought I would be too stiff and sore. I never could understand what the trouble really was, nor how it was that I got over it so easily. Certain it is that the next morning I awoke rested and refreshed, stiff and a bit sore, of course, but only triflingly so by comparison. I got on my shoes all right, and from that time on clear through the trip I never did have any more trouble. I took coffee and corned beef hash in mine after that every time I got a chance, and attribute my later success to those remedies. That one first bruising day—it was a nightmare of a time—made the beginning and the end of the grief. After that the art of shoeing grew easier and easier every day, and the trip more and more delightful. But I have not yet forgotten how Billy stayed with me when I was disposed to lie down and join the golden choir.

The men who first reached the Swan Lake Flats that day saw four elk off to the right of the trail. No other game was seen. Billy and I noticed elk pawings in the snow on the hills north of the Golden Gate, but no very large band was indicated.

The thermometer went nearly to zero that night.

In the Heart of the Mountains.

LONG before the sun had dreamed of touching the top of even Mt. Washburn in the Park, let alone the rocky front of the Obsidian Cliff, which frowned down not far from our snow-bound camp, there was a general unbending and straightening out of the cramped forms in the little shack, and everyone busying himself preparing for the day's march. It was only a little after 3 o'clock in the morning when Sergt. Kellner and his party took the trail. Billy and our men were a little later, as we stopped to give the *skis* a scientific scorching and waxing. A new *ski* is like a new shoe, it needs breaking in. A scorching which leaves the surface browned or almost black seems to lay the grain of the wood. The coat of grease and wax heated in on this surface keeps the grain from being started by the snow, and gives that perfect slipperiness so much valued by the experts and so embarrassing to the greenhorn.

I left the camp ahead of our party, sometime before sun up. The trees were banked with snow, so that one could not see 20yds. into the forest. Where-ever one could get a look through at the mountains he saw only a white silence which repelled and did not greet. We were now in the heart of the mountains and the trip was on. There was a singular feeling of smallness and insignificance which came over one in such surroundings, yet I felt cheerful and happy in the fact that I was not so badly off physically as I had feared, but was refreshed fully by the night's sleep. Moreover, some advice from the boys had set me on better terms with the *skis*. The day before I had had my toe straps too tight, and had been walking with my heel on top of the heel strap. I now loosened up the thongs of the toe straps, put my heel square down into the heel straps and buckled the *ski* fast on. The bottom strap of the heel brace I cut off altogether, as it was too short for the big overshoes. Thus arranged, I found that my foot got a control over the *ski* it had not had before, and I was free of much muscular strain, while the foot worked with far greater ease in the straps.

BILLY'S TURN.

I plodded along alone in the trail of the Kellner party for a while, but not fast enough to keep ahead of Larsen and Holte, who raced on, anxious to get over the nine miles which we had set for the limit of the day's journey. Billy was last to come on, and by the time we joined forces we were some distance on the way. We then went ahead in company for a few miles. Billy was dull and loggy, and at about 9 o'clock he said he was feeling weak and faint. By that time we had run the "Brick Kiln Hill" and were over on the hot country near the "Devil's Frying-Pan,"[46] a couple of miles or so from Norris Basin. Here our shoes had begun to stick again, and we concluded to stop and wax up and make some tea for Billy, who was distressed a good deal, much as I had been the day before, only not so badly. I guyed him a little bit about its being his turn to give out, but after he had drunk about a pint of tea with a little brandy in it, he recovered from his faintness and was soon sassy as ever. We had trouble in getting any good wood here, as the axe was on ahead and the snow covered everything deeply, but Billy with his usual deftness managed to get a fire. We started the snow to melting in our teapot by sinking the latter in one of the little boiling springs near by. As it melted we put in more snow, a little at a time. On all the trip we had to melt snow to make tea or coffee, and we learned that if you crowd snow into your cup so high that it sticks up over the top, the water will taste smoky. The best way is to get a little water first in the cup and then add snow gradually.

WINTER SCENES.

There was a little open lake to the right of the trail here, and a lot of steaming, red hot little geyserettes which had no business to be out there in the snow. A broad strip of bare ground crossed the trail every once in a while, where the underground heat kept the surface too warm for the snow to lie. The melting of the heavy snow often created quite beautiful effects. Moreover, we found an energetic little "paint pot" or so along the trail, where boiling clays kept up an eternal complaint, and the big "Devil's Frying-Pan," with its endless sputtering and sizzling of gaseous hot water, served to make pause for a moment eyes already beginning to get used to the wonders of this unnaturally wonderful country.

AT THE SOLDIERS' STATION.

Private Lockhart, from the soldiers' station at Norris Basin,[47] joined Billy and me as we were finishing our way-side rest, and we went up to the station together, arriving at the soldiers' shack all in good shape. Here I put my feet into a bucket of ice water, much to the horror of Larsen, who thought that was inviting a cold. Yet I found that a short trot barefoot in the snow did not have that effect. We all ate like fiends, and created apprehension in Lockhart's mind, as his rations were running low. He had side meat, flour and canned tomatoes, and we thought that was good enough for anybody. The Norris Hotel was never rebuilt after burning down, and the only accommodation at the Norris Geyser Basin is a lunch house, which is closed in winter. The soldiers' quarters are not public, but we were taken in and given share and share alike. Lockhart was at that time alone. Two men are stationed here all winter, and there are also two horses, two cats and one dog. The horses have a barn, and rarely get more than a few yards away from it, except close along the banks of the Gibbon River, which rushes by near the shack. Between the barn and the house the snow was 6 or 8ft. deep, with drifts of twice that depth. The horses had trodden down a sort of yard, and seemed to be wintering well and to be full of spirit. The thermometer was 45° below here once this winter, but it was above zero when we were there, and in this spring-like air we all took off our heavy wear and unbuttoned our shirt fronts.

THE WINTER PATROL.

It was about the middle of the afternoon of our stop here that Burgess brought in his prisoner, Howell, as I have earlier described. Later on Capt. Scott and Lieut. Forsyth came in, and at 7 o'clock in the evening "Snowshoe Pete," the telephone lineman, who had been over the line in the upper Park, also came in, so that we had a houseful again. All reported soft snow and plenty of it, and very hard shoeing. The two officers were tired enough with their journey of twelve miles from the Cañon that day. Capt. Scott had a bad heel. Billy's heel was also badly blistered, and I had a bad place on my own heel. Here was where I threw away my shoes and took to the moccasins, which I never regretted. Billy stuck it out and got part of his original heel back to the Post at the end of the trip. Poor Burgess, with his frozen toe, was the worst off of the party. Pete, who had come in from the Fountain, had had nothing to eat but one sandwich for the past twenty-four hours. I did not hear anybody complain, and such little aches and pains seemed to be regarded very much as a matter of course, and as a necessary part of the business. My admiration for the U. S. Army and the Park patrol rose still higher. There are men out there who don't need any pomp, pride and circumstance, but who can put on a Mackinaw shirt and "plug" their twenty miles a day on the shoes when they want to. The American public doesn't know the first thing about the U. S. Army, and I imagine that most of the Army doesn't know anything about Ft. Yellowstone and its pleasant little winter service, trying to do what can't be done. I couldn't help thinking of the weary miles of tramping that had been done for this dirty, greasy specimen of humanity, Howell, who seemed so chirk[48] and sure of his early release at the Post. Down the trail, somewhere, were Kellner and his party, making their twenty-one miles that day to get the plunder this fellow had left behind him. Still another party was to follow to bring the stuff out. Here were the two officers and Burgess. The whole Park was full of men for the first time in its winter history, all on account of this fellow, who had been doing something which ought to bring him ten years in prison, but which would really net him only a few days in the guard house. Yet there was not a complaint, not a harsh word to the prisoner, only a quiet, dignified acceptance of duty as it came.

SKI LORE AND SNOW QUALITY.

The next morning Burgess left for the Post with Howell, accompanied by Pete. Capt. Scott and Lieut. Forsyth concluded to make two days of it, and camped that night at the Crystal Spring shack, where we had passed our first night out. The shoeing continued bad, continued falling of snow adding always to the great depth already fallen, and lying light and fluffy on top the settled body of snow. As we learned later, it took Burgess till dark to do the twenty miles in. "Snowshoe Pete," who is a very excellent shoer has really made this twenty miles in three hours and thirty-five minutes. Larsen has made it in four hours and twenty minutes. Sergt. Morrison has gone from the Fountain Hotel to the Mammoth Hot Springs, forty full miles, in half a night and a day. It all depends on the shoeing. To the inexperienced all snow would seem alike, but the expert *ski* runner knows that it is never the same two days in succession. If the weather is very slippery and not freezing, the shoes will slide and not stick. If the thermometer then drops to the point of freezing they will begin to "ball up" and stick horribly in the moist snow. In the morning when the snow is cold and dry the shoes slip nicely, but by 9 or 10 o'clock, when the sun begins to strike the snow, they will begin to clog up before the snow shows any sign of melting. In fresh-fallen snow the shoes do not stick, but sink down deep and make awful going. On the other hand, a very cold, dry, floury snow will stop the shoes like so much ashes. One of the most dangerous things to meet in running a hill is a strip of this fine, dry, drifted flour snow. One can not see it until into it, and it stops the shoes at once, and will give the best *ski* runner a tumble. Still another sort of snow is a crusted snow, and this may again be a stiff crust or a crust which now and then breaks down. The *ski*-goer realizes at once when he has struck a good day, though often he can not tell why the snow is so obliging, and on such a day he travels long and far as he can, resting when the going is bad. Sometimes he travels at night, as we did some of the time later on in our trip. When he hits a deep, light, soft and yet moist snow, with more of it coming, as we found it at Norris Basin that next morning, he looks wise, shakes his head and holes up for the day. We holed up, concluding to exercise only enough to take the soreness out of the muscles. This we did by a trip through the geyser basin, a mile or so distant from the shack.

Geyserland in Winter.

We first went over the east part of the basin, where the wide valley lies out, bare of snow and covered with steam. The rim of this valley as seen by the summer tourist is one of the hills covered with dark pines. As we saw it, it was all white with heavy snow. In many places, as at the outlet of the Great Growler Geyser,[49] the masses of snow assumed the most grotesque forms. Often we walked in among great clumps of snow, high as one's head, with our feet on the bare hot ground. Under each clump, hid deep from sight, was one of the boulders among which the summer tourist picks his way with ease.

The geysers were very accommodating to us, and kept up a great series of spectacular eruptions. The Constant, the Hurricane, and lots of big ones in this part of the basin kept in view nicely, and every way we looked there was a little hell of steam and boiling water on tap. At the edge of one of the smaller geysers we stood close enough to feel the thin rock heave and sink rhythmically beneath our feet. It was a strange, unreal scene about us, and one the world can hardly parallel. No wonder that we put a camera into active requisition.

The Growler Geyser, which lies at the top of a knoll above this east valley, at the side of the trail, is a rare and beautiful sight in winter. As we saw it, its crater was deep in a well of crystal-like snow and ice, out of which came a cloud of fleecy white steam. As the wind changed, it often whipped this obscure cloud away, and gave us a glimpse below our risky footing on the edge of the ice wall. The hot steam melts the snow it strikes. The wind changes, and the melted snow freezes while the steam is busy elsewhere, so all up and down for apparently 30ft. or more, we saw a ridged and wrinkled caisson of many-tinted ice. If you will stick a stick down into the snow and pull it out, you will on looking down into the hole see that the snow seems of a deep blue color. This icy case of the Growler has all that wonderful deep blue tint, but a hundred grades of it, dazzling, bewildering, evading. When we can photograph in colors and reproduce the colors, one may see this picture of a winter wonder, but until then one must take the winter trip to gain a notion of it even the most meager.

We left the Growler finally, passed the many mud pots and miniature hell spouts, till we reached the fathomlessly beautiful Emerald pool. Thence we descended a steep trail the hot water had made through the snow, and examined the mighty Monarch Geyser, which was fretting and fuming, but not making much of it. The Minute Man, and a lot more mud pots and pools of course came next, and the wrongly named "Blood Geyser," which Hayden called the Echina. In some of the little nooks of the hills back of the geysers we got wonderful effects from the snow masses, melted into all sorts of shapes by the heat of the geysers, and of these I got two beautiful photographs, which I prize very much.

The New Crater gave us an interesting exhibition of spurting hot spray, and we spent some time here. There had been an eruption of this geyser apparently about a month ago. It seems to have a habit of slamming out rocks and things to a distance of 30 to 250ft. At the edge of the hot ground around the main vent of this angry funnel there was a clean-cut drift of snow, in which it was easy to read the record of the geyser. Deep down under the surface was the layer of old snow, and above this came a stratum of mud, rocks, etc., which the Crater had spit out. Then snow had again fallen several feet in depth, and over all, not so very far beneath the top of the snow, had fallen a many-colored deposit of liquified clay, rock, and what not, which had apparently been thrown over a strip of country 200yds. across. This geyser is a corker when it gets down to business, and when it is having a busy day I would just as soon be somewhere else. It is liable to drop a chunk of rock about the size of a piano on a fellow, anywhere from 25 to 50yds., and disfigure him.

On top of a hill to your right as you return to the Gibbon River from the basin, is the Congress Geyser, so called because its new crater was formed at the time, three years ago, when a congress of geologists was visiting the Park. This open pool is without bottom apparently, and is of a gracious opaline hue, with indescribable blending tints of yellow, blue and pearl.

In the distance, on Schurz Mountain, we could see the gleam of the Monument Geyser basin, some miles distant, but we did not go over there, for we had more wonders than we could handle right at hand. I cannot, of course, attempt any actual description of this weird region, additionally wonderful and startling as it is under the disguising robe of winter, for the main purpose of these articles is different. I can only say that even those to whom the geysers are an old story in summer became enthusiastic over them in this winter aspect, and even Billy was eager to go over the entire basin again. To Billy, of course, much of our pleasure was due here, for he knows every geyser thoroughly, and is a most interesting and thorough and enthusiastic guide. If I had a friend wishing to make the Park trip, I should by all means advise him to get Billy to go along, for he knows the Park inch by inch, and even its scientific features and scientific history are not strange in the least to him, since he has been so much associated there with parties of scientists of all sorts. Billy could talk of rhyolite and algae and silicates in a way to make your head swim.

In walking over the geyser country we left our *skis*, and picked our way along the hot water streams which traversed the country so generally. Once in a while we had to plunge through snow waist deep to get from one geyser to another. Our feet were soaking wet in spite of our overshoes when we again mounted our *skis* and took the tidy run down hill to the soldiers' quarters by the Gibbon. We had done enough work among the geysers to earn a good night's sleep.

OFF FOR THE CANYON.

Those who visited the Hunter's Cabin at the World's Fair[50] probably saw Billy Hofer curled up on the settee, reading a novel describing the trials of the Lady Evalina,[51] or something of the sort, and thought he was plenty lazy. That is correct. All mountain men are lazy when at home. It is the delving lowlander who gets out before breakfast to plow com. But on the trail I found Billy an energetic and tireless commander-in-chief, always alert, but alert for all and not for himself alone. About 3 o'clock in the morning of the following day, about the time I was just fixed all right in among my blankets, Billy crawled out and began waxing up his *skis* for an early start. Our breakfast of bread, coffee and bacon was soon over, and we each made a sandwich for his lunch. We were to do the twelve miles to the

Cañon that day, and needed to make an early start, for the shoeing was found to be bad. The light was barely gray when Billy
and I pulled out, Larsen and Holte not starting for half an hour
or so later. I broke trail for a mile or so and found it hard work,
the shoes sinking down into the soft, light snow nearly a foot
at each step. Then Billy and I alternated for a time at breaking,
until at length Larsen and Holte came up and went ahead for
the rest of the day.

A Lunch in the Snow.

Even Larsen and Holte found it bruising work, and at 11
o'clock in the morning, after hours of choppy hill work, where
we could only average about two miles an hour, they turned out
of the trail and asked for coffee. Billy did not like to stop, but
we out-voted him, and so made a wayside camp. The snow was
so deep on all the level that we could not find bottom with the
snowshoe pole, but we got along all right with the fire. The little camp axe soon had a dead pine tree in lengths, and these we
corded crosswise on the trodden snow, making a platform on
which we built our fire. Around this, with our feet down in the
hole, we sat on the edge of the snow pit, with logs and boughs
to keep us from sinking. Our packs we threw off and left standing on our *skis*. Noticing how picturesque our little camp appeared, Billy backed out and made a shot at us with his big
camera, though the light was dim and the shadows very heavy.
In that section the pine timber was very dense, nearly all of
straight, slim trunks about 8in. in diameter. Over it all the snow
hung in great flakes and rolls, like strips of cotton batting. One
could not see into the woods for any distance. The silence was
simply oppressive. There was no sign of life except the track
of an occasional pine squirrel or of the big-footed "snowshoe
rabbit." Everywhere was whiteness and silence, the gravity and
dignity of nature, in which a jest seemed almost out of place.

BAD HILLS.

We had some hard hills to climb on this day's march, the first of these being the Cascade Hill, that winding, reckless eminence down which the Gibbon River leaps and plunges so beautifully summer or winter. At this hill we had the hardest sort of corduroying and a slide backward would have been dangerous. The snow was much higher than the rail on the roadside and from there it filled the entire cut with a great drift which slanted far up the mountain side to the left. We had to climb, and climb along a risky sidehill of snow, too, and the best of the shoers could not help distress at such labor. I waited till the others had gone on and took my time on this hill. Time and again I slipped and fell, and every time I went down I took more than ten seconds before I came up again. I learned that the only way to do was to lie still and rest when one got a tumble, and not to wallow and work too hard, or try to do it all at once. It may have been half an hour or three-quarters before I got to the top of this hill, and I was mighty glad when I got to where I could see over.

"Is this the worst hill we've got to-day?" I asked Billy with what little breath I had left.

"Well," said he dubiously, "the Blandon hill is longer.[52] It's about a mile climb up the Blandon."

Of course this made me feel real good, but when we actually came to the Blandon hill I found I was worse scared than hurt. Larsen and Holte walked right up it, on end, only corduroying in a few of the steepest pitches. Billy told me to put on clogs here, so I tied a good knot of gunnysacking under each shoe and went ahead. To my delight I found I could go right up the hill, and raising my toe high and slapping the *skis* down hard I made great time and caught the two privates resting at the top. They complimented me on my increased skill and pulled on out as soon as Billy came in sight. Billy was having a hard time with his heavy camera and complained of a coal of fire between his shoulders. We took off the head-strap of my Lake Superior pack bag and arranged it so he could ease his shoulders by passing the strap across his forehead. Which reminds me, now that I think of it, that Billy has got that head-strap yet, and I wish he would send it back, as it is part of the combination of my pack bag and worth more than all of his old camera, as I will later show. Billy and I rested a moment at the hot country, eight miles from Norris, but we did not drink at the stream where we saw the others had stopped to drink. Billy warned me again that to take a drink of cold water was the most weakening thing I could do on the trail. He said also that men who drank liquor on the trail always paid for it with an early exhaustion. We did not touch our brandy supply that day, nor for many days afterward, and neither of us suffered from exhaustion to any extent. I had lightened my pack by leaving some under-clothing and other articles at Norris Basin and was now rapidly hardening up and getting into the work, so that I got along all right.

"We haven't very far to go now," said Billy as we paused at the top of a long and winding hill. "At the bottom of this hill is Cascade Creek,[53] and beyond that we have to climb the Cañon hill, about a mile, then we're there. You go on ahead down this hill, and I'll come after you, so that if anything happens to you I won't have to come back up the hill. It's pretty steep."

Of course, this made me feel real cheerful, but there was only one thing to do. My spine sort of crept a little, but I turned loose, and away we went on a lovely, swimming, sliding, sailing flight down the winding mountain trail, which was indescribably exhilarating, and like most dreaded things, not so bad after all when you go ahead into them. I disappointed Billy by not even getting a fall, though this hill is not really a bad one.

The Flowers that Bloom in the Spring.

Billy noticed that the boys ahead of us had not followed the usual trail down to the bridge, but had taken a short cut through the woods. We followed their trail foolishly enough, as it proved, for it took but a few moments to see that they had had no idea what they were going into. Their trail led across a series of ravines and steep, choppy side hills, covered with dense timber. We could see where they had fallen time after time, and where they had taken some risky slides. It was finely reckless *ski* running of them to turn loose through such a country, but it was poor judgment, and we found it poor judgment to follow them. It was an awful bit of travel, and we had a rough time of it, hanging on to the side of the mountain and trying to keep from toppling over, or from smashing into the trees on some of the sharp little runs.

It was here that I met with what might have been a very serious accident, possibly one that would end the trip at once unfortunately. I was trying to get around a jutting bit of rock on the mountain side, when my pack struck a tree and I got a fall, sitting down hard and swift on the snow. My *ski*, purposely left a little loose to avoid injury to the ankle in such rough work, slipped off my foot, but I shoved my *ski* pole through the strap as it started to glide away, and stopped it.

"Look out there!" cried Billy; "for heaven's sake don't let your shoe get away from you here!"

It was too late, for even as he spoke the pole slipped as I reached out for the shoe, and the evil thing started by itself down the mountain side.

At first the *ski* slid smoothly and gently, front end first, by some miracle avoiding the trees as if it were alive. Then it got on speed, and began to leap and jump and glance down the steep slope, leaving a fine white skit of snow behind it as it flew. At last it took a final leap, and disappeared from sight over the bluffs which we knew lined the creek at the bottom of the great ravine below us.

I was in dismay, for to be left helpless in that way 30 miles from a settlement, in snow so deep and soft as that, is by no means a laughing matter. Men have, perhaps, perished from such accidents, when having no axe to mend a broken shoe.

I have heard of a man who bound pine bark on his hands and knees, and so crawled half a mile to his own home. I have heard also of a man who made a pair of *skis* out of barrel staves, and of yet another who cut off the splintered end of a *ski,* and so traveled on a *ski* and a half—not so difficult as it sounds. But to travel 30 miles, or one mile, on one *ski,* in such a country as this, was something impossible, and I grew suddenly contemplative as I realized this. I didn't want to sit there without anything to eat till spring time, and as no one would be apt to be along before then, the flowers that bloom in the spring would have had, in my opinion, entirely too much to do with the case, tra la, because they would be growing over a discarded and forgotten journalist long before any relief expedition could have found him. Tra la, again.

"Did she smash into any tree?" sung out Billy.

"No, I think not," said I.

"Well, sit down on your other shoe and slide down after it," said Billy.

I was just warm enough under the collar to slide down anything about there, so I obeyed directions and slid, hanging on to the straps of the remaining shoe. The grade was awfully steep, but the snow that rolled up between my legs broke the *facilis descensus,*[54] and I found I could manage it and also could keep in sight of the trail left by the flying recreant ahead. At last, with a final plunge and slide, I found myself clear at the bottom, by the side of the creek. Clear across the creek was a great white drift of snow, and in the side of this I saw a narrow slit of broken snow. The *ski* had jumped 50ft., clear across the creek, and in that drift, after some digging, I found it, saved from splintering by the cushion of snow, and saved by the luck from absolute ruin on any one of a thousand trees, past which it had glided on its bullet-like flight.

In a Hole.

Billy, plucky and faithful always in time of trouble, started on down the mountain side after me, and after a while succeeded in getting way down to the creek, over an awfully rough little gully. And there we were, down in a well of snow, on each side of us slopes so steep that it seemed a goat couldn't go up them.

"Never you mind," said Billy, "I'll soon show you I know right where we are. We're three-quarters higher up the creek than the bridge at the falls, so we've saved just that much climb if we can once get up out of this cañon, and I think we can."

Out of the Hole.

We did get out, after an hour of the toughest work we had on the trip. The further side of the creek was bare of trees after we got up a bit, but it was very steep. We had to zig-zag up, rail fence fashion. Of course this meant a turn at an acute angle every once in a while, and at every turn some one would get a fall and a slide. But finally we struck a draw which offered easier going, and soon saw the great roof of the Cañon Hotel crowning the ultimate hill. It was far after 2 o'clock when we got in. Larsen and Holte had had a rough time on their trail and were just in. Soon we were all about the big stove in the kitchen, all talking with our mouths full, and all very happy.

The Park as a Winter Resort.

There are three hotels of the magnificent chain of hostleries established by the Yellowstone Park Association which have keepers left in them by the Association all through the winter. None of the hotels is open to the public after the close of the season. It was a great courtesy, then, of Manager Deane,[55] the acting and efficient head of the Association in the Park, to give us permission to stop at the Park hotels when we found that convenient. At the Lake Hotel Mr. Fletcher and his wife

Photographer F. Jay Haynes on his skis. MONTANA HISTORICAL SOCIETY RESEARCH
CENTER, PHOTOGRAPH ARCHIVES, HAYNES FOUNDATION COLLECTION

spent the winter. At the Fountain Hotel John Schmidt has been winter caretaker for some time. At the Cañon Hotel[56] is John Folsom,[57] the best snowshoer in the Park, and by reason or his horribly lonesome life, absolutely alone for more than half the year, grown to be one of the most taciturn men on the earth, just as he is one of the kindest-hearted and most obliging. In all the time I was with Folsom I never knew him to speak a word unless addressed. He has books, a cat, a flute and a little organette to help him break the awful monotony of the winter life alone in such a region—a calling most unique and trying among the singular ones followed by the sons of men. His chief duty is to keep the roofs free from snow and to exercise a general care over the buildings. The winter keeper is generally a carpenter as well. He must also be his own cook, laundryman and chambermaid. At all these turns of work John Folsom proved adept. Thanks to Mr. Deane, we got a home in the kitchen, a good bed to sleep in and supplies for continuing our trip. The value of all this can readily be appreciated. We thus avoided the carrying in of heavy supplies of food and lightened the hardships of the trip most materially.

THE PLOT THICKENS.

We were now thirty-two miles into the Park, all well and hearty, and so reported to Capt. Anderson by telephone, as quick as the wire began to work, receiving hearty good wishes in return. We felt contented and comfortable, knowing that we were now within a day's march of the buffalo and elk, and with the most interesting and exciting portion of our trip ahead of us. It will be in due order now to tell about our camps on the Hayden Valley, and about our experience there with the great game of the Park.

MIDWINTER IN THE MOUNTAINS.

THE morning following our first night at the Cañon was bright and clear, thermometer 2° above zero. John Folsom went up-stairs to see about something and took his *skis* along. He found it easier to slide out of the second story window than it was to walk down stairs. The snow was 25ft. deep on one side of the house, and its level at the lowest part caught the downstairs windows at about the middle. Back of the kitchen a great drift 10 or 12ft. high rose up sharply and we had to cut steps in that to get over it. Every way from the hotel the sheer white cover-ing sloped sharply down in steep rolls and pitches of descent. To the falls of the Cascade Creek, at the bottom of the hill, was a good mile. To the left of that point the black line of timber swept, and down in that somewhere was the Grand Cañon of the Yellowstone. From the hotel top we could see away across the Cañon, could see the steam of the Falls, and that of the geysers beyond the river, the latter rising white and sharp in the winter air. To the southwest we could see out over the Hayden Valley,[59] and with the glasses could see that it was storming in the valley, the snow blowing in blinding drifts. We could see the direction of the great natural game trail across the Park, which the elk follow in going from the Hayden Valley to the Soda Butte country in the northeast corner of the Park. Fol-som showed me where the U. S. troops in the Nez Percé pursuit crossed the Yellowstone, warping their wagons down into the gorge by ropes. Some of the trees that were skinned by the ropes can still be seen scarred up to to-day. To man unskilled in mountain travel it would seem impossible to get any sort of vehicle through here.

Nature's Cold Storage for Thrills.

The Haynes party were expected to arrive that day from the Lake, and Billy started out to meet them on Hayden Valley, hoping to join forces and locate the buffalo. He went quite alone, not a very desirable thing to do in that climate and country. I wished to see the Cañon and the Falls, so took my camera, and accompanied by Folsom, Larsen and Holte, put in the morning along the wondrous Yellowstone, a privilege which has been accorded few travelers of all the world under conditions such as these.

From the hotel to Lookout Rock,[60] below the Grand Falls, the distance may be something like a mile, for the most part a rather easy slide on the *skis*. After the first run to the edge of the timber we worked along the little hills, through the straight young pines, till we came to what seemed to be a sort of trestle or bridge, over the gulch near the Point. This was all covered 10ft. deep under snow. From that point to the jutting crag known as Lookout Rock there was a succession of gigantic and irregular drifts of snow. Folsom went all over this calmly without taking off his *skis*. I confess that in the worst places I dismounted and went over on my hands and knees, with my hands in the toe straps.

Lookout Rock we found to be a great white heap of snow, standing out over the fathomless and unthinkable depth of the cañon. What the footing was we could not tell, but supposed it must be solid out to where the ragged tree was standing on the verge, so we trod a way waist deep out to that, and stood silent in full view of one of the wonders of the world.

I suppose thousands have stood grasping the stem of that

same sturdy, ragged tree, and have looked in silence as we did. They have seen the Cañon in summer, and I wish they might all see it also in the depth of winter. Now the glorious colors of the walls were gone, but the peaks and cross and pinnacles were there, free of all color, but done in a clean, perfect white. It was "frozen music"—the diapason of nature's mightiest and most mysterious anthem all congealed in white, visible, palpable, authentic. No thinking man could stand there and not feel the exalted and compelling theme go thrilling to his heart.

Against the monotone of the snow the evasive blue-white clouds of steam arose from the little hot geyserettes along the river's brink. Above us the great veil of white mist which shrouds the Great Falls by winter shifted and swung and halted and paused and towered as the wind said, rising high up to the level of the forest. The ice bridge nearly spanned the Falls at the time of our visit, and down both sides of the Falls, wherever the spray struck the clinging snow, there were broad columns of ice, which at our distance, looked white and dull, but which close at hand must have been prismatic, radiant, glorious in the bright light of morning. It would have been worth one's life no doubt to risk the descent into the Cañon, as a snow slide would have been almost certain. We therefore made the photographs from the ragged tree, whence I suppose thousands of Kodak shots have been made by the summer tourists. The white of the Falls and of the mist made a difficult subject against the white background of the snow at so great a distance, and I got only an indifferent view, partly for reasons which I will later on set forth. There are many fine summer negatives of the Falls extant, but I believe the finest amateur negatives I have seen were made by Dr. Gandy, post surgeon at Fort Yellowstone. Dr. Gandy has put some of his beautiful Park negatives at the service of FOREST AND STREAM, and they speak highly of the possibilities of this pleasing art. I am not sure that Mr. Haynes got a winter view of the Falls on his trip, but if so, it was of course good. I know of no amateur negative made in winter except the one we got that morning. There was so much snow piled up on the edge of the Lookout Rock that it was difficult to get a shot down into the Cañon. I made one or two exposures over the edge with the others holding on to me for safety reasons, but had meagre luck of it.

Leaving Lookout Rock, we skirted along the river hills and went up the river about a mile and a quarter or more, to a point directly above the Upper Falls. Here we could see only a blinding steam of mist coming up through the reverberant roar of the cataract. The masses of snow kept us from going very close, but we were able to see down into the caldron of the Falls. Of the rapids above the Falls we had a beautiful view, and I stopped to make some exposures here, of course, though it was coming on cold and windy. Here, after a shot or two, my camera, which had been working very badly all the morning, broke down entirely, the film tearing clear across, for the second time already on the trip. Nothing was left but to quit and go home. Folsom told me we could get up a dark room, and I thought perhaps I could tinker the camera into something like shape.

It took us something like three-quarters of an hour to make the mile climb from the Cascade bridge up the Cañon hill to the hotel. It goes slow on *skis*, and I imagine there are folk who couldn't get up it in a hundred years. It takes about two or three minutes to come down, according to the condition of the snow.

We all had rude appetites, which John Folsom proceeded to appease in the small but cosy kitchen. Water we got out of a barrel full of melting snow.

Re-enforcements Arrive.

At 3 P. M. heavy snow began to fall. At 5 P. M. Billy got in, and I was glad of it. He had not met the Haynes party, and had *cached* his camera in the woods in Hayden Valley. At 6 P. M. the Haynes party, Mr. Haynes and two men, Sergeant Morrison and Bobby Burns, a Post attaché, got in, all in fair order except

Burns, who had lost his glasses and was suffering badly from snow blindness, the black handkerchief he had worn across his face below his eyes not having been efficient. Billy told him to keep a hot-water compress on his eyes, and by morning he was much better.

Not an Easy Job.

Mr. Haynes reported only fair luck at photographing game, as he had met a great deal of stormy, cloudy weather. It would seem a simple thing to go right into the Park and begin to photograph buffalo and elk, but it is really extremely difficult. One must first locate the game. Second, he must not let it get sight or scent of him, else it will stampede and leave the country. Third, he must have a clear day or he will get no sharpness to his pictures. Added to this he must have a long distance (or narrow angle) lens, and lastly he must have a combination of ready skill and ever-present good luck, for the chances come only for an instant at a time. Let any one undertake to arrange this combination, at the end of a 50-mile *ski* tramp with a heavy sack on his back, and he will learn a great deal about the difficulties of this task.

Mr. Haynes had hard luck at the Lake, and had traveled 60 miles for nothing trying to get a picture of the poacher Howell's tepee and cache. Troike, the private who attempted to find them, was unable to do so. I offer this as one more instance of the incredible difficulty of patrolling this tremendous country in winter. This man had been with Burgess when Howell was arrested and was supposed to be able to go back to the place. A fall of snow came and he was three days in finding it, do his best. How about setting out for a 75-mile jaunt on *skis*, and under pack, to find a poacher no one has seen or located? When people talk to me now about how "Capt. Anderson ought to be able to stop all the poaching, with two troops of soldiers and nothing else to do," it makes me hot clear through. Such people have no idea what they are talking about. It is easy to be wise and critical with your feet on a stove. Stick them into *skis*, and turn yourself loose in the Yellowstone Park in winter, and I'll bet a thousand dollars to a last year's banana peel that you think a whole lot different.

GAME IN SIGHT.

Mr. Haynes had seen game as mentioned below: On March 10, 2 buffalo, 6 foxes, 48 elk, all on the Hayden Valley. On March 13, 1 bull elk, 1 cow elk, 23 elk in herd, 31 buffalo and 6 buffalo, all on Hayden Valley. On March 14, 1 black fox, 1 red fox, 3 mink, on Hayden Valley. On March 16, 19 elk, 2 foxes, 6 buffalo, all on Pelican Valley (where the Howell killing was). On March 17, along the Yellowstone, he saw 12 swans, 18 foxes and about 300 ducks. (The Yellowstone does not freeze.) Billy and I had not yet gotten into the winter game country, but we were now right upon the edge of it.

We all concluded to join forces for a day or so in the matter of trying for big game photographs, so that we would not hurt each other's chances by frightening away the game.

Mr. Haynes used a simple 5X7 box—a Waterbury, if I am not mistaken—but he had a $125 Ross lens, and he went to all the trouble—a very great one—of taking in glass plates, which he said far surpassed any film. He got beautiful results, and thus added largely to his perpetuation of the beauties of the Park, whose skilled and tireless artist he has been for years. He expresses himself satisfied, as well he might be, with the results of his first attempt at photographing wild game. I spent a time to profit in a talk with him in the hotel kitchen the evening of his arrival at the Cañon.

VALUABLE ADVICE TO AMATEURS.

"It is a very common mistake of amateurs," he said, "to think they must always have the sun at the back when making an exposure. If you get to one side and catch the shadows, you get a Rembrandt-lighted picture which is much prettier, not so hard and with proper contrast.

"Now, if. you try to photograph a geyser in action you will get nothing if you make the picture with the sun at your back, because you will have no contrast between the steam and your background. But you make your exposure right square against the sun and the light shining in against your cloud of steam will give you a contrast and you will get a sharp, clear negative.

"Another common bugbear of amateurs is the question of focus. Now, with the right sort of lens, you don't need to bother about focus. I never touch my lens, and it cuts sharp and clear at any distance from 25 feet to half a mile. It will get relative distances and perspective into a picture. Cheap lenses will not do this, and they have to be changed in focus continually to avoid blurring the negative. Success with one of these must be largely a matter of success in guessing distances. It pays to get the best lens possible. Glass is better than film. One should get out of the habit of snapping at everything, but wait till he gets what he knows will make a good picture. Then with a good lens, good plates and good care, he knows he has got his picture when he presses his button.

"Of course, a short-focus lens is quicker in action than a long-focus. If you narrow your field, getting a long-range camera, you get a slower lens. Yet with quick plates, I should think a machine made on the principle of Mr. Hofer's here, would be the best for this sort of work, where you don't want too wide an angle, but want size to your figures." (Billy had plates also for his machine, and used some of them.)

As Mr. Haynes is one of the best and best known photographers of the country, the above advice may be taken as *ex cathedra*.[61]

Tried for Buffalo.

On Monday, March 19, Billy took Larsen and Mr. Haynes took Morrison, they going over on the Hayden Valley, six or eight miles, for a try at the buffalo. As was feared, it came off stormy, and they got no pictures. The shoeing was sticky and very hard.

Progress in Ski Theory.

By this time I was beginning to study into the theory of *ski* running still more deeply. I had noticed in coming up the great Cañon hill, which was largely a case of "corduroying," that the heels of my *skis* hung lower than the toes, and so were always dragging down behind in the side-step. I held a consultation with John Folsom, and the result was that we cut 5in. off the heel of each of my *skis*, set the straps back 3in., and planed off a lot of useless wood from the tops of the *skis*. We took off about a pound in weight from each shoe. After that I noticed a startling improvement in my ability to get up hill. It is only by experience one learns.

I noticed that Folsom's *skis* were of ash, but channeled and worn thin by several seasons of hard use. Folsom told me that Norway pine made the best shoes, as they did not stick like ash, though they were apt to be brittle if made too thin. Hickory, he said, made fine, springy *skis*, with good grain, but a trifle heavy. Ash was pretty tough and light, but needed more care in waxing. The best wax for shoes was made of tallow and beeswax, but if you get in too much beeswax, you would get your *skis* so slippery and glassy that you could hardly use them, especially in going up hill.

Eight Miles For Fun.

On Tuesday Billy was tired and his sore heel hurt him, so he curled up on the bed in the kitchen and read a novel, declaring that he had had enough of travel for awhile. All the rest of us except John Folsom went out for some fun on the *skis*. The thermometer continued about zero, which temperature seemed pleasant. The snow was in good order and we had a good run, doing perhaps eight miles or more for the fun of the thing. We had a good run down the Cañon hill—fortunately not running off the trail at the sharp angle near the bottom, where even so good a shoer as Folsom has failed to get around and narrowly escaped a headlong plunge into the depths of the ravine below. We then crossed Cascade Creek, with its beautiful falls buried out of sight under the snow, and followed the Hayden Valley trail out for a mile or so, to a place where the mountain slopes rose up high and bare, offering a good place for a long and swift *ski* run, which was what we were after. We worked up the slopes for a mile, perhaps, getting as high as we could, and going forward all the time, until we reached a high peak or point, bare of timber, and swept with a keen wind, which packed the snow almost into ice. Below us lay the level of the valley of the Yellowstone, and on the bank of a little creek we could see far below us a little cabin, built for the summer use of the troops, and now just visible above the level of the snow. The leaders of our snowshoe brigade thought it would be a good thing to jump off the earth from the top of this bare peak, and land somewhere down there by the cabin, three-quarters of a mile or more. For my part I was not enthusiastic over this proposition, but by this time was getting sort of resigned. One after another dropped off over the edge and shot down, and, holy mackerel, how they did fly. A man seemed to condense and shorten up like a telescope as he sank down and down, instant after instant, so that he wasn't over half size when he reached the foot of the hill. When I let go I had no definite idea of what was going to happen, but as I wasn't particular where I went it didn't make much difference anyhow. Again I experienced the exhilaration of the astonishingly smooth and easy motion of the swiftness of which the *ski*-runner himself has no just conception at the time. To my surprise, I kept in the tracks of those ahead and arrived all standing, with only the temporary disgrace of having "ridden my pole" on the last sharp drop, at which there was loud protest from the others. Then we all went in for *ski*-jumping for an hour or so, making a lovely jump out of a snow drift on a steep hillside, so that we could clear 30ft. or so. At this we found our Skandinavians, Larsen and Holte, easily superior, they having had long experience in the winter games of Minnesota and Wisconsin. In *ski*-jumping the jumper does not carry his pole, as he would almost certainly injure himself in landing after the jump if he kept hold of his pole. It is a matter of nerve and equilibrium. Most of us seemed a little shy on the latter, but we kept on jumping till we were all in coats of white and a glow of heat from head to foot. Then we went home and ate John Folsom out of the place.

OFF FOR A CAMP ON THE VALLEY.

The next morning, Wednesday, March 21, was keen and cold, below zero. We all joined forces and started for the Hayden Valley, feeling that it would be better to get closer to the game, in order to take advantage at once of any bright weather suitable for photographing. (The light in that country at that altitude and in winter, is about 20 per cent. "faster" than in this, and is fine for instantaneous work on any clear day. Such a day is, however, rare in winter, and when the snow is falling and the clouds are dense, the light grows too dim for one to think of photographing, as at best one could not get a picture with any sharpness or "distance" in it). We concluded to make a camp somewhere on the Hayden Valley, and to act from there as headquarters.

It was with feelings of the liveliest interest, one may be sure, that after the sharp five miles or more of *ski* work across the hills between the Cañon and the Valley, I turned from the Yellowstone with the party, crossed Alum Creek, and made out toward the middle of the broad, white, dazzling expanse of the Hayden Valley. Here we were no doubt to determine the success or failure of an important part of our work. Somewhere, behind some of those long tongues of timber which pierced the five miles square or more of open whiteness, there were without doubt numbers of the greatest and the rarest game of the American continent, which we had come so far to see at home on the winter range, and to enable others to see, if we might be so fortunate.

Billy and I went on up to the point of timber toward the middle of the valley, where he had *cached* his camera two days before. The rest of the party kept on up Alum Creek a little further, it being the understanding that they were to make as good a camp as they could in the timber or some one of the slopes making down to that stream. It was still early in the morning of what was to prove a very eventful day, followed by a night not less so.

No. 8.

THE HEADQUARTERS ON HAYDEN VALLEY.

BILLY went straight through the thick woods to where his camera was *cached*, and taking it along we skirted the edge of the island of timber, out in the open where the keen wind was whirling the fine hard snow across the country in wisps and strings. We concluded to cut straight across through the timber toward Alum Creek, intending to intersect the trail of the rest of the party, and not go back the way we had come, following it in from the point where we had left them, as this latter would make a longer journey. We traveled for apparently three-quarters of a mile through heavy pine forest, whose boughs, heavily laden with mats and masses of snow, formed almost a continuous roof of white above us. It was very white and silent in the forest. We saw no signs of life except where the porcupines had gnawed off the bark some of the young trees, and except one elk trail, old, but deep and wide, as though a steam plow had gone through.

We followed the gently falling hillside until we came nearly to the Alum Creek level, and still found no trail, nor could we hear the sound of an axe. We therefore turned back to the right, toward the point where the party had first entered this motte of timber,[62] but though we went nearly half a mile in that direction, climbing a little again, we did not cut the trail. At length Billy smelt smoke, and finally we found the camp, away up near the center of the timber. We had gone half around it, as the party had not gone in so deep as we had expected.

We found that the others had dug a hole in the snow down to the ground, the level of the snow being about even with one's face as he stood on the ground. The hole was about 12 feet across. Around the edge of this, following Billy's general advice given earlier, they had stepped a number of poles, cut from young pines, about 18 or 20ft. long, there meeting at the top lodge-pole fashion. On the inside of these poles was stretched in a semicircle the light lodge-lining which Billy had brought all this way for this express purpose. This lining was about 5ft. high. Above its height there was absolutely no covering at all, as the lodge poles were not numerous enough to make any covering or wind break. A fire was built in the center of this "tepee," if such we could call our extremely well ventilated winter house, and the boys had cut a plenty of wood. A stairway, made by treading short logs into the snow, enabled one to get downstairs into the hole in the snow, which constituted the salon, dining room and sleeping apartments of the edifice. Billy looked at it critically and said it would do as long as it didn't rain. Then we all went downstairs, melted some snow, made tea and coffee, and were happy. In the heavy timber the wind was not much felt, and down below the level of the snow it was hardly perceptible, though we could see the tops of the taller trees swaying, and could hear the talking of the pines where the axemen had jarred off the snow.

THE FIRST SIGHT OF ELK.

The advantage of experience now made itself felt. Billy knew right where to go to find the elk and buffalo, that is to say, the general direction and probable distance, subject of course to the limited movements of the game on its winter feeding grounds. He said he would not need to go far up Alum Creek, and as it was still early we hoped to do some work if the weather would only clear.

At noon the sun came out and at once we were off up the valley. Larsen and Holte, who complained of wet feet, were left at camp, all the others taking the trail.

At a half mile from camp we saw a hand of thirty elk feeding below us, close along Alum Creek, but as we saw no antlers passed this herd by without disturbing them. At two and a half miles out we saw three big bull elk lying down in the shallow snow close to the creek, where the ground seemed warmer. We left these to the right and kept on up the creek, hoping to strike the buffalo. We saw still other elk, but did not stop, as we wanted to use the light we were having on the rarer subjects, the buffalo.

Buffalo.

At length Morrison, who was slightly ahead, pushed back from the summit of a ridge and motioned to us to get down. He had sighted five buffalo above us. We tried to get the attention of Billy and Burns, who were off to the right, and finally succeeding we all began the stalk, taking the benefit of a wind which happened to be in our favor. We made a long swift detour through the hills, taking one or two runs on the *skis*, and after about a mile of this we came out, breathless and eager, on the point of a hill directly above the buffalo and not more than 100yds. from them.

There were five of the huge creatures, looming up large enough against the white background. They were all lying down and did not see nor scent us. It was a magnificent opportunity, a great chance among those chances for which we had come. Billy and Mr. Haynes silently and swiftly got their cameras ready, and we all crept close to the edge of the hill, which brought us about 50ft. above the buffalo, which seemed then to be almost directly beneath us.

The buffalo seemed not to notice us. Not so, however, with a band of ten elk, which were lying down about 250yds. from us, beyond the buffalo. These trailed out on the run, leaving the creek and making into the deeper snow after a little. Then the buffalo rose, stupid and bewildered, and apparently uneasy but unable to locate the cause. As they stood, humped up and undecided, Billy and Haynes both got a fair shot. Then, as they located us and lumbered off down the creek in that odd, ungainly but speedy gait of theirs, Billy lay flat on his back on the brow of the hill, and with his camera between his knees industriously took shot after shot at them as they ran, using the sights which he had had mounted on his long box like peep and globe rifle sights. The buffalo followed the trail of the elk, and as the latter turned to leave the creek, Billy got a shot at the whole procession, thus accomplishing the rare and probably unduplicated feat of photographing wild elk and buffalo at the same time running.

The reader may now have fair idea of the necessities in success at this work. One must get near the game, wait for a proper light, then locate the game, finally stalking it far more carefully than if one were hunting for a shot with a rifle, which could be taken at much greater distance. Lastly, at the critical moment he must not get nervous and forget the requirements of a camera, a much more complicated weapon than a rifle. He must act promptly, for the opportunity lasts but for a moment—a camera does not carry as far as a rifle. These being the conditions, it may be seen that success does not come as a mere matter of course. The successful man at this must be something of a photographer and very much of a hunter. All through the work of that and other days, Billy Hofer's great experience and rare skill as a stalker of big game came into valuable play.

Various Ways of Crossing a Creek.

We were all very much pleased with our good fortune here, and concluded to push on further up, toward the "hot country," or Violet Creek, hoping to locate the main herd of buffalo, of which we had yet seen no sign, though the shallow snow along Alum Creek was all yarded and pawed up by elk. We took a long slide down an accommodating hill, and brought up along-side Alum Creek. The next question was, how were we to get across the creek? Billy said he knew where there was a little island in it, and at that place he thought we could get over.

We found the island, and extending out to it was a thin bridge of snow ice, the main channel, broad and shallow, be-ing in too much of a hurry to freeze up. We went out to the verge of the island and made investigation. We threw our *skis* all across and prepared to jump, the distance being 10 or 12ft. Billy cleared it, using his *ski* staff as a vaulting pole. Morrison followed, and barely got over, leaving an ugly break in the fringe of ice which made the landing place. My turn was next, and as I stepped back to get a start, smash! I went through the thin ice bridge behind, which had been strained with too much weight. I landed ankle-deep in the ice water. The thermometer was well below zero, and camp was miles away. Under the circumstances it did not take long for a fellow to make up his mind what to do. I sprang forward over the island into the main channel, plunged through the shallow water and crawled up the icy bank beyond, considerably alarmed about my feet, which now had a first-class opportunity to freeze about as solid as those of the Chicago stat-ue of Christopher Columbus or the Montana silver statue of Jus-tice—though I do feel rather bashful, in a way, about comparing my feet with those of Miss Rehan, or even those of Columbus.[63] However, thanks to the high-tongued overshoes and the tight leggins, I escaped without getting wet through—I was only in for a couple of steps—and though my feet and ankles were soon cased in solid ice, the excellent footgear prevented them from freezing. There was small chance left for Mr. Haynes and Burns to get a jump. Not daring to risk a slip into the water, they both had to strip off shoes and stockings, and wade across barefoot—a most cruel thing to look at or to think about. As quickly as they got over we fell upon them with their own rough stockings, and rubbed their feet and legs until they were red. Then they put on their shoes, and we all went on after more buffalo.

A Shot at Elk.

We soon got into a region of tremendous hills and valleys, which gave us hard climbing and swift running on the *skis,* for a distance of perhaps two or three miles in all. We could not get trace of the buffalo, even on the steaming hot country beyond Violet Creek. Billy complained that he had never seen so little game on the Valley in all his life. He thought it was because recent haying operations by the transportation companies had cut down the feed on the limited strip of country where the game can get down through the snow in winter. We saw nothing for a long time but one lone bull elk, which, under Billy's guidance, we stalked until we were above it on a high steep hill. Arranging a signal, Billy and Mr. Haynes both let go and sped swiftly down the steep slope, sweeping around to the right at the foot of the hill. The bull turned back, and they saw not one but three bulls, grouped together. Mr. Haynes was ahead, but did not get a shot. Billy got a shot, and got a nice picture of Mr. Haynes and the three elk, one of the most interesting of our series.

More Elk.

We now soon swung back toward camp and were gratified before long by the sight of a band of elk, which we knew to be the same we had started when we saw the buffalo because there was one cow and one calf, a little fellow among ten bulls. They had come back into the hills from Alum Creek, following the valley of the little hot stream, where the snow did not lie deep. With a swift *ski* run down hill we got right on to them before they could escape. They broke across the little creek and plunged single file into the heavy snow of the hillside beyond, not 50yds. from us at first, a magnificent, but somewhat pitiful sight, the great creatures were so helpless in the snow. I can say truly that one feels no disposition to kill under conditions such as these, the emotion being much rather one of pity. Yet the power of the great beauties was admirable. They plowed a trail

4ft. deep through the snow, and made a pretty decent gait of it, though rising and plunging and stumbling shoulder-deep in the treacherous snow. As we noted when we had started this band before, the old cow led and the baby elk came far to the rear, with an old bull behind it. After a time the cow got too tired and fell back, a bull leading the way in turn. The band at length turned down the hill toward the creek, plunged wearily through the deep snow till they got a footing on the "warm ground," and then rapidly made off down the creek, after having afforded fine chances indeed for photographing. Billy here got a very interesting picture of the band in full course of plowing single file through the snow. A better opportunity would be hard to get.

THE BUFFALO LOOKED PLEASANT.

Our good luck was not to end here, it seemed, for it was not long thereafter till we located a solitary buffalo bull, standing apparently wrapped in thought down on the bank of Alum Creek. He was over half a mile away, but the wind was right, and under Billy's skillful stalking the cameras were soon on a steep knoll above him, about 250 yards distant. Here Billy sat down in the snow and deliberately took a few shots at the old fellow, who seemed entirely ignorant of what was going on. At the critical moment Mr. Haynes found that his plates were with Morrison and Burns, and they were not visible. He turned back to find them. Meanwhile I crawled up to Billy, and we sat watching the old bull for fully five minutes. He was standing broadside to us, with his head hanging down, quite motionless, and was probably asleep. When at length Mr. Haynes had found his assistants, he made an exposure or two on the bull, then Billy, he and Morrison got their *skis* ready and whisked down the hill to get a closer shot. They got actually right up to the bank of the creek beyond which he stood, not forty yards away, and got a close side view. Then Morrison tossed a bit of snow at him, and the bull, stupidly turning around, stood looking at them, directly head on, as if to ask what the mischief it was all about.

Both the camera men improved this second chance for a view, and still another success was scored before the sleepy-headed old fellow deliberately turned and slowly rolled himself away out of sight around a point of timber. This buffalo was close to the creek, and no doubt the noise of the running water drowned the faint noise of the *skis* on the snow. The little contretemps made a singular and rather ludicrous incident. It was a most obliging buffalo, to stand and look pleasant while it was having its picture taken. Usually they will not do that.

Barefooted, Below Zero.

We were now again at Alum Creek, but on the wrong side of the creek, and a long distance below the place where we had crossed it going up, even had we wished to undertake a second crossing there. There was no way of getting over without going five miles down stream, which would throw us far out of our road to camp. The stream was at that point about 10 or 15yds. wide and about knee deep on the ripple near which we stood. It ran through a bare valley, and there was no way of getting a footbridge over it, even if we had had an axe. Nothing remained but to wade the creek, and to strip for it, for if we went in with our shoes on and got wet, our feet would freeze in a very few moments after coming out.

It was now well on toward evening, and the day had been steadily growing colder. Comparing the temperature with that observed at the Cañon that morning, we thought it to be about 9° below zero, probably a very moderate estimate. I noticed that Morrison had tied up his ears, and Billy had cautioned me to be very careful or I would freeze my ears. I noticed also that we chilled very quickly after we stopped traveling. On the whole, the idea of sitting down on the snow, taking off one's shoes and stockings, and deliberately stepping into that ice cold mountain stream, was something not altogether inviting at first flush. I remember I looked at that black, wintry, cold-looking stream for a moment, and wishing it were not quite so wide. I would rather have done almost anything else right then than wade that creek. Still, we had to wade, and a fellow can do a lot of things when he has to. Everything in life is relative.

We sat down on the icy bank, unbuckled our ice-stiffened foot-wear, stripped our feet bare to the skin, and then rolled our trousers up as high as they would go, as we knew it would be a near thing at that, for mountain streams are deeper than they look. We had to carry our *skis*, overshoes, etc., etc., balancing these on one shoulder and using the free hand with the *ski* pole to steady the footing in the rushing stream.

Any one who does not wish the trouble of an experience just like the above can tell how it goes, I imagine, by inserting his feet in an ice cream freezer and leaving them for an hour or so. The water was cold and swift, and the rocks were cold and slippery, and one had to go slow and carefully to avoid a disastrous mis-step—which under the circumstances might fairly have been fatal, for to get one's clothes wet meant to freeze stiff in spite of all. Yet one by one we emerged on the other side without mishap. Poor Billy, with his camera and all, could not get all over at one trip, and as I did not notice this till we were over, and so did not take part of his load, Billy had to go back after his *skis*. By that time Mr. Haynes had jerked on his stockings, and as Billy got about midstream on his way back, Mr. Haynes called to him to hold still while he got a picture of him. Billy posed patiently, out in the ice water, and Mr. Haynes made a careful shot. The result is a very interesting picture, showing Billy in the creek, with others just putting on their shoes.

When the wind struck our wet feet and legs [as] we came out of the water, it cut like a knife, and we had to hurry in drying our feet, or they would have frozen. I know that while I was rubbing one foot, the toes on the other began to stick together. When I get so far along as the lacing of my leggings, my fingers stuck to the metal hooks, as they will to iron on a very cold morning. Yet not one of us got chilled, and not one of us felt the worse for it ten minutes afterward. Not one of us touched a drop of spirits, and

Crossing Alum Creek. From left to right: Emerson Hough (seated), Sergeant Morrison, Bobbie Burns, and Billy Hofer (fording the creek).

indeed could not have done so had we needed to, for there was none along. Not the slightest ill effect ever followed for any of us. In fact, the system gets so tuned up on a hard outdoor trip like this that it will take almost any hardship without injury.

MORE BUFFALO PICTURES.

Soon after we crossed the creek, we saw on the hills above us the same five buffalo we had started earlier in the afternoon. Morrison and Burns made a long detour, and as the buffalo saw them come up on the other side, they turned and made back down the trail they had trodden in going up, giving us a good chance for some more flying shots at them as they approached the lower level where we stood. Seeing us, the buffalo left the trail and began milling [on] the top of a little knoll, not over 35yds. from us. I believe neither camera got a picture of them at this point, or until they had again lined out on the trail. As they plunged up and down in the deep snow, with only half their bodies visible, they looked huge and formidable. It was noticeable that they seemed of a gray color, not black or brown, by reason of the snow matted in their hair. They live and feed and lie in the snow, and get snowed on so much that their hair is full of it.

The buffalo at length broke away from the knoll and started a new trail, off for the top of the ridge. They went slowly, laboriously, painfully, almost tired out and helpless, powerful as they were. It seems to me that only one emotion is possible at such a sight to-day. No man could have the thought of killing one of these great creatures under such circumstances. He could only first admire and then pity them from the bottom of his heart. It is a hard fight they are waging now for survival. Can not Congress, can not humanity, help them?

CAMP "FOREST AND STREAM," 21 BELOW ZERO.

We were now about four miles or so, perhaps, from our open-work tepee in the island of timber below, and as fast as we were able we made for that point, it being late evening when we got there, though the twilight is very long in that latitude in winter. Billy and I had all the packs of our party along, but the total of bedding was just one single blanket and the light sleeping bag. The thermometer was steadily falling, and it was already very cold. The majority of the party determined to return to the Cañon Hotel quarters, not risking a night of sitting up around a fire. We had had a hard day of it, traveling I suppose, at least eighteen miles up to that time, and it was about six miles more back to the Cañon. Billy and I concluded to chance it at the tepee, and we were the only ones who did. The rest bade us goodby, and went away jokingly telling us that they would come and thaw us out in the morning.

"We can't sleep in this place the way it's fixed now," said Billy, after the others had gone. "We've got to shorten those poles, so the lodge lining will lean over us a little more and throw some of the heat down." So saying, he went to work with the axe and proposed to make a more woodsmanlike tepee than our friends had done. He cut about 4ft. off the end of each pole and rearranged them all at the top. This left them closer together at the top and not so high above us, with a much less acute angle at the top. Then we cut pine boughs and filled in all around between the snow wall of the lodge poles and put chunks of snow back of that, so that the wind would not suck down the wall behind us. After that we tied the light lodge lining around inside, and the tepee now being smaller, the lining met at the door, so that we had a fair wall around us, though no roof to speak of. The lining pitched forward pretty well, making a circular "lean-to" wall, which would throw the heat of our fire in and down. We got in a lot of wood, and of course built our fire in the center of the tepee, of necessity not a very big fire. Under the lining we laid down the side logs of our beds, of which we made two. Between the logs we piled in pine boughs for bedding, as many as we could find out in the snow, for we had now been working an hour and a half, and it was about as dark as it ever would be that night.

Billy and I had some of the product of the lowly but useful

hog for supper that night, with a little bread. Billy melted snow and made tea, and I melted snow and made coffee, being plenty scared about tea after my experience with it the first day out. It took more than a quart of coffee to scare me that night, however. We had had a hard day and were pretty well tired down.

We hung up the cameras on horizontal limbs and stood the *skis* up on end in the snow, so the porcupines could not get at the straps, and not long after supper we turned in, if one may call it so. We put on all the extra clothing we had and crawled into our scanty bedding, hugging the saving fire as closely as we dared. To-day Billy's sleeping-bag has a long scorch on the back, where I got too close to the fire at one stage of the game.

It was an odd night, and I shall not forget it. The forest was absolutely silent, not a creak of a limb or a whisper of a bough falling on the ear. The sky was blue and cloudless, and through the meager rafters of our house the great stars shone brilliantly down. Our little fire snapped and smoked, and flared and fell, and continually craved food to keep away the spirit of destruction. How shall I describe it—this feeling that there was a Spirit of Cold about on every hand, eager to destroy? One could feel it tapping, tapping, for weak places in one's covering and in one's vitality. There were silent, spirit fingers feeling all over one to find some point of stealthy assault. A veil of cold lay upon the face. One felt, vaguely, restlessly—and in sleep one dreamed it half fearingly—that above the bed of these violators of the wilderness secrecy there bent a white-winged, stony-faced Spirit of Cold, with fingers creeping, creeping. A tiny rent in the sleeping-bag felt like a hand of ice all night long. Every thin place in the covering was tapped, tapped, incessantly, remorselessly, by those invisible and persistent fingers of the frost.

Of course, had we had proper bedding, we should hav[e] had not so much of an experience of it, but we were very poorly equipped, and had we not made proper use of the facilities at hand, we would have frozen to death. The cold of the mountains is not the same thing at all. Billy curled up under his single blanket, and hunched as close to the fire as he dared. Once in the night he got up and went out into the snow after more wood, some of which remained piled up outside. We put on a stick or two every once in a while, of course. We built the fire at right angles, so that each of us had a long, burning stick extending up and down parallel to his backbone. Again, I noticed that though I got cold, just as I was in wading the creek, there was no chilling through, no rigor, such as a tired man would very likely have in such circumstances in this climate. I am willing to aver, though, that pine boughs are about as warm to sleep on as so many icicles. Also, I would have given $4 an inch if Billy's sleeping bag had been about a foot or so longer. It caught me just below the shoulders, and do all I could, I couldn't keep my shoulders warm. We had to tie our silk handkerchiefs over our ears to keep our ears from freezing, but I didn't have anything to tie over my shoulders. At last I hit on a happy thought. I took my Lake Superior pack bag, spread the flap down under, and poked my head into the bag, pulling the whole thing down over my head and shoulders. It was dark in there, and a trifle close, but it was warm. Before this I had learned another trick, of which a fellow perhaps wouldn't think unless he were in a camp cold as this. The skin of a wildcat isn't very thick, and it let the icy coldness of those *frappé* pine feathers through until I thought my hips would turn to ice.[64] I put my big mittens under me, but they wouldn't do. At last I put my broad-brimmed hat under me, and that kept out the cold, and I was all right after that; with my hat under me and my head in the bag. I don't want to hear anybody poke fun at the Western hat any more after this. Where would a fellow have been with a derby hat in a case like that, or a silk hat?

Thanks to Billy's skill in arranging the camp, and to his unselfishness and care all night through, we both finally got through the night and got some sleep, too. I can not say that I was really very cold. We kept just this side of that. Still I have been hotter and I shouldn't wonder if Billy has. We must have been two rather grimy and tough-looking characters when we turned out in the morning, with our eyes full of pine smoke and our faces black with cinders. Still we could cut a caper or two, and felt pretty good. With our knives we cut each a cake out of the hard snow, which gave out the crisp, ringing, crinkly sound it does of a very cold morning. These cakes of snow we rubbed over our faces and we let it go at that. We had no mirror, no soap, no towel and even the solitary comb was lost somewhere in the packs.

For breakfast we had beef and coffee. The beef was raw, so we blew the ashes off the coals and slapped it right down on the coals, where it broiled nicely, and without any smoky or woody taste. We had a very scanty breakfast, but we ate another one when the party came in from the Cañon with more supplies.

When the morning was well advanced, about 9 o'clock, perhaps, we heard the whisper of *skis* on the snow, and soon the face of Larsen peered curiously over the edge of our pit in the snow. He smiled gladly, as if surprised to see us alive. Larsen had frozen his ears coming over from the Cañon that morning. Every man was covered with a deep white rime of frost as he came up. We could hardly believe it when they told us that it was 21° below zero at the Cañon that morning. We had judged it to be about 6° below. From this we thought it must have been about 6° below when we crossed the creek the day before. When Billy and I learned that we had put in so cold a night, we looked at our late tenement with more respect, and called it Camp Forest and Stream. Mr. Haynes made a picture of it. Any one lost on Hayden Valley is welcome to the use of the poles, which will probably be standing for years, unless the elk rub them over.

The story of how we found more buffalo, and how we at length crossed the Continental Divide, will do for another day.

STILL MORE BUFFALO.

THURSDAY morning, March 22, we left our camp for further efforts at locating the buffalo, no large band of which had yet been seen. The parties separated. Billy and I intended to cross the Divide after finishing our work in Hayden Valley. The Haynes party returned to the Cañon, and we did not see them again until after our return to the Mammoth Hot Springs. Haynes took John Folsom along as a guide to find the buffalo. Billy said nothing much, but I think had an idea we would find the buffalo over on the Mary's Mountain hot country, which we would not reach until the following day. We intended to pass the night at the shack on Trout Creek, west of the valley proper.

Our party had been on the trail for an hour or two that morning, when we sighted buffalo away off to the northeast, on top of a ridge near Alum Creek. They were so far as to seem mere specks. We pushed on without leaving our course until we came to a little spit of timber running out into the open valley, and here made a temporary camp, taking off our packs and building a fire. Larsen and Holte had never seen a buffalo[65] (they had not been with us the day before), and we concluded to let them go out with Billy while I kept camp and made tea against their return. It was decided that they should circle around the buffalo and turn them down toward the creek if possible, so that they would pass Billy, who was to make off to the left and go down one of the draws which ran down to the creek in that direction.

The buffalo were about 2½ miles from us. Billy's experience taught him that when disturbed in that part of the valley they would usually run over to the Mary's Mountain country, which would accord well with our plans for the next day. Accordingly they three set out, going in divergent directions.

Sign.

I found the young trees in the timber point almost worn bare by the elk, which had evidently made that a favorite scraping spot for the hardening of their horns after the season of velvet. Still larger game, too, it seemed, had found this a cool and shady spot in summer, for on digging away the snow for a place to make a fire, I found quantities of buffalo chips. Of these I made my fire, and I imagine this was the last camp-fire in America ever built of the old-time *bois des vaches.*

The Surround.

From my place at the timber point I could see the buffalo feeding along the ridge where we first sighted them. There were eleven of them. At length I saw two tiny figures appear away off to the right, unseen by the buffalo, and these I knew to be Larsen and Holte. Billy I could not see. Larsen and Holte went clear beyond a ridge and I could see them no more, but knew they were making their stalk close up to the herd. Larsen afterward told me that they got to the top of the ridge, within 40ft. of the buffalo, which were feeding just below the crest on the other side. "They didn't like that deep snow," said Larsen, "and they wouldn't run. They look at Pete and me, and shake their heads and say 'moo!' down deep. Pete and me thought they was going to run over us. That scared Pete and me. I think that was a good chance for one of them pictures."

The Stampede.

That was what Larsen and Holte saw. What I saw was a whole eruption of buffalo come boiling over the top of the hill back of my eleven buffalo, and go tearing down the hill toward the creek. Their speed appeared to be very great, and there was a great idea of power conveyed by the way they plunged ahead through the deep snow. I counted them as well as I could, about thirty head, including the two bunches. The boys had found another bunch beyond the hill on which I could see the eleven head.

THE SHOT.

What Billy saw was both these two bunches and also a third one of about forty head, which was invisible to all of us at first, but which was picked up by the stampede as it crossed their feeding ground lower down toward the creek. The whole outfit, about eighty-five head in all, passed close by Billy where he lay concealed with the big camera, and got several shots at them as they strung by.

All this took five or six miles of *ski* work and two or three hours of time. The men were all tired when they got in, and we freshened up with lunch and tea.

HOW THE BUFFALO FEED IN WINTER.

Billy remarked on having seen a great many wolves while he had been gone, on a piece of country back of where he photographed the buffalo, and not far from our line of march, and said he came near getting a photograph of some of them. We saw one or two coyotes at a distance, over in that direction, soon after we took the trail after lunch. We now were on the natural winter feeding grounds of the buffalo. The snow here does not lie so deep as it does in the forests, because of the warmth of much of the ground, and because of the winds which in places strip the open ground nearly bare of snow. Moreover, there is good grass over this valley country—or would be if the thrifty haymakers of the transportation co[mpan]y would let it alone as they should—and once in a while we saw the tip of a shrub or two which may or may not afford the buffalo food. As we kept on our course, which now made a chord to the wide arc of Alum Creek, which bent off to our right, we met abundant proof that the buffalo and elk were using on this part of the valley. We crossed several "yards," where the snow was torn up as if by tremendous plows. The snow was only about 3 or 4ft. deep here, and for a space of 200yds. or more square it had been worked over carefully as the dirt of a placer mine. (The elk paws the snow away in feeding. The buffalo thrusts or roots with its head, throwing it from side to side in working down through the snow.) Deep trails connected the different yards. The sign appeared to be rather old, but we saw a big fresh lynx track, which seemed to be lining out just about the way we were going, and we also saw a mountain lion track, which seemed headed in much the same direction.

The Find of Butchered Buffalo.

We pushed on in this direction for half a mile or so further, and as we topped a long ridge which bounded a wide valley making down into Alum Creek (I think it was near Trout Creek proper), we saw ahead of us about half a mile of country that was literally all tracked up with game.

It was all sign of flesh-eating animals. Our lynx and lion had been here, and so had a wolverine, and apparently thousands of wolves, coyotes and foxes. We saw a coyote or two and two foxes go skurrying away across the open for the timber as we came in sight. Further on we struck the trail of a very large bear, which surprised us, as it was very early in the season for bear to be out.

The trails seemed to converge toward certain little heaps of snow, and as we saw this we knew why the animals had gathered here in such numbers. We ran down to the nearest snow heap and found beside it a deep pit dug 4ft. or more in the snow. At the bottom bones and torn flesh were visible. On the snow lay wisps and curls of buffalo hair. In all we saw eight heaps, and supposed that eight buffalo had been killed.

This was where we made the discovery reported last April in FOREST AND STREAM, one of the items of the Park news which attracted wide attention over the country. As was stated in a later issue, Capt. Anderson sent Burgess down on the strength of our story, and from our description of the spot he was able to locate the killing, as he thought. Burgess made out only four dead buffalo, and thought the other holes were to be accounted for by the fact that the wild animals had dragged off parts of the carcasses to a distance. The latter hardly tallies with my notion of the case, as the diggings seemed to be so far apart that it was hardly likely large portions of a carcass would be dragged so far. Burgess may or may not have hit upon our find, but in any event the matter was bad enough, for some time after that John Folsom discovered ten head more of dead buffalo in that same part of the country. That a killing of considerable extent had been made does not admit of doubt. The strange thing about it was that none of the heads or hides had been taken. Here is a bit of unwritten history of the Park in this, and no doubt after a while the facts will come out.

We had no means of digging in the hard, packed snow and so could not learn much about our discovery. Moreover, it was now 4 o'clock in the afternoon and we had still a long march ahead of us and a camp to fit up for the night. We left the place feeling a new indignation against the contemptible butchers who had been violating every law, civil and natural, in the destruction of these few remaining specimens of a nearly extinct race. Even Larsen and Holte were angry at it. Nothing would have pleased these sojer boys more than to arrest a poacher, but I am afraid the poacher would have been received at the Post in bad order had they run across him in the Hayden Valley that day.

HEADED FOR CAMP.

The country we were now traversing must be in the summertime a very beautiful one, and even in winter it was not unpleas-

Some of Yellowstone's elk herd in 1894. MONTANA HISTORICAL SOCIETY RESEARCH CENTER, PHOTOGRAPH ARCHIVES, HAYNES FOUNDATION COLLECTION

ing. The open, rolling hills were crossed by occasional strips of timber which diversified a landscape which at that point could hardly be called mountainous, though the hills were long and often steep. Finally the "Valley," as this large extent of open hills is called, began to dwindle down and thin out into long arms of open country, running far up into the timber. We followed up one of these long, narrow glades, having some amusement at a puzzled red fox which was studying us from the other aide of the glade. We kept climbing a little bit, always remembering the *ski*-traveler's maxim of getting elevation wherever possible, and never losing it unnecessarily, just as a civil engineer works when laying out a railway line. One arm of the valley dwindled out into fingers, and one of the fingers became a gorge. We turned to the left, under a sharp run down, and were in the lovely cañon known as "Trout Creek," wrongly so, as it is really Alum Creek, Billy says.[66] Up this we traveled for half a mile, until finally we came to one of the littlest, tiniest, snow-coveredest and best hid little miniature log cabins in all the world—the "Trout Creek shack," built by the U. S. Army for the use of scouting parties and known only to a few of the patrol and to a guide or two like Billy. This small structure was set in against the rock wall of the cañon, of which it seemed a portion. The sweep of the continuous drift of snow that lined the mountain side took in and enveloped the cabin as it went, leaving nothing visible except the end and door. Inside was a fine white drift of snow, and the chimney was full of snow, and the windows were blocked with snow, and the roof was loaded with snow, and the woodpile was many feet deep under the snow. Still, we didn't mind that, and to our eyes the little cabin seemed a most acceptable abode.

WINTER LUMBERING OPERATIONS.

A great trouble here was the getting of firewood, which we could only obtain at a distance of about 300yds., and far up the steep snow-covered hillside. Billy and I spotted a dead tree away up the cañon wall, and laboriously made our way up to it on the *skis*, but after we had it in lengths the worst of it was not over. The short logs sunk in the soft snow, and would not roll down hill. I wallowed shoulder deep in the snow in getting the logs down, riding a pine branch part of the time to keep from sinking too deep. Then Billy started my *skis* down to me, and at last tried to slide my *ski* pole down. The latter took a dive into the snow, and cost us a half hour's hard work. We found it 6ft. under the snow and 30yds. from where we thought it was, it having slid under the snow like a snake in the grass. After finding this we called out Larsen and Holte, who were busy at the cabin, and we all got on the *skis* and packed logs in on our shoulders. It took us an hour to get in our wood, and the sun had long since gone behind the further cañon wall. Water we got this time out of the creek, Billy locating an open hole by a deep dimple in the level expanse of snow which filled the little cañon. We dug down here and found a sweep of open water about 6ft. below, which we reached by buckling our belts together and letting down a tin.

A Soldiers' Snug Harbor.

We fixed the chimney so it would not smoke by cutting a thick-foliaged young fir tree and standing it up alongside the chimney. This was a scheme of Billy's, who is a good deal of a schemer around a camp, and we found it worked all right. The little fireplace in the corner was not very big, but it was active, and it kept us warm all night. We had a good chance to dry out all our wet footwear and to put our *skis* in perfect order. Of course we had no bed clothing except the meager outfit earlier mentioned, but we passed a warm enough night, for the little cabin was so covered by the snow that it was nearly air-tight. We were all tired enough to sleep soundly, and we got a good night's rest.

Off for the Divide.

The next morning, Friday, March 23, found us up and busy before the sun had begun to look over into our little cañon. In summer I should like to follow up that cañon, for I imagine it leads into roughish country, but it seemed we were to go in the other direction, to find an easier approach to the great divide, on whose edge we now were. The maps show the main Continental Divide as south of where we were, and the mountains there are rougher, yet from Two Ocean Pass, below the south line of the Park, it is practically all divide along the crooked range clear up to where we were and beyond. Alum Creek, on which we were camped, flows east into the Yellowstone, which empties into the Missouri. Nez Percé Creek, which flows west down the opposite side of the range, drains a watershed of great area into the Firehole and Madison, which in turn reaches the Missouri, it is true, though by way of a water system entirely different from that flowing to the east. The forks of the Snake, of course, lay to the south and west from us, across the Divide proper, whose further waters find their way to the Pacific. It was our intention to work up the east slope, across the hot country of Mary's Mountain, and then to make down the Nez Percé Creek and the Firehole to the Fountain or Lower Geyser Basin. This necessitated a journey of something over twenty miles, which had to be made all in one day. We burned our bridges behind us, taking only enough food for one meal, and storing away our single blanket and sleeping bag in the tin-covered box, which Uncle Sam leaves as a mess chest in every one of these patrol houses. This lightened up our loads considerably, and we were glad of it, for we knew we had hard enough work ahead. We intended, if we had any luck at meeting the buffalo on Mary's Mountain, not to return to the shack, but to keep right on. If we did not find the buffalo, we intended to hold a council, make medicine and form further plans later in the day.

Billy and Larsen started on ahead, Billy telling Holte and myself not to start for half an hour or so, in order that the approach to the buffalo might be made more quietly and a better chance given than if the party were larger. Holte was complaining of his eyes, he having carelessly left off his glasses a part of the day before, and contracted a very good chance for snow blindness. We did everything we could for the eyes that morning, after we had put out the fire and put everything in military order about the shack.

AGAIN THEY GET THE BUFFALO.

We followed the trail left by Billy and Larsen until we had climbed up to the "hot country." Here there were numerous wide strips of bare ground, too hot for the snow to lie upon, where the buffalo evidently were in the habit of yarding. Abundance of sign was all about, and we saw deep fresh trails where there had been a stampede, so we knew that Billy had started the buffalo, whether he got a shot at them or not. I could see that part of the herd had plowed their way east back to Alum Creek, and part had gone straight ahead to the higher buttes into the dense forest and apparently in the direction of the heaviest snow, though we later saw that there was more hot country further up the mountain. As I learned from Billy later, he had had a splendid opportunity that morning. He surprised the whole herd on the lower hot strip of Mary's Mountain, and stalked them to within 40yds., as close as he cared to get. The light was good and he made several shots deliberately before the herd took fright. When they did start they went like a volcano, or an earthquake, or anything that is big and in a hurry.

THE BUFFALO ESTIMATED.

Billy thought that these were no doubt the same buffalo that we had photographed on Alum Creek the day before, and barring the six head we had seen lower down on Hayden Valley, we were quite sure that this constituted practically the entire Hayden Valley herd, from 80 to 100 in all—85 head as exactly as I could count it. We concluded it was not worth while to trouble these same buffalo any further, more especially as Billy had had fifty-eight shots at buffalo alone with his camera. The work on Hayden Valley seemed done. We took the Haynes report as to the game on the Pelican Valley, and decided not to make the long trip into that region in search of what we were practically certain not to find. The poacher Howell said there were only a few buffalo left on Pelican. We were now well settled in the conviction that the number of buffalo left alive in the Park was not one-half or one-third that generally supposed, and from what we had seen we feared that the killing had been heavier than anyone had dreamed. I would state here that I think our view of the case was conservative and fairly accurate. One knowing the country less thoroughly than Billy might have supposed that the buffalo seen this day and the day before were two distinct herds. Believing this, his report would declare the number seen and actually counted to be just twice what it really was. Let us wait till some one has seen in one day and in one herd 200 buffalo in the Park before we ever again believe there are so many as that left. I do not believe there are 150.[67] Of course I have not given all the little details of our investigations on Hayden Valley, but they were really thorough. We worked hard and crossed the valley from end to end and from side to side, and I do not think we missed a bunch of any size. Now we had seen the product of the hot country on Mary's Mountain, about the only other possibl[e] wintering ground of consequence remaining to be visited. If our search had not been thorough, I think it will be long before one is made that is more so. As only a few portions of the Park are or can be inhabited by the large game in the winter season, we felt that now a great part of our work was done. It remained to take a look at the Nez Percé Valley, where occasionally a few head of buffalo drift in, and after that to return to the north and go over into the northeastern corner of the Park to see about the elk wintering there.

A Glorious Privilege.

The immediate thing to be done, after Holte and I had overtaken the others—at the end of five miles' hard shoeing through the heaviest timber on Mary's Mountain, where time and again Holte declared that Hofer was "sure lost and goin' clean wrong," though we stuck to the trail of the shoes ahead, or followed the arrow marks on the snow-covered rocks when the trail crossed the hot ground—the immediate and pressing thing to be done, however, was to get to the top of the divide as quickly as possible, and then get down again on the other side to the kitchen of the Fountain Hotel as fast as possible, or a little faster. So we pressed on up the grades of the east slope, only stopping for a moment for breath when we paused at all. In spite of the hard work and the hurry, I could not help pausing once in a while to look back at the majestic panorama which unfolded more and more as we climbed higher and higher up the mountain. It was a rare and noble picture that lay unfold-ed, and one that I shall cherish many a year in memory. The Hayden Valley and its setting-clasps of timber points lay like a jewel of the range before us. Beyond it the mountains faded into the sky, white peaks rising saliently between. Nearer at hand the summits and cañons were more distinct. Below us, in the immediate foreground, lay the black forest, with masses of shade and all the contrasted high lights of the incumbent snow, dazzling under the radiance of a brilliant winter morning. It was a glorious sight—a glorious, glorious privilege to see it!

THE VIEW WEST FROM THE DIVIDE.

We crossed the last of the upper buttes of Mary's Moun-tain, with the many strips of hot country between, and at length came out upon Mary's Lake, directly on the summit. This body of water was now simply a level plain of snow. We found that by digging down a few feet in the snow we could get water, all the lower level of the snow seeming to be soaked full. We drank but sparingly, and pushed on hard as we could, for wherever the sun struck the snow now it was growing sticky, and we had many a weary mile before us yet. We did not follow the water trail which makes out for the west from Mary's Lake, but cut across a little ridge and finally worked out upon the west side of the Mary's Mountain summit or divide, from which we could look all over the Nez Percé Valley,[68] down which we were to go. Here we paused and spent a long time in the view. Fifteen miles to the west and south we could see the two low, round-topped buttes which mark the Firehole Valley near the Fountain Hotel. The white course of the creek valley lay like a broad ribbon between, apparently running directly in under the foot of the mountain on which we stood. Between us and the foot of this summit there stretched a black forest of pines, through which no *ski* runner, no matter how daring, could run down direct, yet somewhere through that bristling wood, and somehow on that rugged mountain side, wound the single trail by which we could get down. What the run was to be, one can imagine. Five miles of it was to be very fast, then the gradual slope of the water grade down to the Firehole Basin, about 10 miles more.

SOME CIVIL ENGINEERING.

The reader of this has perhaps traveled mountain trails, cut into the side of a declivity, and built on a grade so steep that a horse could barely go up or down. In that case it is only a question of the up and down angle, for the wheels sit flat or the horse goes on a level keel. But now suppose we blot out the entire trail with a fall of snow which fills up the cuts and buries all the fills, and makes the whole mountain side a slanting sheet of white. The *ski* runner, mounted on his glassy-bottomed snow skates, has before him two problems and two angles to be considered. He must take the down grade, but must cling to the side of the hill as he goes down. He must not slip or fall, and so get a broken back in course of the headlong roll which would ensue upon that. He must not steer too high up the side hill, and get into a box out of which he could only escape by a straight down grade too sharp for him to consider. None of these things must he do. He has in coming up gained elevation and held it jealously as long as he could. Now, a civil engineer in flight, with but the space of a wink to form and carry out his decision, he must throw away his acquired elevation just as rapidly as he can with safety. He must lay a course with as sharp a gradient as he dares. This was the problem before us, and as I looked at the sharp downward sweeps of the west aide of the divide, I was willing to admit that mistakes in taking that run were likely to be costly. We had had some sharp spins in getting this far down, but now the trail to be taken made one bold sweep down, out on open ground, then doubled sharply back into the black forest, as steep as a set of cellar stairs. Beyond the forest line no deponent said anything.

A Leg or Two Is Nothing.

All this writes pretty well, but we didn't talk about it very much. We cleared off the bottoms of the *skis*, and set the straps right and wondered how far we could slide before the snow got too sticky. Then Larsen, who was ahead on the trail at that time, quietly turned loose, setting on brakes with his pole as sharply as he could. With the indescribable, smooth, even motion peculiar to the *ski* run, he settled, shrank, condensed, shortened, seemed to grow smaller rather than go further. There was a light crust on part of the hill, and he flew over this and hardly broke it. Then he crunched through snow crust the sun had weakened, but tarried not at all. In the light snow we saw him throw up a long skit of white behind him. Then he leaned heavily over, got around the sharp bend and vanished like a flash into the forest, gathering a speed which showed what sort of a grade it was there.

Holte followed Larsen and Billy took their tracks. Holte and Billy both got slight falls, but made the bend. I got around the corner myself in their wake, and then nearly lost my breath at the jump downward the trail took as it turned into the wood. I could not by any means stop the speed. I sat astride the pole, but the momentum tore the end out of the snow and I got no brake of it. I jumped one hole in the snow where some fellow had had a tumble, and at length, taking one of the dozen corkscrew turns, I went bang! into a bank and came a great cropper right where Holte had done the same thing. On a run like that a fellow doesn't much care what he does or where he goes. My dignity suffers when I reflect how we all ran the last of the steepest grades, yelling like demons, and wishing, I do believe, that the snow was a little smoother and the gait a bit more keen. The first plunge of a sharp *ski* run is the only trouble. After that the impending loss of a spinal column or a leg or two doesn't seem to disturb one very much.

WINTER HOME OF THE BEAVER.

We made rapid time till we got into deep woods and soft snow, and then the shoes began to stick. The snow got worse and worse, and we had to waste over two hours in the middle of the day, waiting for it to mend. We built a fire, made a little meal, and gave our *skis* as thorough and scientific a roasting and waxing as they got any time on the trip. At this camp poor Holte forgot his revolver, and had to go back after it, a mile and a half and return, all of which made him swear very cordially of course.

When we came to crossing the Beaver Creek, we found it no easy matter, for the beavers have a dam here, and this had backed the water up into a dozen different channels, each so wide that it was next to impossible to jump on the *skis*. The water seemed to be from warmish springs, for it was mostly open and running, though often nearly covered by the deep drifts of snow. There is a Government postal shack here, but we found it half full of ice and water, as it sits in the willows on the level of the natural bank. After managing to get over the beaver waters, we built another fire, and again touched up our *skis*. It was here that we waited for Holte's return. That youth was in a bad fix, showing a little disposition to tire down, a tendency to snow blindness and a pronounced inclination to profanity. He was, as the saying among *ski* folk goes, "quarreling with his *skis*," which is natural, whether it does any good or not.

Hard Plugging.

Across the Nez Percé lay mile after mile of nearly level snow. It was just straight ahead, hard "plugging" here, the sort of going the *ski* man dreads most of all. We kept up a pretty steady swing till we got along into the Firehole timber. Here Billy's sore heel began to pain him seriously, and his big camera was nearly killing him. I traded loads with him, as my pack was now getting lighter, and was below 20lbs. We left Billy on a snow-covered stump, calmly examining his sore foot, which he had bare in the cool evening breeze. He said he would soon overtake us, but we were quite a way down stream before he did. Then we found a log across the river, and knowing we were now only a couple of miles or so from our objective point, we strung out as fast as we could, finally crossing the open valley of the Firehole on a crusted snow and in a sharp wind, for it had turned cold. It was black night when we stumbled into the kitchen of the Fountain Hotel,[69] with a good deal of the starch out of us, but still alive. Each man was made to dance a jig before supper, just to show that he was feeling good and lively. We had traveled over 20 miles that day, with all sorts of shoeing, most of it pretty bad.

Nez Perce Buffalo.

From the summit as we looked west we saw on the Nez Percé Valley what we thought to be three buffalo, but we could not confirm this when we got down to the level of the valley. The buffalo do sometimes cross the divide about where we did, and work between the hot country of Mary's Mountain and this sheltered little valley. They have not wintered on the west side of the divide in any numbers for a considerable time.

Struck Some Charms.

At the Fountain Hotel we found John Schmidt in charge, and he took the best of care of us. I am disposed to believe that he felt a mild surprise at the appetites we showed.

At the Fountain Hotel we proposed to stop for a couple of days, enjoying ourselves and seeing the geysers. We were at this point forty miles from the Mammoth Hot Springs, and we felt as if that were nothing, and as if the trip could not fail of being a success in its main purposes. Barring Holte, whose eyes were paining him intensely and who seemed to have gone a little stale, we were all in perfect health, with vitality keyed up to a pitch which made the mere breathing of the air of heaven a keen and subtle pleasure. Let those who will, loiter languidly through the Park in summer and comment on its beauty from a carriage seat. That is better than nothing, but the best is the trip on *skis*, if one really wants to see what wonderful things the Wonderland can do for one in winter. Certainly, it has spells, magic, charms for rest, for healing, for delight.

THE EFFECTS OF SOLITUDE.

IF it be true that it is well for man to be much with nature, it is equally true that is not well for him to be too much alone with nature. No hermit is absolutely sane. No Western sheep herder ever passed beyond seven years at his solitary calling without becoming mentally affected, and in the West the class is notorious for "cranks." Surrounded by the tokens of man's handiwork and presence, under a roof and within communicating distance of other men, the case of the solitary man is different, yet even such environments will leave visible effect. The winter keepers of the Park show the marks of their calling. I have spoken of John Folsom as the most silent man in the world. At the Fountain we found John Schmidt, the winter keeper, quite the opposite of this. He was delighted to see us, and talked freely with us on all sorts of topics. He would sit and talk on and on, and while I presume he never knew the difference, his voice had a low, even monotone; no doubt the reflex voice of his monotonous, solitary life. I said solitary, but this should be qualified. Mr. Schmidt had two enormous house cats and a dog. The two cats were bitter enemies and fought on sight, but each loved their keeper as much as he did them. One of them would crawl up on his lap and put its paws around his neck, and he would sit and stroke it by the hour. For the dog we visitors had no affection because that animal had a habit of sitting up all night and barking at the wolves and foxes which every night came in about the hotel kitchen where we made our abode. Often the dog would come running in and barking full voice, and then we knew he had struck something bigger than a fox, and wondered what it was. Meantime we did not sleep.

Our little stop at the Fountain was very pleasant, the more so because John Schmidt was an efficient hand at getting up good and frequent meals. We enjoyed rude appetites and were all in perfect health except Holte, who practically fell out of the trip at this point. He had neglected to wear his glasses on the last day out and was now nearly blind as result, besides being pretty well tired down by the long march. Holte was only a boy, barely 21, and though a good shoer he was too slight to stand the work as well as his mate, Larsen. Both were good cheerful boys and we could not have asked better. We let Holte go back in to the Post with one of the men from the Firehole station ahead of us, the others staying on for the trip through the geyser basins.

Died Alone In the Snow.

The dangers of winter travel in this wild region were painfully brought to view for us during our stay at the Fountain Basin. Sergt. Moran and one man had just gotten in from Riverside station, the extreme westerly patrol station of the Park, distant 15 miles from the Fountain or Lower Geyser Basin. Moran was asking anxiously for news of his other man, Alex. Matthews, who had started for the Fountain two weeks before. Matthews had not been heard from at either end of the route, and the hard conclusion had to be accepted that he had lost the trail and died alone in the snow. Capt. Anderson, knowing well the risks of shoeing in the Park, has issued strict orders that no soldier shall go out alone and no sergeant in charge of a patrol station has authority to send out a man alone. Moran was very uneasy and explained that Matthews had insisted on going alone over to the Fountain after the mail. He had been over the trail before and laughed at the idea that he could not make the trip in safety. Moran went to the top of the hill with him, 4½ or 5 miles, and from there the trail was easier and should have been plain. Matthews had a lunch with him and some matches, but nothing else by way of supplies. He might possibly have gotten through two or three days and nights, not more. What probably happened is that he was caught in some sudden storm, which blotted out all landmarks and left him with no idea of the points of the compass. Wandering from the trail, frightened at the awful situation which faced him, he no doubt exerted every energy to keep up the highest possible speed, and so became heated up. When night came with its added horrors, he was forced to stop. Perhaps he built a fire, but he had no blankets, and worn out and discouraged as he was, he perhaps dozed by the fire. Then came the dreaded chilling through, the stupor, the rigor. The wolves would soon find him then. Private Matthews's bones, last witness of another of the hidden tragedies of the mountains, may perhaps some day be found by the searching parties which sixty days later had proved unsuccessful. His bones may be found to the left of his trail, down in the Madison Cañon, or may be to the right, in the lower mountains, or perhaps he may have wandered miles back into the inner ranges, where men never go. His actual fate may perhaps always be a mystery. Desertion from the army was out of the question for him, equipped as he was, indeed an impossibility, for he would have been obliged to pass by some station for supplies. Heavy snows had wiped out all trails at the time we saw Moran, and later, after the thawing and sinking of the snow, the raised trail of the *skis* could not be found where it was expected Matthews had gone. He no doubt lost his head early in the day and got entirely out of his course. At the time we left the Park he had not been heard from, and since then I have not learned other news. Private Matthews enlisted at Cleveland, O.[70]

Moran wished to report to Capt. Anderson at once, of course, but the wire was down. On this account the man was sent in from Firehole Station, Holte accompanying him. They found the break near Norris Station, and the message reached the Post before they did. At the Fountain all we could do was to look sadly at the white mountains to the west, which held their secret tranquilly and coldly. Had it been two days instead of two weeks after the non-appearance of Matthews, something might have been done by searching, but as it was we all knew search was utterly useless, and so did not make up any party for it. Capt. Anderson duly sent out a search party on receipt of the news, but no one of the detail had any hope of success.

Among the Geysers.

Billy and I spent a couple of days resting and seeing the geysers, and of course, being new in the Park, I took the keenest interest in the wonderful spectacles of that weird region. We put in a half day in hard work with the camera, and made views of the Fountain Geyser, the Paint Pots and several of the minor geysers. I had also a good view or two of the hotel, half buried as it was in the snow. I can remember very clearly that afternoon, when toward evening the clouds broke and gave us a hint of the glories of a mountain sunset. The white armies of the snow were marching in endless file across the wide valley, and the same winds which drove them made endless involutions of the mystic mist veils of the geysers, made tenfold more distinct by the contact with the frostful air of winter. Near by us the breath of the mighty Fountain Geyser had congealed in a thousand prankish forms upon the trees nearest to it. Away in the background the sun was struggling bravely with the opposing clouds, and to the right of where it was sinking, appeared the high front of Mt. Holmes, just cut in half by a white snow-bearing spirit of the storm. I do not know what other time or what other region could produce a scene parallel to this. It is one of the panels of the majestic panorama which in my dreams I still can see to-day.

OFF FOR THE UPPER BASIN.

After seeing the main points of interest at the lower Fire-hole Basin, we concluded to visit the yet more wonderful scenes of the Upper Basin, and on a beautiful bright morning set out from the Fountain for that purpose, taking Larsen along with us. We made fine time with the *skis* till we reached the middle or Midway Basin, when the snow began to stick. We cared little for that, however, for the beauties about us compelled forget-fulness of physical exertion. Here we saw geysers and geysers and geysers, all sorts, all colors, all shapes. One of the most startling of the features of this district is the Prismatic Pool,[71] a beautiful great pool, whose surface is bordered by a wide band of deposit which in regular and sharply defined lines shows al-most every color of the rainbow. This prismatic ribbon extends quite around the pool, and is as evenly laid on as though by the hand of a skilled painter. It is well known that the different col-ored algæ form in different temperatures of the water, and this accounts for the different colors on many of the geyser terraces, but to find this regular parti-colored band showing the lines of color so vividly demarked is almost too startling for scientific theorizing. I like better to call it the alchemy of nature used in sport, the bubble-blowing of the Titans, the chemistry and the art of elves.

The great Excelsior Geyser,[72] whose tremendous crater could swallow up a troop of horse and not feel it, was not play-ing, of course, for it has not been active for years, but all the interior of the vast crater was a blinding mass of white steam. Out of this crater ran a brook of boiling water, which fell into the Madison River after its course of a few yards.[73] In its palmy days the old Excelsior when spouting threw out a boiling flood which raised the Madison a foot in height. Some years ago a trooper was fording the Madison when Excelsior was in action, and his horse was caught by the hot flood of water and so badly scalded that it died. Excelsior is the largest geyser in the world.

What its future is to be the grumbling, hissing crater would not tell, but all students of the Park hope it will resume activity after the present business depression shall have passed.[74]

WILDFOWL IN WINTER.

While at the Midway Basin I saw a flock of seven wild Canada geese flying down the Madison. In the Prismatic Pool I found the bones and feathers of a wild duck, which no doubt had been scalded to death. Wildfowl often light in the hot pools and are fatally scalded before they can escape. The foxes make quite a good thing out of this, and enjoy the luxury of game not only caught but cooked in advance.

A LOVELY STREAM.

After we left the Midway Basin we followed up the valley of the Madison, which is here a lovely stream. We saw numbers of ducks in the river, and were near enough to have shot them, but not near enough to photograph successfully. All along the Madison there are little hot steam peanut roasters of geysers, busily engaged in making steam for the sake of the landscape, and at some of these the frost effects, where the steam had condensed and congealed upon the foliage of the surrounding trees, were so beautiful that we could not resist the temptation to unpack and use a camera. Especially good views appeared as we neared the Upper Basin, and I have one view of the rapids on the Madison with snow masses and clouds of hot steam opposed to each other in the middle distance, which is one of the most prized landscapes in the series that I made.

SUMMER IN WINTER.

At the lower end of the Upper Geyser Valley we quit the direct course and went wandering on foot among wildernesses of geysers, hot springs, steam vents and hot streams of water. The hot rivulets cut long labyrinths of channels through the deep snow, and among these we wandered for a long time, seeing so many wonderful things they fairly ceased to impress us. Here also we got some pictures. I was just busy making a shot at a tiny hot pool, the formation of whose edges interested me, when Billy and Larsen called me to come and see a porcupine which had just come down to the river's edge. I did not get a picture of the porcupine, but I got a very good one of the pool, *sans* color. If only we could photograph in colors, as presently we shall.

We found a tiny stream of water, ten feet down between banks of snow, and in the water, green in the midst of all the whiteness, flourished a bank of tender water plants. It is an odd land, this Park country, with its summer in winter. There is no other like it on the earth, and it should be kept forever as it is.

A SNOW-SHOEING ACCIDENT.

There is no habitation at the Upper Basin except the lunch station of the Park Association, a small building which is closed at the end of the season. We intended to pass the night here, and had brought along enough provisions to last us for that time. It was a little after noon when we got to this silent and as we supposed deserted building. Larsen was in advance, and as he opened the door he heard voices within. Knowing that no keeper was ever left here, and not knowing of any other party being so far up in the Park, he naturally suspected poachers, and went on in with a heart full of hope and a handful of revolver, expecting to make an important arrest. We found the occupants of the little building to be Sergt. Van Buskirk and two men, Brown and Kuhr, the detail of the Shoshone patrol station, the southern-most of the military outposts which patrol the Park, and one located beyond some of the wildest and roughest country, that near the Teton range. These men were on their way to the Post, but they looked in bad shape to finish the journey. They had just gotten in to the building, and it appeared doubtful whether they would ever all get out. They were all more or less snow-blind, and Brown had an ankle so badly sprained that he was really a pitiful object. His foot and leg were horribly swollen, and

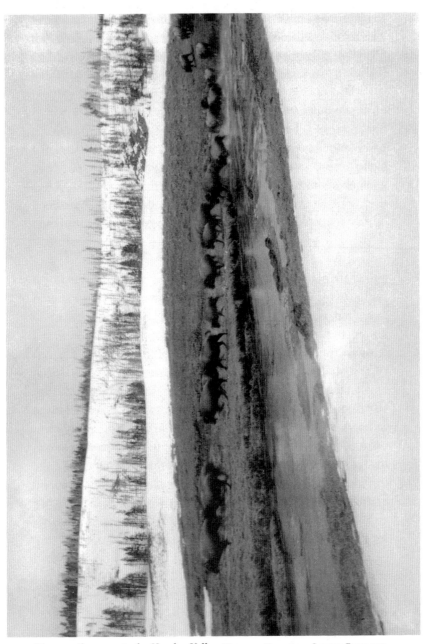

Bison on the move in the Hayden Valley. Montana Historical Society Research Center, Photograph Archives, Haynes Foundation Collection

he was suffering acute pain. The others were in better shape, but none too good, for they had all had a sad time of it. They were out there three days from Shoshone station, and had spent two nights without blankets, huddling over a fire. Brown had sprained his ankle in a bad fall in running a hill, and the little party had really been in serious trouble. The others kept with Brown till the provisions ran out, and then at the last camp, eight or ten miles back, it became necessary for one or both to go ahead and leave Brown on the trail till food could be brought back to him. Brown did not like the idea of being left, and so summoned up courage enough to make the last stage of the journey in. As there was no possibility of his receiving care at the place where he now was, he had to face the thought of a still further journey on the following day, to the Firehole station, nine miles more of absolute misery.

PUBLIC IGNORANCE OF THE PARK SUPERVISION.

Such are some of the incidents of the winter patrol of the Park. It is easy to sit a[t] home and say how it ought to be done. The actual fact is that it is wonderfully well done, with a commanding officer whose equal for the task could perhaps not be found, and by men whose courage and fortitude could not be duplicated if asked of any other class. No one knows of this. No one knows anything about the Army. No one knows how the Park is watched either in summer or in winter, at what cost of privation, of hardship, of simple courage, at what expenditure of care, of vigilance, of energy and thoughtfulness. It is easy to sit at home and criticise this, but I hope that if any such self-appointed critic may happen to read something of this, he will in simple justice to himself take counsel of his ignorance hereafter and criticise no more that of which he knows so little. I have seen nowhere except in FOREST AND STREAM any fair statement of the facts, and I do not for a moment pretend to be able to set forth the facts in such way as would show the difficulties of the service asked. Perhaps the story of Burgess, of Brown, of poor

Matthews, may give some idea of what one winter may bring of misfortunes to the men in the humbler ranks of the service—misfortunes felt keenly enough by those higher in authority. For Brown, it will serve to say that he managed to make the journey to the Firehole Station the next day, and that ended the trip for him. He never got any further all the winter, and was forced to wait until the snow was gone before he could travel the remaining forty miles to the Post. At the Fountain Van Buskirk got the mail for his detail. They had not had any letters since October and it now was March.

Could Wax their Skis.

We now numbered six men at the Upper Basin, but we managed to get along very comfortably, finding an excellent place to cook coffee and wax *skis* on the big range in the abandoned kitchen. The fire we built in the front rooms started a number of leaks in the roof, which was badly strained by the great mass of snow resting on it.

It is not within the actual province of these articles to attempt description of the scenic wonders of the Park, for space alone would forbid it, but none the less Billy and I enjoyed thoroughly our unique privilege of seeing the greatest geyser basin of the world in the depth of winter. Thousands have stopped where we did and have seen Old Faithful, the Lion and Lioness, the Giant and Giantess, the Castle, the Bee Hive, the dozens of others of notable geysers of this great group. Of all these the world already knows or should now, and all who have not seen them should do so. I am a bit ashamed of Americans who go to Europe before they go to the Yellowstone Park. Singularly enough, in Europe the Park has a more distinguished reputation than it has here, and a very large per cent. of the travelers who visit it are foreigners.

Obliging Geysers.

When the geysers knew the FOREST AND STREAM party was in the valley they all put on their Sunday clothes and did their best to entertain us. Old Faithful, the Giantess, the Lioness, the Castle, and a lot of lesser lights, played long and well for our inspection and we gave them generous applause. The camera came into use once more, and we spent the afternoon very busily.

The "Forest and Stream" Luck Held.

On the following morning we were all astir early, as we knew the shoeing would be better early in the day. Van Buskirk's party led ours by some hours. Billy went next, as he was anxious to get photographs of some Clark's crows,[75] for which he had put out bait on a shed at the Fountain Hotel. I kept Larsen and stayed behind, hoping for a clear morning by which to get better opportunity to make pictures of the Geyser Valley. The FOREST AND STREAM luck held, and I was more than rewarded for the wait. I saw the Geyser Valley at sunrise of the clear winter morning. Ah! but that was a glorious eight, a strange and glorious sight! Never in my life can I hope to see the like again, for I will hardly take the winter trip again. What good fortune, then, that I am able to show my friends a portion at least of this rare spectacle. The FOREST AND STREAM luck held, and the best photographs I made in the Park I made right here. Remembering the expert advice quoted earlier, I went down to the lower end of the valley, so that when I looked back over the view I was facing the sun, which was just rising above the wooded mountain rim. The air was radiantly clear, and the snow was sparkling and dazzling in contrast to the somber black of the surrounding pines. All over the valley rose columns and sheets and veils of white steam, sharp and distinct in the brilliant light which shone through them from the east. I made my pictures with the camera turned squarely toward the sun, and I caught geyser after geyser, as sharp and keen as though they had been frozen, to say nothing of many beautiful cloud effects. I even got one picture which shows geysers in action and also shows the full disk of the sun, clean cut and round, on the unfogged plate. This singular photograph seems to me one of the most valuable of the lot, and I look on it as quite a triumph for the Eastman film, a roll of which I was using out of Billy's Smithsonian Institution supplies, having discarded the less successful film made by another firm. This free, unsolicited praise I can easily give as I look over the results of that fortunate morning's work.

After I had concluded my picture-making, Larsen and I pulled out for the Fountain. We overtook Van Buskirk's party still two or three miles out. Larsen went in with them, while I left the trail and went out alone to secure photographs of the Peat Fountain[76] and Black Warrior Geyser, which two solitaries are at some distance from the main.

It Looked Like Night Traveling.

We were having a delightful time at the geyser basins, and I could have enjoyed a month of study there, but we had to shorten our stay and prepare for the completion of our journey. We lightened our packs here still further, discarding every article not positively necessary. Our needful laundry work we did at one of the hot springs just at the foot of the hill. It was a beautiful washtub, about 15ft. across, but the water was too hot to bear one's hands in. While we washed one handkerchief in this boiling fluid, its predecessor in the process would be frozen stiff on the snow near by.

On account of the bad shoeing we had been having, we determined to travel at night, making our start for the journey not later than 1 o'clock in the morning. It is rather odd, snowshoeing at night in the mountains, and about this I will try to tell something in the following article.

A NIGHT MARCH ON THE SKIS.

ON the morning of Tuesday, March 27, we began our journey from the Fountain Basin to the Mammoth Hot Springs. We had found the snow too sticky during the last few days to warrant trying a long march in the day-time, so we resolved to make the forty miles in two journeys of twenty miles each, making the half-way stop at Norris station, and traveling both stages as much as possible during the night time, when the shoeing would be easier.

We had little sleep the night before we left the comfortable quarters of the Fountain Hotel, for we arranged to have John Schmidt call us at midnight. I hardly believe any of us needed much awakening, for John Schmidt's dog had kept us all awake in his nightly pastime of barking at the wolves and foxes. I was sorry to leave John Schmidt, who had shown himself cheerful and expert in making us comfortable, but I was glad to be separated from John Schmidt's dog and his reverberant and redundant voice. Anyhow, Schmidt and his dog got us out of bed at 12 o'clock midnight of the blackest sort of night that ever fell on the mountains. We ate breakfast at 12:15 A.M., and having our packs already pretty well arranged we had our *skis* in order and were outside the kitchen at 1 A.M., in an air quite keen and shivery. An obscuring sort of white, misty darkness seemed to prevail in the midst of the black darkness. This was caused by the reflection from the snow. It was a black night in a white country. We said good-bye to Schmidt, and his dog eloquently bade us farewell as we turned our toes to the northward. Then each gave a push with his pole, and on the instant disappeared down the great icy drift which sloped from the hotel down to the level of the valley. As we slipped ahead the dark ring of the pines which encircled the hotel became plainer, and in a moment we had slid through and were out in the little open plain which lies between the hotel and the patrol station, out of which one or two hot springs bubble up. All around us was a baffling, puzzling, impenetrable veil of gray, through which we could see only a short distance about us. The short night was at its very darkest, and for a time the outlines of the peaks and forests about us and ahead of us were indistinguishable.

SAW A BEAR IN THE NIGHT.

The Fountain Hotel is always a great place for bears in the summer time, numbers of those animals being attracted by the offal pits. Our trail lay not very far from one of the stamping grounds of these familiar and impudent beasts, though we had no thought of any bear being out so early at that season of the year. One old fellow, however, it seems, was making an early spring reconnaissance that morning. Larsen first called my attention to him, just as we got to the foot of the little hotel hill and out into the open near the hot spring. Billy was off to the left, trying to pick out a trail through the trees, and did not see the bear, but Larsen must have been within 30 or 40yds. of him. In the gray fog of the night the creature seemed to loom up about as big as a court house. We left him holding down the Geyser Valley, as none of us wanted him. Larsen had his six-shooter, but Billy and I would have had a hard time getting a bear if we had been hungry, for we had only a butcher knife apiece. Besides, this bear was illegal.

A New Lesson in Ski Work.

The snow was crusted over hard and firm, so that we did not break through, and I found that I had still another lesson on the *skis* ahead of me. The *skis* slipped ahead all right, but they also slipped sidewise with equal cheerfulness, and when I took a step forward with one shoe, the other would be going backward just as busily. It took me a few moments to get the hang of this, and to learn that crusted snow takes an altogether different *ski* theory from soft snow. In the ordinary *ski* step the pole is held with both hands, the outer end touching the snow at quite a distance from the feet. No great force is gained then, and the pole is used practically only for steadying the *ski*-goer in his stride—and a wonderful help it is, too. On crust matters are quite different, and the inexperienced one finds himself straining and laboring where all ought to be easy sliding. If the inexperienced one will grasp his *ski* pole in one hand, and setting the end in the snow close in by his feet, push forward with it in the line of travel at every step, he will find a vast improvement in his progress. One can take a staff and push himself forward on skates upon the ice, and the principle is the same with the *skis* on crusted snow. Given a smooth, hard crust, with no "ash snow" blown across it, and the *ski* traveler should make his best time, because the shove from his arm on the staff gives him an impetus which lengthens each step a number of inches, and it is the added slide of the *ski* beyond the natural step which makes time in traveling. His step thus becomes much more like a skating step, and he moves on with an easy roll of his weight from one leg to the other, with less friction under his feet and with the added propelling power gained from the muscles of the arm. Crust going is the easiest of all for an expert and perhaps the hardest for a beginner. Until he learns the hang of it, the latter will rack and strain himself trying to keep up telegraphic communication with his feet, which take to themselves the most surprising absences from their post of duty.

What Makes a Good Walker.

If one will take the trouble to observe the persons he sees walking on the streets, he may notice that the great majority walk with an up and down, straight back and forward motion. They do not advance the body alternately side and side, as Aunt Susan does when she carries in the basket of washing from the laundry house. In other words, the majority of people will walk with a knee action instead of with a hip action. Yet no great walker can ever be found who walks with a knee action, and this any long distance pedestrian will tell you.[77] Some horses are born with a pacing action, apparently, and some men have naturally that looseness of the hips which makes possible the easy rolling gait, the rapid long stride without effort or "over-stepping" which are present in the natural walker. If you will try this, rolling the body sidewise at each step, you will see that you can step further than when you face square to the front and stick your foot out square to the front. If you can do this hip step easily and keep it up, you will seem to be "walking all over," but you will be making time. If you can keep it up, you can beat any up and down, knee action walker, for your step will be longer than his and just as rapid. An acquaintance of mine, an ex-professional pedestrian who has done 110 miles in twenty-four hours, steps 36in. in his stride with perfect ease, and can keep it up. It is simply impossible for a knee walker to keep near him. Some wise men of science say that a rolling walk betokens a weakness of the muscles of the sides, but the wise men often make mistakes. The ungainly contortionist walk of the professional has its reasons for being.

If then no man can succeed on the sawdust if he has a bound-up hip conformation, I should think the same would be true as to his success on the *skis*, where the rolling of the weight from side to side is even more essential to get that coveted little gain slide at the end of each step. Your good *ski*-goer does not quicken his step when he wants more speed. He keeps his easy, steady swing, but increases his sliding stride, getting his added momentum out of the transfer of his weight and the push of his rearward foot, plus the push from his staff, whatever that may amount to. I often watched the loose-jointed, shambling, rolling, hip action of Larsen and Holte on the march, which was so noticeable that it sometimes looked like lameness. Yet both these boys were fine shoers, and their shambling gait was taking them easily forward, each step a little further than a straight ahead step would.

A TOBOGGAN-SLIDE IN CURL PAPERS.

I had plenty of time, or at least plenty of cause, to figure on some of the foregoing things as our night journey went on. Billy and Larsen, who just reveled in crust running, hit an awful gait, and I surely thought they would kill me before even we got across the Firehole River. At the end of the first mile I was in a reek of perspiration, though the temperature must have been near zero. About that time I hit on my theory, and thence-forward I walked about as much with one arm as I did with both legs, and rejoiced exceedingly. I could not see the others more than 40yds. ahead of me out in the open, but when we got into the dense forest even this distance was cut down. Mile after mile, in that black, mysterious, unpromising mountain night, I swung on rhythmically, trying to keep the toe of my *ski* just at the rear edge of the slim, phosphorescent streak of light which came back from under Billy's shoes. This faint glow of the snow was quite pronounced, and could be seen at a distance of several yards, while the figure of the man ahead was only the dimmest of outlines. The effect of it is very weird and odd, and one of the main features of the night march, for we could for a long time see only the blackness of the shadowy forest about us, and the faint white reflection that hung close down along the surface of the snow. I give it up how Billy kept the trail, but I supposed he was a plenty good guide, and did not venture any advice as to which way any place or anything was, because I didn't know. There might be hills, forests, mountains, streams, in that country, but I couldn't see any of them and had to take it all for granted. I was sure I was walking in a wild, unreal dream. The forest was absolutely silent, and from on the trail ahead there came no sound (*ski* travelers do not talk, needing all their breath). Only the soft *s-zit*, *s-zit* of the whispering *skis* could be heard, and only could be seen that uncanny fire that came out of the icy snow. Surely that must be a dream.

Trusting to chance, it seemed to me, Billy turned aside from the trail and took a short cut across country, heading for some place that he knows more about than I do. We caught an awful climb in course of this cut off, and I presume we were half an hour getting up that one hill. I suppose I fell about fifty times getting up there, but I had plenty of company. Then we went ahead some more over some open, rough hills, and at last pulled up at the top of what appeared to me to be the bottomless pit. It was simply a black hole, down below us in the universe, and how deep or how big it was we certainly could not see from where we were.

"This is the big 'S' hill. You'd better ride your pole here, old man," said Billy, soothingly, in that gentle, off-hand, try-to-be-unconscious tone of voice he always used when he knew a fellow was standing on the edge of an air-tight cinch for breaking his neck. Whereat, being on to Billy by this time, I groaned, and got my straps ready.

"There's two or three pretty sharp turns in this hill," said Billy, deprecatingly, as if he had made the hill and wasn't quite suited with it, "but they might be worse, and you can ride your pole hard at the turns." So saying, Billy turned, stepped forward, and disappeared in the dark below like Mephistopheles, leaving a train of fire behind him for a brief instant as he flew.

Turns in that hill! I should say there were, several of them. The only thing I can liken that hill to is a half mile of toboggan slide done up in curl papers. I don't see how they got all the turns in, and for my part am confident I skipped some of them.

Not knowing the trail in the least, all I could do was to get my *skis* in the tracks ahead and let go. Of course I could not tell when there was a bend ahead, but as I usually went end over end at the turns, I suppose I found a good many of them. I don't know why such falls don't kill a fellow, but they didn't seem to jar very much, and at last I rolled the last stretch of the spiral chute and emerged not much the worse for wear. I didn't consider it etiquette to ask the other fellows how many times they had fallen, and they didn't ask me. I couldn't have told them accurately if they had.

THE NIGHT RUN DOWN CANYON CREEK HILL.

We plodded along in the night, making pretty good time over a country which did not seem to be so very difficult for *ski*-work, though once in a while we struck slopes up which it was sore labor to climb. After the first four or five miles our crust left us, and toward morning the snow began to have a creepy feel, which made us fear sticky work when the sun should come out. We made very good time till we got to the top of that long two miles of grade known as Cañon Creek hill. (Billy took the old trail and did not go by the new trail, past the Gibbon Falls[78]). Here the light had grown perceptibly stronger, though we could not see with perfect distinctness at any very great distance. Here again Billy intimated carelessly that on the whole I might as well ride my pole, when we got to the last sharp, where the hill spills itself into the valley of the river. Down to this point on the hill we had come by a succession of easy grades, whose pleasant slides had made us think that snow-shoeing wasn't such hard work after all. At the last pitch Larsen went ahead, dropping out of sight like a bird in flight. As he turned into the forest around the first bend we heard him give a great shout, and supposed at once he had met something in the trail. This turned out later to have been a red fox, which for an instant tried to keep ahead of the *skis*, but gave it up and disappeared in the forest a very much scared fox as the yelling Scandinavian swept close up to it. When Larsen yelled Billy started off after him, and giving Billy time to get clear, I dropped off in turn, having by this time a clean-cut trail to travel in. I rode my pole, as per Billy's late advice, or tried to do so, though the hind end of the staff insisted on jumping up out of the snow and giving the *skis* a better run for their money, evidently thinking it a shame to spoil a good hill. The last short hitch of that hill was like the roof of a house, and moreover, it had a compound curve in it which must have applied a severe torsional strain to the backbone of the mountain. Lastly, there was a drift about 15 ft. deep at the bottom of the hill. This latter I could not see, for in that dim light the surface of the snow seemed to have no inequalities at all. I found the drift, however. Coming down the chute of the last grade, the first thing I knew I was entirely buried in the drift, my shoes going into it before I was aware of any difference in the level. Billy was standing beyond me, in the woods away off from the trail. Larsen also was off the trail, and was pulled up by the river, above the bridge. The last run of the Cañon Creek hill is a screamer, and it is said that no shoer of the Park except John Folsom has ever run it and made the bridge across the river without flying out of the trail. Snowshoe Pete has twice run into the river here, and I am inclined to think he would not have done that purposely.

It was still too dim to see well the full glories of the Gibbon as we passed up it, but enough of its snow-clad steeps could be made to prove of interest. The Gibbon hereabout is an ideal stream for the angler, but there are no native trout above the falls, I believe, though plantings have been made which are yet to be heard from.

At daybreak we built a fire on the bank of the river, made coffee and ate our little breakfast with keen relish. At this point there was a beautiful series of rapids, and altogether it was a fine place for a breakfast in the snow. Snow began to fall as we sat at breakfast and the morning broke gray.

After breakfast I started out up the cañon ahead, but I found to my surprise that in the short time of our halt some mysterious change had taken place in the quality of the snow. That which we dreaded had happened. The snow had begun to stick! I turned back and found the others already waxing up their *skis*. In turn they now set out and left me alone at the fire waxing my shoes. I gave them a good going over, taking a quarter of an hour to it perhaps, and set out after the others, hot foot. By the trail I passed one of those great wonders which are so common in the Park that they seem almost unable to attract notice—the Beryl Spring,[79] a great caldron spring of bubbling, beautiful, gem-colored, boiling hot water, which pours a brook into the Gibbon, over which a culvert is a necessity. I paused here alone for quite a time, until I felt obliged to hurry up the trail. The shoes were sticking frightfully.

A NARROW ESCAPE.

Of course the Gibbon does not freeze at any time of the year. It is here a rapid, rushing mountain river, as I remember it, about 20yds. wide and perhaps 3 to 5ft. deep, though it is no doubt deeper than it looks. The foot trail for Norris crosses the Gibbon hereabout by means of a foot bridge,[80] the latter being constructed of two logs. On top of these two narrow logs, which had no hand rail to them, the snow lay in a long white ridge, about 2 or 3ft. deep. Along the top of this ridge of snow I could see the *ski* trail of Billy and Larsen, who had incontinently walked right on out on to it, in child-like confidence that everything was all right until proved otherwise. I noticed that the snow bridge had sagged and cracked beneath their weight, but what was I going to do about it? There was that river, and I had to get across. Therefore I stepped out boldly in the tracks of my predecessors. I had gone out to near midstream, when crash! down went a whole section of the snow ridge under me, and down I came to bed rock on the logs, fortunately astride the logs, but with my pack hanging down to one side, down stream, my *skis* just hanging to my feet and just barely clearing the rushing water, and my whole center of gravity entirely lost in the confusion. I presume that was the nearest I came to a serious accident while in the Park. Had I gone into the river I could hardly have hoped to get out. Had one of my *skis* slipped off, as I feared each moment it would, it was on the instant gone beyond all chance of recovery. Thanks, then, to muscles well toughened. Slowly, it seemed to me an age, I gripped with knee and hand until inch by inch I got back over the logs, with that ton's weight pack above me, and not dragging me down. Then, lying face down along the log, I twisted my feet under and got my left *ski* off with my right hand and the right one off with the left hand, being careful to keep my toes turned up stiff, so the *skis* would not get caught by the water. Then I put them on the broken snow ridge ahead of me, and every moment expecting another break and tumble, crawled the rest of the way on my hands and knees, with my hands in the toe straps. I was perspiring some and plenty scared when I got over. Some folk never get scared. I do. I don't want any more midwinter carnival of athletics of just that sort.

Not far beyond the Gibbon I found Billy and Larsen sitting by the wayside, on some hot ground about a miniature set of geysers which kept up a great fretting and fuming. They had built a fire and we all now waxed up our shoes, remaining here for quite a while, as the snow was now in horrible shape, though it was still early in the day. After a time we got into our packs again and plodded on to Norris Station across the beautiful Gibbon meadows and in over the Geyser Basin. We saw no game whatever either on the Gibbon meadows or in the Elk Park.[81] We thought the haying operations might possibly have driven the elk out. We each took his own gait, as we knew we were well in. Toward the last the snow became very soft and wet, and in this condition it did not stick to the shoes, this showing another phase of the infinite variety of *ski* travel. We reached Norris at 11 A.M., having been on the way ten hours, though not traveling all the time. At noon a heavy snowstorm was in swing at Norris Station. Here we stopped and spent the afternoon and the night till midnight. At 1 A.M. of Wednesday, March 28, we were again on the *skis* and off for another night journey, the last between us and the Post.

Night Stage from Norris in.

I will not weary readers with a minute story of our journey in, as all that can be wished is a presentation of features enough to show the character of the trip, and not a story of personal exploits or experiences except as the latter are incidental and so useful. We made this last night stage of twenty miles in good shape, and it was more of a pleasure than that of the night before, much by reason of the greater strength of the light, it not being cloudy, but clear and very cold. It grew colder as the night advanced, and for almost the only time except on Hayden Valley we tied up our ears and faces. The thermometer was no doubt well below zero. Our clothing was covered with a white rime of frost.

The night continued bright and pleasant and we ventured an occasional jest as we pushed along. Every fellow was now hard and fit, and the fatigue of this journey in was very different from that felt on the same ground coming out.

At the Crystal Springs we thought we might see one of the mountain lions which are known to lurk in the rough country thereabout. We did not see our lion, but we saw his tracks along the trail ahead of us, as if he had been following along a *ski* track, in curiosity to learn what made it.

At the Swan Lake Flats we had a great privilege—that of seeing perfect winter sunrise in the mountains. The sun broke glorious over the mountains making the eastern rim of this level glittering plain, and slowly, one by one, we could see the tips of the peaks on the west of the flats grow pink, purple, white, under the advancing rays. Electric Peak, Trilobite Point, Antler Peak, Mt. Holmes—all these look well in summer, so they tell me. One can vouch that in the winter and at sunrise they are simply glorious. We stopped and looked at the lovely panorama for many moments. As usual, the coyotes were saluting the morning sun with a series of ragged, thin-edged howls. It sounded as though there were a hundred of them.

THE LAST RISKY RUN.

On Swan Lake Flats we found the snow crusted, and on the great descent of the Golden Gate hill we found it still more crusted. Here the snow had thawed and frozen, and presented a surface which we knew would make it risky running the great hill on which we had counted so much for an exciting but pleasant run. Each fellow got down after his own fashion, but there was no fellow who kept on the trail, or who got off without fall and risk of limb. Larsen had his shoe get away and go down into a cañon, but fortunately the crust bore him up so that he could get down after it. After that he seems to have turned everything loose and gone down the rest of the grades helter-skelter and haphazard. He missed the trail in many places. I often caught Billy riding slopes sitting down on his *skis*—an act which we were now almost ready to call unprofessional conduct. I was close behind Billy, getting down the slowest I knew how, when finally I saw him stop at the top of a long, sharp slope, and peer curiously over. Evidently Billy was thinking, and I slid over to ask him what he thought. Just before I got to him he swung astride his pole, slid off, and was out of sight. The next moment, as I happened to look off to the right of the trail, when I got to the place where Billy had started, there was Billy three-quarters of a mile below, away off to the right of the trail and headed for the Post meadows. He wasn't longer than a lead pencil, and was whizzing like a bullet, doing his best to come to anchor. For my part, I wished I was down where he was. That was an awful run. I could not keep the pole down in the snow for a break, do all I could. I lost control of the shoes entirely, flew from the trail, and went at terrible velocity down the mountain side. The hard, glassy crust gave no bite on the snow at all for the shoes. What should have been a pleasure ride became a wild and risky flight on a pair of runaway *skis*. My education as a *ski* man was to be rounded out, and a trifle of my conceit removed. This the runaway *skis* seemed to say to me as they clocked together, going side-ways and every other way, utterly beyond my control. We jumped all sorts of things, the *skis* and I, and I kept my feet, leaning back on the pole heavily. At length, a group of trees appeared, directly in the course and they got bigger and blacker every half second, and the more unwelcome as I realized that I could not avoid them. I saw that one tree was square in my line, and felt that to strike it meant bad disaster at least. Unable to do better I threw myself on my side and went rolling on down instead of sliding. The force of the bullet-like flight sent me bounding up into the air, pack and all. When I stopped at length the heels of my *skis* were just where the toes ought to be, and my feet were doubled under me. Saved by the FOREST AND STREAM luck once more, I got out of an awful fall with nothing worse than a game ankle, which was nearly well before I left the Park. That tree is still standing. If I had ever hit it it wouldn't be, and I have no doubt Capt. Anderson would have had me arrested for defacing natural objects of interest in the Park.

It was Capt. Anderson himself who at 8 o'clock that morning was welcoming us back, and asking me what I thought of America, and how I liked snowshoeing in general. I was glad enough to surrender without conditions, and though at first a little timid about soap and water, not being used to them, I gradually got around to where a private soldier would look at me without pulling a gun. The main trip through the Park was over.

YANCEY'S TO FOLLOW.

I have already spoken of our trip to Yancey's, twenty miles northeast of the Post, after the elk. Of this rather interesting part of our game explorations I shall wish to speak a bit more fully in the concluding article of this series. On this, the last journey of them all, we saw more game in two days than we had seen in the whole Park up to that time.

THE COUNTING OF THE ELK.

EASE WITH DIGNITY AT THE POST.

IT was very comfortable at Ft. Yellowstone in the good hands of Captain Anderson, the commanding officer, and for my part I did not care to leave either the Park itself or that portion thereof in which I was then located. There was a comfortable willingness to lie still a day or so, and a cheerful disposition to obey the command of the ranking officer to keep still, retain my clothing on my person and take it easy for a while before doing any more snowshoe travel. Very valuable also were these days of rest at the Post, for during them I learned still more of the thorough method by which the Park is governed, of the perfected system in force, and of the painstaking and conscientious labor performed by every branch of the military body to whose care the great preserve has been handed over. At that time, March 29, it should be remembered, there was no law by which a poacher or violator of the Park could be punished, except as under military regulations. The latter, though acknowledged to be inefficient, were naturally construed as severely as possible. At that time the poacher Howell was reposing as deep in the guard house as Capt. Anderson could throw him, and Capt. Anderson, with some quiet chuckles, told me how sometimes Capt. Scott, whose troop was stationed, in the tourist season, at the Geyser Basins of the upper Park, had found occasions to make some exuberant bridegroom, who had written his name and that or his beloved on a geyser formation, walk back twenty miles from the next stage station and scrub out his immortality by means of soap and brush.

Our rest, however, was not of long duration, for it was thought best to make the trip over to the wintering ground of the elk, so that a personal investigation could be made as to their numbers. This would take us over toward the northeast corner of the Park, to the country about Yancey's, and the East Fork beyond Yancey's. The distance to Yancey's was twenty miles, to be made in one journey. A Chinook was on, and the shoeing had now become simply awful. Mr. Haynes had been over to Yancey's, and described it as the worst time he had ever had in his life. With this outlook we did not feel exuberant over the trip.

To get some sort of notion of that country, in the absence of a map, let us suppose a large letter V. The legs of the V are made of the Yellowstone and Gardiner rivers. Ft. Yellowstone we may call located near the apex or point of the V, and we will say Yancey's is at the base, calling it about twenty miles across the base. Yancey's is, however, on the level of the Yellowstone River. These rivers here all run down hill, and they run at the bottom of deep valleys or cañons. The Post being located outside of the V, that is to say, on the left hand side of the Gardiner Valley, there were, in *ski* talk, three "hills" to be accounted for in this trip (in reality there may have been 3,000). The first was the west side of the Gardiner, or from the Post down to the Gardiner River, maybe a couple of miles or less. Then came the climb up so-called "Gardiner Hill," two miles or so more, to an elevation much greater than that of the Mammoth Hot Springs. This would bring us to the great plateau—a very broken and hilly one we found it—which we will say lies between the two arms of the V. Across this plateau was ten or twelve miles, and we would then be within five miles of Yancey's, that is to say, at the top of the left side of the Yellowstone arm of the V.[82]

Yancey's, being at the level of the bottom of the valley, would of course be far below, but once at the top of the hill we were the same as there, it was said, for everybody agreed that once at the Devil's Gut at the top of the Yancey Hill, it would take us a very short space of time to get to the bottom, always provided that we could keep up with our *skis*.

It will be seen that we had only one "hill" to climb going east, the Gardiner Hill leading up to the plateau. Coming back, we would have two "hills" to negotiate. Capt. Anderson very kindly offered us a solution of a portion of our difficulties. He thought that as the snow was going so fast at these lower altitudes, he could set us in an ambulance across the Gardiner River and pretty well up the Gardiner Hills behind.[83] He further promised that if we would set a day for our return he would have the ambulance meet us as far up the Gardiner Hill as it could get on that day. All of which was not only kind but valuable assistance, as it would save us one run down and one climb up, on a locality where the shoeing was very bad.

It was about 9 o'clock of the morning of March 30 when we left the Post for Yancey's. Billy took along his big camera, and we both had along in our packs the necessary articles. We had along this time private Hunt, Capt. Anderson having detailed him in place of Larsen—who had started early the night before for the Lake Hotel with the detail sent out to bring in the buffalo heads stored there by the first party out of the Howell plunder. This would give Larsen 140 miles or so more on top of what we had traveled, enough to get him in condition, anyhow.

I have often had occasion to admire the skill of the real Western mountain teamster, which is something no tenderfoot driver can appreciate without seeing. A tenderfoot teamster would have turned back at the end of the first half mile and called this road impassable, for the mules were breaking through, plunging and wallowing shoulder deep in the snow. Our teamster took it all coolly, never hurried his mules, and let them take their time. Those beasts seemed skilled and sapient also in this sort of work. They seemed never to get rattled when they went down nearly out of sight in the snow, but lay still and took it easy till they got their breath, and then slowly and carefully tried it for a few yards further on. By this curious illustration of an adaptation to environment, we got on slowly even so far as the Gardiner River and a little way up the hill beyond, to a point where the snow was too deep for the mules, and apparently hard enough for the *skis*. The snow was melting along the ground and not on top, as we learned by slumping through into streams of water when we got out to help the mules. We did not dare take many chances about getting our feet wet in the valley flats, but here on the hill the snow was not so hard, so after leaving the team we walked on foot nearly to the top of the Gardiner Hill. The mail carrier, Church, perhaps the most skillful winter driver in that region, had taken his team with a sled up this hill. Church took a buckboard to the point where we left our team, then left the buckboard and took to his sled. When he could get no further he hitched his horses and took to his *skis*. He carried the Yancey's and Soda Butte mail, and was rarely behind in any weather. How he did it was a mystery. The snow he passed through and over was from 3 to 30ft. deep, and it probably averaged 6 or 8ft. He managed to find bare ridges and get along. As I have stated, the snow does not lie so evenly in this part of the Park, being blown about more.

We found Church's trail up the Gardiner Hill of much service, as it packed the snow so that it would bear our weight that morning without the *skis*. We found that the best place to step was about 4in. inside the track of the sled runner, where the snow seemed to be compressed most. If one stepped on the ridge between the horses' tracks he was apt to break through. When he did that he would sink down full-leg depth, get a bad jar, and have a hard time regaining his footing. Repeat this a hundred times, and the result is annoying and tiring. It was noon, and we were tired enough already, when we topped the long, steep and winding Gardiner Hill, and turned out into the timber just above the beautiful Gardiner Falls[84] to eat lunch and put our *skis* in order. We were now what is called five miles on our way, and at the edge of the plateau, if the succession of mountain spurs and foothills can so be called.

As has been earlier taken up, there are certain gentlemen who profess to be anxious to build a railroad through the Park to Cooke City, up the Yellowstone, or that is to say, up one arm of the V of which we have been speaking. It may be that railroads can be built with ease over a country where a good *ski* runner can't go, though I doubt it. Anyhow, we knew it would be impossible to get up the proposed route of the Cooke City air line, and took this easier route, away back from the sharper dips and cañons close to the deep valley of the Yellowstone. I should say that our route, being the easier of the two, would be the better one for the Cooke City air line. It would be necessary, however, for the line to be equipped with a vertical elevator of sufficient power to lift the railway trains three-quarters of a mile straight up into the air. This would be simple, and would bring the right of way up to the level of the "plateau." I think they would then be plenty busy enough to get a grade across that interesting country, which is about as level as the fingers of your hand when you stick them up straight. I will not say that a road could not be built across this "plateau" if a company had a few million dollars, but it certainly would have to have an elevator on each side of the plateau, at the Gardiner Hill and at Yancey's. I don't know of any road so equipped, so the Cooke City Air Line, when built, would be in a manner unique. It could get a good deal of advertising out of its mile-high elevators, and I advise the Cooke City men to build the road, by all means. People would come a long way to see it, and to ride up and down the elevators on the trains. The road in this way might be built, and this might be called a practical scheme. Of course nobody really thinks that a railroad could be built up the Valley of the Yellowstone, and no engineer has ever called that a practical route. Some roads are built along a bluff, and some roads are run on top of a bluff, and some roads are backed only by a bluff. The Cooke City Air Line is one of the latter sort. But I wish the gentlemen would consider my elevator scheme. It might give new life to their project, which I understand to be in rather a languishing condition. Some of these things occurred to us as we looked over toward the tremendous landscape which hedged the Yellowstone, a landscape mostly set on edge.

Awful Going.

The country we were now crossing was high and cold, nearly bare of timber near the trail, something like the Hayden Valley, but much more broken, I should say. It was not such very hard *ski* country, but the condition of the snow made the going simply awful. The snow was, in some places, crusted hard enough to bear us up on the *skis*, and in others so soft as to let us sink down below the surface. Then there were strips of country along the ridges quite bare, or so nearly so as to compel us to take off our *skis* and go across on foot—something which the *ski* runner declares tires him more than five times the distance of straight travel, because he does not like to stoop over and fix his straps, or to carry the slippery *skis* over his shoulder. Of course the condition of the snow depended much on the way the sun struck it, so that one side of a hill might be soft and the other with a hard crust. Again, the hour of the day had much to do with it. The snow was melting underneath and settling fast, but at mid-day this did not matter so much. In the afternoon, however, a crust began to form, and this crust was just strong enough to break through about every few yards. When it broke down the unfortunate *ski* man would find himself a couple of feet below the surface of the snow. Attempting to step out, he would break in again. Struggling still further, he perhaps would thrust the toe of his *ski* far under the unbroken crust about him and have a fine time in getting it out again. Breaking up the crust by treading it between his feet, he might make a last try for liberty, only to slip back into the hole at the last instant.

The continual straining and struggling we found very wearing. To make it all worse, Hunt was having trouble with his shoes, which were sticking badly. We stopped twice to wax up, building a fire and melting snow at one place, and thus getting a drink of rather smoky water.

IN THE ELK COUNTRY.

We could now see plenty of evidence that we were getting into the elk country. We could see trails and pawings in greatest abundance in every direction. The elk seemed to be more numerous in the section about the Blacktail Creek. We saw one band of 48 elk, distant perhaps half a mile or more on the left of the trail. Being well pushed for time on account of the fearful shoeing, we did not leave the line of march to look up any bands of elk, indeed, it was not at that time thought there were so many in the Blacktail country.

THE RUN OF THE YANCEY HILL.

It was 6 o'clock in the evening, and time to be getting somewhere, when we at length found ourselves at the summit of the Yancey Hill. Billy was ahead here, and disappeared from view on a long, gentle, curving slide around and down the last hill that side of the deep gash through the mountains known as the Devil's Gut.[85] I followed, with a serene sense of relief at the easy, gliding motion of a down grade and good snow. All at once the whole earth seemed to fall out from in front of me, and all I could see was blue air below. My serenity vanished, and I hurriedly got across the *ski* pole to put on brakes, but before I had time to do that fully, I was at the bottom of the chute, where Billy stood looking at my look of astonishment. This was the last sharp drop down into the Devil's Gut. We all got handsome croppers here, but the snow was soft and it didn't matter.

"We're in the Gut now," said Billy, "and just the same as at Yancey's. It's five miles, but every inch of it's down hill."

With this latter statement we were later disposed to agree,

but with the essential statement that we were as good as there, we had cause to differ. We had a frightful time getting down that hill, and were heartily glad when this part of the day's journey was over.

I suppose the Yancey Hill is riskier to run than the Golden Gate Hill, because on the Yancey Hill some of the grades, though shorter, are very steep indeed. The descent is by means of a series of sharp pitches or steps, with now and then a long run nearly level between them. For five miles this goes on, the drop being tremendous down to "Pleasant Valley," as Uncle John Yancey calls the sheltered bight of the mountains which he has made his home. I do not know the difference in elevations, but, roughly speaking, it seemed to us to be about five miles forward and one mile down.[86]

Given a good snow, and the run down either the Golden Gate or the Yancey Hill would be pleasant to a good *ski* man. But here the snow was in the worst possible condition. It was covered, in these deep defiles, with a glassy crust, over which light snow had drifted in places. Moreover the team of the dare-devil mail carrier Church—by what means let somebody else explain—had been down this hill and cut up the snow into rough hillocks along the trail. The crust would hardly hold one on foot. To run it on the *skis* looked like doing five miles of nutmeg grater glacé. Still, we had to do it, and each man did it in his own way, plunging down as best he could and falling probably fifty times. The falls hurt us all, too, because the crust was hard enough to cut.

More than once I was astonished to see the ease with which the *skis* took the inequalities of the surface. Dashing down the steep pitches over the rough tracks left by the horse team, I could feel the *skis* jumping and jarring beneath me, and could see a long stream of holes and hillocks go by and back of me, but the *skis* kept on jumping and jumping and going ahead and down, over country where one would expect them to be brought up standing any minute. The good luck did not last forever, though, for in one of these rough stretches my toe got into or under something and I got a nasty fall, which did my game ankle no good, and made me mighty timid for a long while. Hunt was carrying Billy's camera part of the time, and I believe he went down the Yancey Hill as much on his back as on his feet. Anyhow, it was good rolling and sliding when a fellow couldn't stand up, so we all got down someway, Billy of course much better than Hunt or myself, who had not so long a schooling on the *skis*. On the last steep pitch just above Yancey's, Billy took to the woods, and sitting down on his *skis* slid down through a thicket of quaking asps. I walked or plowed down the steepest part of the run, coming on Hunt, who was lying on his back in the snow, resting after a tumble. From below there came a hearty peal of laughter at his mishap, and I knew that at last we were at the end of the march. We then all got upright on our *skis*, and ran down with a flourish to the two log cabins, in front of which stood the entire population of "Yancey's," consisting of Uncle John himself, proprietor in general; Taswill Woody, the well-known mountain man and guide; Brown, the cook, and old Bill Jump, who has a cabin just back of Yancey's, and a stable for the mall carrier's horses. Nor should I forget Uncle John's two staghounds, Pinkie and Green, fine specimens, albeit of touch-and-go temperament. Bill Jump has a dog also, which may or may not be a staghound. Pinkie and Green lick him so easy that he is afraid to call his soul his own, and so takes it out barking at strangers.

THE POPULATION AT YANCEY'S.

The population, now nearly doubled by our advent, adjourned indoors. We were at home again, and a very pleasant home we found the cosy cabin, with its blazing fire, its abundant hearty food and the general air of free and easy Western hospitality. There were some saddles and saddle-blankets on the floor, and the fellow who was willing to fight Pinkie or Green for a blanket could make himself hugely comfortable in the warm corners back of the fire. Here we went into executive session of story-telling, and few parts of our stay in the Park were pleasanter than the days at Yancey's.

Uncle John Yancey[87] is one of the features of the Park, just as much as the geysers or the Cañon. My impression is that he was there before the Cañon was finished. He is one of the few persons who are allowed leases in the Park, it being in his case thought well to have a place in that part of the Park where some sort of accommodations could be had by travelers. Here there is a little garden, a cow or two, and always a bed and a good plain table. Some of the very best trout fishing in the Park is near Yancey's, and the place is one of the prettiest and pleasant[est] of all the possible stopping places.

Uncle John is a Kentuckian by birth, long a citizen of the West and by far the leading attraction of Pleasant Valley, if only you strike him right. He has a wholesome contempt for tender-feet who get too "peart," and a hearty respect for the mountain qualities of manhood. Some of the tourists irritate him very much.

"They're sech fools," he said frankly, "some of 'em. Onct one rode up to the door here and ast me how fur it wuz to the Mammoth Hot Springs.

"'It's twenty miles,' sez I.

"'The book sez it ain't,' sez he.

"'I don't give a dash what the book sez,' sez I. Then I went right on in and shet the door, an' left him out thar a-settin' on to his hoss."

One time a citizen still more seriously offended Uncle John, who didn't like the way he acted around the house.

"I wuz a great mind to kill that feller several times," said Uncle John calmly, in telling about it. "I reckon I would a killed him on'y I didn't want him layin' around here until I could git word over to the Post an' have some one come over an' remove him. I felt very hostyle to that feller."

Uncle John loves a good joke, and can tell one on himself

if needs be. He tells one about an experience of his which happened when he was younger.

"I wuz livin' in Mizzoury then," said he, "an' I reckon wuz a kinder wild young feller. You see, I wuz goin' to town one day, an' I had to cross a river, an' they wuz on'y one boat there, which wuz owned by some folks who lived clos't by the river. The owner wuzn't to home, but his wife wuz. She wuz a great big woman, 'bout six feet high and big proportionate. She wuz a young woman, but savager any young woman ought nacherl to be. I ast her fer the boat, an' she said 'No!' ez if I wuz a insultin' of her. That sort of riled me, an' I 'lowed I'd hev to take the boat anyhow. So I goes down an' I lays hold of the boat fer to push it off. The woman, she gathers a club, not sayin' a word, an' she comes fer me. She wuz big ez three of me, an' I didn't know what to do, so 'lowin' I'd quiet her down a little whil I wuz thinkin' it over, I hit her a whack hard ez I could over the head with a oar. She set down pretty hard an' kept quiet, an' I went on acrost the river.

"When I come to find out, I learned the feller that wuz that woman's husband wuz a touchy sort of feller, an' I 'lowed when I seed him I wuz apt to have trouble, an' I s'posed nothin' would do exceptin' I had to kill him or him kill me, which wuzn't pleasant nohow. Well, one day I met him. We wuz both on horseback, an' I saw him ridin' on down the road towards me. I got all ready, 'lowin' the shootin'd shore have to begin, but not thinkin' it wuz egzacktly perlite to hit a man's wife with a oar an' then begin shootin' over it befo' he did. Well, he rides on up towards me, an' we both stops, I a-bein' mighty careful like, a' the upshot of it all is, I out an' tell him the whole story, 'lowin' his wife hadn't treated me no ways right. The feller he listens to me all through, an' says he, 'Stranger,' says he, 'I wish to God you'd done that sooner to that there woman. She's been a different wife to me since then.'

"That kind of relieved me, you know. Yes, it shorely did relieve me."

Elk in the Hayden Valley. MONTANA HISTORICAL SOCIETY RESEARCH CENTER, PHOTOGRAPH ARCHIVES, HAYNES FOUNDATION COLLECTION

The Second Silent Man.

I have mentioned John Folsom, winter keeper of the Cañon Hotel, as the most silent man I ever knew. The second silent man is Taswill Woody. During the whole of our stay at Yancey's Woody hardly spoke a word unless accosted. He spent hour after hour and day after day playing solitaire. Woody is a man of large stature, over 60 years of age and quite gray. I think he has more natural dignity than any man I ever knew in any walk of life. He is a well known mountain guide and has been much out with Mr. Roosevelt and his friends. He says Mr. Roosevelt is the best big-game shot he ever knew. Woody was born in Missouri, and has long lived on the front. He was a '49er, has been to the Australian gold fields, and, in short, has seen all the wild life of the world and all the glories of our now faded West. Of his experiences as scout and Indian fighter it was extremely difficult to get him to talk. Acting on Uncle John's advice, I tried to get Woody to tell me something of the fight on Bouvier (?) Creek (on the present Crow reservation), where he, Charlie Cox and Hubbell holed up in a willow thicket and stood off probably 1,000 Sioux all day, killing eight or ten of them.[88] I waited for a whole day, till Woody and I were alone, climbing up the mountain side to go over and see some elk, and then I said, carelessly:

"How about that fight you were in with the Indians, over east, here. Wasn't it a pretty close thing?"

"What fight?" asked Woody, calmly. Then he relapsed into silence. The above was all the description I could get out of him about that fight. Later on, however, making an evident effort to be communicative, he told me a few things about Indian fights in general. He claimed that the Indians were very poor rifle shots, and that the closer they were to you, the less apt they were to hit you. At long range they were better shots. "They seem to get excited and trembly, close to you," said Woody. ["]A lot of 'em shot at me and a Dutchman one day. They rose up not 50ft. away from us, and ought to have killed both of us. I stayed back with the Dutchman, and we stood them off.["] (I could not learn whether the Dutchman was hurt or whether Woody himself was hurt). The solitaire game always broke up the talk.

In the Heart of the Elk Country.

We learned that we were now in the heart of the winter range of the elk. From the cabin door we could see a little band of elk feeding on top of the bald ridge which rises at the upper end of "Pleasant Valley." Learning of our purpose, Woody quietly told us that he could take us to a point within two miles where we could see over 1,000 elk at one sight. As I shall later show, he did it, too.

GAME IN THE SEGREGATION STRIP.

THE WINTER HOME OF THE ELK.

ON Saturday, March 31, the first day after our arrival at Yancey's, we found ourselves tired enough to spend the day in loafing and resting up. Billy fished out a bandage from a hidden pocket, and showed the ability to bandage an ankle as well as a surgeon. I learned then that he had taken the precaution to carry along a bandage or so, and also a few screws, which latter, however, he explained were intended for use in case of a broken *ski*, and not of a broken bone.

The next day was Sunday by the calendar. It was observed by a general cleaning up. After that we concluded not to wait longer, but to go on out after the elk. Woody kindly acted as guide, and took us to a point about a mile and a half northwest of Yancey's, to a high butte, or rather a high rock wall overhanging the Yellowstone Valley. From this vantage ground we saw a spectacle truly remarkable and magnificent, one hardly to be duplicated in America or in the world to-day.

Below us lay the Yellowstone, even at that depth of distance clearly visible. Its color was a brilliant green, and its re[g]ular foaming on the rock ridges which crossed its path as it came out of the sharp defile at our right had all the apparent substance and rigidity of solid substance. Down to the Yellowstone ran a sheer drop of white, and all the forest for miles to right and left of us was clad in white, this being the north slope of the mountain. Across the Yellowstone, between the Cottonwood and the Roaring Fork and beyond them, there stretched a vast and rugged picture of wild mountain scenery, broken by cañon and crag and defile, by long gentle slope and by wooded depths at whose profundity we could only guess.[89] All the colors of winter were there, the intense white of the snow, the varying blackness of the forests, but added to these were a hundred of the reds and browns of mother earth uncovered. This was the south slope of the range at which we were now looking, and sun and winds combined to strip many of the slopes of snow. Apparently half the surface was bare or nearly bare of snow, one could see great streaks of bare brown ground running away up on many of the ridges, without apparent cause. The character of the ground was very rough and broken, and how the Yellowstone was to find its way through the wilderness of mountains that crowded in on the left was matter of vague conjecture to us as we stood and looked across the great peaks beyond the stream and to the westward. A tremendous and impressive scene it was of wild nature at rest. One can remember few spots in the Park where he would more keenly feel that he had intruded where he did not belong. This feeling was the more heightened by the way we came upon the spot, the forest being dense up to the very edge of the great wall on which we stood.

THE ELK WERE IN HUNDREDS.

But not alone the physical characteristics of the country entitled it to our wondering admiration. The picture was not a picture alone. It was replete with life.

Below us we saw some dark figures outlined against the snow. They moved and we looked more closely. A dozen elk came out from behind the point of timber in which they stood, and looked curiously up at us on our lofty perch, but they did not take alarm. Then beyond the river, on the bare ground, we saw another group, and another, and another, and then dozens of others. In singles, in pairs, in groups, in small bands, the elk were feeding in hundreds and hundreds, scattered all over a strip of country five miles across. The whole further bank of the Yellowstone, here laid open before us as though by special plan, was alive with elk. In all my life I had never seen so much game at one sight. For the first time in the Park I felt an absolute thrill of amazement and delight at seeing the great animals in such numbers, in such content, in such apparent security and freedom from suspicion. There are few hunters who have seen enough of the more fertile game countries of the now barren West to remember any such sight as this. There is no other part of America where such a sight will ever be seen again. Here, protected by the Park, these noble animals had chosen out a ground where nature had provided opportunity to feed through-out the winter, and had gathered in by hundreds and hundreds, as if purposely to go on show for those who wished to see them. The FOREST AND STREAM luck held. We had found the elk just where we thought to find them, and in numbers which set at rest all theorizing as to where or what was the winter range of the elk of these mountains of the Park. Here was their range, below us, before us, around, on every side of us, and the elk were there, there not only in hundreds, but absolutely in thousands.

Woody said nothing, but sat down with his back against a tree, and with the long and powerful telescope we had along began to sweep the opposite hillsides over carefully and slow-ly. Once in a while a low exclamation escaped him, and he would say, "There are four hundred in that band," or "there they are again, over by the bare peak," or "just take a look at this bunch." We took turns in taking looks, both with the tele-scope and the field glasses, and before we got through we were all more or less excited. Billy pointed out a big bunch he had located before we came out on the point of rocks, and with the glass we studied these long and carefully. They were lying down, feeding, moving about, quite at home and unconscious of our being within three miles of them, and cognizant of their every movement as well as though the distance were not more than a quarter of a mile. In these might be 250 elk at least. How many there really were we could not tell with any exactness, for they were continually coming into and going out of view on the strip of bare brown ground over which they were feeding. How many elk lay unseen on those miles of brown hills and valleys no one can tell. How many were on the opposite sides of the ridges from us or in cañons and valleys into which we could not see, no one of course could tell. "You can only see one-half of this country at one time," said Woody, "that is, the side of the hill to you." We located one great band of 500 to 800 elk, as nearly as we could estimate the number, and guessed roughly that we must have in view 1,500 elk in scattered bunches at distances from half a mile to three miles. In all, seeing only "half the country," we concluded that there must be 2,000 elk at least within reaching distance of the eye at one time before us on the north bank of the Yellowstone alone. Doubtless there were 3,000 or 4,000 on that ground, could we have seen them all. In stating these figures I am taking the estimate of Woody and Billy, both used to seeing large numbers of game, and not given to emotional estimates.

IT WAS ON THE SEGREGATION STRIP.

It was the purpose of the FOREST AND STREAM expedition in coming into this part of the Park to look into the game supply fairly, not bringing to the task any preconceived ideas whatever, and not seeking to uphold any theory, although there was not the slightest occasion to doubt the report of the Park superintendent, Capt. Anderson, which assigned large bodies of elk to this very section of the Park, and which was accordingly reviled by the local Montana press, or rather the Livingston press, as being untrue and unreliable. The Livingston press would have it appear that there is no game in that part of the Park which they want cut off. I purposely do not have Capt. Anderson's report before me as I write this, but I can state very briefly what we actually found over here in the segregation strip (i. e., that part which it is sought to cut off from the Park). We found a rough country, not a smooth one, one of the wildest and most broken character. We found a country only half covered with snow. In some parts, especially the upper flats, the snow was 5, 8, perhaps 10ft. deep, though many of the ridges were nearly bare. On the lower levels, on the south slopes, in the creek and river valleys, on the tops of the ridges and often over great patches and wide areas of the mountain sides, the snow did not lie so deep, but could be easily pawed through by the game. For miles, I will say, there were hills and stretches of broken ground which were entirely brown and bare where the sun struck them or where the wind had sweep. In the valley of the Yellowstone, on the north slopes of the hills, in all the cañons and the deep rock country, of course, the snow was deep and heavy.

We found, in our first morning out from Yancey's, taking the estimate of experienced mountaineers, than whom there are no better in America, 2,000 elk in sight at once, and probably 4,000 or 5,000 in all within reach of the eye had all been visible by reason or the lay of the ground. We saw every one of those 2,000 elk on the north side of the Yellowstone, wholly on ground that would be cut off from the Park under the proposed segregation act. We found as many more elk that same day, partly on the south side of the Yellowstone and along the East Fork, partly on and partly off the segregation strip. On the second day following we saw probably 800 to 1,000 elk, the majority of which were on the proposed segregation strip. In two days we actually saw somewhere between 5,000 and 10,000 elk. We can not claim that we saw half of all that were on the country. We do not claim to have examined all of the line of the proposed railway. Had we done so I think we should have seen more than twice as many elk as we did see. If you draw a circle about Yancey's, with 10 miles radius, you will take in 10,000 to 15,000 elk this winter certainly, perhaps twice that number. If you make the radius five miles I will guarantee you take in over 5,000, probably 8,000. If you make it four miles you will take in over 3,000 elk certainly. I do not consider these figures guess work, but accurate so far as accuracy is obtainable by actual investigation in the winter time, and by unbiased and skillful estimate. I do not offer the estimate as mine alone, but I saw all the game that the others saw, and I will testify on honor or on oath that these statements are accurate and fair to the best of my knowledge and belief.

THESE ARE FACTS.

Now, gentlemen wish to build a railroad through exactly this portion of the Park. Has this story up till now spoken of seeing any such numbers of game in any other part of the Park? No, for the game winters nowhere else in such numbers. Gentlemen ask us to believe that building this road (if it could be built) through exactly this part of the Park, through exactly this winter range, through exactly these great bands of game, "will not destroy or disturb the wild game of the Park." Shall we believe them? Not until the American public is made up altogether of idiots and fools. We went into this country in the winter, and studied it, and I know what I am talking about absolutely, and I am glad that for this paper I can say these things out publicly and unhesitatingly, and in such way as does not admit of any successful or trustworthy denial. These are not assumptions, but facts. They are not surmises, but facts. They are not one-sided assertions, but facts. On these substantiated facts let the public make up its opinion as to the harmlessness of a railway through the heart of the greatest game preserve on earth. Let the public ask the friends of segregation for their facts, and not for their assertions, or their hopes, or their guesses about the facts. Then they can turn to FOREST AND STREAM, which says that the elk are there now, but would be there no longer if this road were built. Build the road, and then there would be for boundary not the wild wall of mountains which we saw to the north of the Yellowstone—so desolate and forbidding that even now it is thought there may be a few head of bison left over beyond the Bison Peak—but a narrow public path of accessible grades, of no barriers insurmountable to the traveler by foot, of no obstacles to prevent digression on either hand. The hunter now is fenced out of the winter range. The railroad would lead him direct to the heart of it. The first year the road went through, 10,000 elk would be butchered. The next year, 1,000. The next year, there would be no elk in this part of the Yellowstone, or the bare ground north of the Yellowstone, or the open valley of the East Fork. Driven back into the big snow country, they would have escaped the skin hunters only to starve and perish by hundreds, as even now they every year starve and perish by hundreds in the less favored and more inclement parts of the Park.

Let the elk alone, they can take care of themselves. Let the Park alone, it can take care of itself. In the name of humanity, of decency, in the name of the honor of the American people, let the Park and its inestimable treasures, animate and inanimate, alone forever, a heritage of growing value to this people and to the world.

A Vivid Panorama.

Our morning with the elk made up an experience unique and vivid in every particular. In the great mental panorama which will during my life remain the greatest treasure resultant upon this winter journey, there will, I fancy, long continue bright and sharp this picture of the white and brown hills sloping down to the Yellowstone, dotted with their thousand heads of game. I shall long see, I hope, the keen green of the Yellowstone, its transverse ribs of white, and the fathomless depths of the snow in the black-sided cañons. Not less impressive was the reverse of this picture, for as we turned to descend the great hills up which we had laboriously climbed, there burst upon us the full glory of the mountain scene which we had had at our backs as we came up, eager only to find the elk ahead. We were perhaps at a third of the full height of the rise to the upper plateau, and hence at an elevation quite sufficient to see unfolded much of the glories of the inner Park, whose peaks and cañons now seemed grouped and composed for our special benefit. In the center stood the great gleaming peak of Mt. Washburn, which from the opposite side of the Park we had seen before, always central and commanding. It was as if this mother mountain stretched out her hands to bless the heads of small mountains, who crowded up about her knees. To oblige us, the sun came out gloriously, and lit up the whole majestic landscape with a light more brilliant than ever yet fell on any artist's studio, or than ever yet had reflection on any human canvas. The artist who could paint this compelling brilliance would be derided as gone wild. If he should paint the purples of the mountain sunrise and sunset as deep as they really are, he would be denied credence and called a cheap pretender at effect. Thousands of artists have been drawn to the mountains and have tried to show them in their more friendly moods. I do not know of any artist who has ever attempted to depict the great range in the depth of winter. He who tries it will try in vain. He cannot catch this serene fatefulness, this terrible calm, this supreme indifference to Life and Time. The mountains are infinite. Study the differential calculus, and when you get to the end of the indeterminate equation, you may know the meaning of the mountains and so be able to portray their thought. I could imagine an artist going insane should he sit day after day trying to fathom the meaning of the mountains, always different, always the same, always beckoning indifferent, fascinating, terrible, immutable, calm. The mountains are at peace. They have outgrown change. The bestowing upon them of human names is indignity. Mt. Washburn, we say! Who was Mr. Washburn, and who will he be? But if we should call this enduring monument the Mount of Supreme Calm or the Mount of the Ultimate Rest, we might at least please the Indians, who have better taste and more delicacy than we in many ways—less compliment to us.

More and More Elk.

It took us only a short time to slide down to Yancey's, and pausing there only for lunch we set on further east toward Junction Butte, that high mesa-topped elevation which masks the union of the main Yellowstone and the East Fork.[90] Woody did not go with us in the afternoon, but he told us we would see plenty of elk all through that section. We certainly did so. I counted twenty-one bands of elk to the left of our trail to the Butte. The whole country was full of elk. There were elk on Specimen Ridge. There were elk on top of Junction Butte. The East Fork valley was full of elk. The main valley of the Yellowstone showed band after band. They were so common that they almost ceased to interest us. They were in greater numbers than I ever saw cattle on any range. There were hundreds and hundreds and hundreds of them, how many in all I shall not say, because accurate count was an impossibility. The snow was now breaking up sufficiently to allow the elk to get about with comparative ease, and there was even a considerable amount of ground almost bare, though not so much over here as we had seen on the north side of the river in the morning. We found that the elk could easily get feed all through this section, and also discovered that they could easily keep out of our way so that we could not get a good shot with the camera. The slopes were too long and open to give much chance for stalking. We were rarely closer than a quarter of a mile to the game.

The Center of the Winter Range.

We found the Yellowstone a grand, powerful stream at Baronette's Bridge,[91] where we crossed it. From Yancey's the Junction Butte did not look to be across the Yellowstone, but we found it a comfortable climb on the other side. It was quite a sharp climb up the last escarpment, but for some reason the butte was barer at the top than lower down, and we got up, carrying our *skis*. A watchful old cow elk, which Billy anathematized cheerfully a dozen times as we were climbing up, stood on the edge of the mesa and spied upon us, so that we could get no stalk on the band which was feeding on the top; though we got up within 100yds. of a small bunch which were lying down on some bare ground, and which ambled off easily down the steep side of the butte as we came into view on top.

From the top of Junction Butte we had a view only short of that of the morning, so far as the quantity of the game was concerned. We could with the glasses command a great range of country. A great many elk, startled by our coming, were running across the snowy valley below us, making for the timber beyond. Along the main river there were many large bands feeding without thought of danger, and we had all the opportunity in the world to see the wild animals at home.

We discovered that the elk were breaking up into small bands of cows and spikes.[92] The bull elk were beginning to shed their horns. We saw only two bulls with horns that afternoon. We found dropped elk horns on top of Junction Butte.

We were now fairly in the center of the main winter range of the elk. We make no claim to have covered all of it, nor half of it. We saw it was not necessary. We had learned all we wished and felt that our work was practically done. We could have duplicated these sights of game hour after hour on up the East Fork country toward Soda Butte, but knew that it was needless.

The shoeing was now growing soft. The snow was going fast at the bottom and settling. Uncle John Yancey thought the break-up would soon come if the snow was melting below.

We saw many horses wintering in this part of the Park. They cannot winter in the Upper Park, and neither can elk, except in certain portions. The horses were on the segregation strip.

FIVE THOUSAND ELK NORTH OF THE SEGREGATION LINE.

I asked Woody directly how many elk he thought there were wintering wholly on the country which would be cut of[f] by the proposed railroad. He said, after thought, "At least 5,000." I offer the figures given, let me repeat, as to the head of game, not as my own, but as those of better authorities. I believe them to be correct.

CAUGHT IN A MOUNTAIN STORM.

[I] had taken such a fancy to Uncle John and Woody that I didn't want to go home at all, but had a notion to just quit my accustomed life and finish out the living business right here in this quiet and beautiful corner of the mountains—a spirit of rebellion which is sure to strike me every time I go into the mountains. But we all decided to pull out for the Post Monday morning, April 2. Billy set this date conditionally, as there were threats of a storm which might stop us. When the morning came, Billy did not want to start, for he could see by looking at the tops of the peaks about us that it was storming up above, even though in sheltered Pleasant Valley it all seemed quiet and peaceful. It looked like a bad snow, Billy said, and he advised holding up for the day. We would much better have taken this advice, as indeed most of Billy's advice on such matters, but I was getting uneasy about being so long in the Park, and besides was afraid Capt. Anderson would send out a team to the Gardiner hill to meet us, in which case I thought we ought to be there. I therefore insisted on a start, and that we did, though Billy was none too willing.

For some reasons I am glad we did start, because I got a chance at the one remaining mountain experience which we needed to complete the eventfulness of our journey. I had heard of the storms of this region, whose violence and intensity were such that the traveler was entirely bewildered and forced to stop where he was, unable to tell the points of the compass or to see any landmark. Of course, I had read all about Dakota blizzards and I had been in a blizzard on the Western plains hard enough to "drift" all the range cattle for fifty miles, but I could not say that I had ever seen a blizzard quite bad enough to warrant the timidity which all these mountain men seemed to feel about the storms up in the Park. Billy seemed to think that being caught in a storm was about the only real danger there was in this winter voyaging, but that one thing would always make him serious. He was serious as we said good-bye at Yancey's and started up the first hill. At that time there were a few flakes of snow falling.

When we topped the first pitch and reached the ledge, from which we could almost toss a stone down on the cabin roof below, our few flakes of snow had become a few thousand and we saw that the storm was coming. We pressed on for a quarter of a mile, perhaps, and the storm thickened so fast that we could hardly see.

"Have you got enough of it," Billy asked, "or do you want to go ahead?"

"Go on ahead," I said, "it can't snow this way very long." Billy grunted and went on. I could not see him 30ft. ahead of me. The trail of his *skis* filled almost as fast as he passed. We made the top of still another little hill. It seemed only to reach another level of the storm. Raising my head, I tried to look ahead, half-blinded, but all of which I could become conscious was an advancing wall of thick, smothering white. There was no landscape. I could not see a tree. The trail had no sides, no end. There was no distance, no direction. Everything was swallowed up in an eddying, whirling, impenetrable mask of snow. There was no atmosphere. It had all turned to snow.

"Have you got enough?" Billy asked again, calmly.

"No!" I said, idiotically proud and ashamed to go back. "Go ahead. We'll hole up over the next hill and wait till it blows over."

Billy was dead game, and once more turned forward. I suppose we went to the foot of the next hill. I lost him in the snow, and could only keep the trail by looking close down at my feet. The snow was damp, and came down in sheets rather than in flakes. I never knew before how snow could fall. We were all wet through in a few moments. We could see nothing and hear nothing. At every breath I was learning how a fellow could get lost in the mountains, how in a storm like this, which might last for days, he would lose all sense of direction and wander he knew not whither; how he would become wet through; how he would chill in the cold following the snow; how he would try to build a shelter and perhaps fail, perhaps succeed; how at last he would sit down by his little fire, perhaps, and give up, and be buried by the snow and perhaps never seen again, even though close to the trail. These things I thought of before we got to […] the next hill. We never got over it. I met Billy coming back down the trail.

"We can't go on," he said, decisively. "It's simply awful up there. Hurry on back to Yancey's now, fast as you can, before the trail fills up."

At once we did what I ought to have been willing to do at first, and turned back down the trail. We were not much too soon. Our trail made coming up was blotted out entirely. The deeper ridges of the old trails were all that showed us the way, and these we could only follow by looking close down at our feet. Without this aid, Yancey's might as well have been a dozen miles away as half a mile. When we got to the ridge above the houses we could not see their roofs. The whole valley was full of blinding, driving, suffocating snow. The trail took us to the door.

We spent the rest of the day drying out. I had seen a mountain storm. I cannot describe the helplessness in which it leaves the traveler. The *ski* party caught in such a storm at night might have an awkward time of it. Even nerve and good woodsmanship might not get them through. The length of the storm would have everything to do with their safety. No one not familiar with these mountains can have any idea of the character of such a storm, or understand the great depth to which snow can fall in a single night. Words give no idea of such a situation as that of being caught by such a storm. When you go into the mountains you go into a region of large distances, large value, large impressions. But the mountains in summer do but dimly shadow forth the mountains of the winter.

TRIED IT AGAIN.

Tuesday morning we tried it again. Nature had whirled her weather wheel again. The wet snow was frozen into a solid crust. We did not use the *skis*, but walked more than half the distance of the climb up to the Devil's Gut. The morning was bright and clear and we had some glorious mountain views as we looked back on our climb near the summit. In the middle of the day the shoeing was not good, but Billy hit out an awful pace, and we made good time. At the Blacktail Creek we stopped for lunch and fixed up the *skis*. The snow here was very deep (the drift on the side of the creek was about 30ft. deep), but with his usual ingenuity Billy got a fire, this time on top of a fallen log, and we were happy over our lunch.

STILL AMONG THE ELK.

All the way in, especially from Geode Creek[93] to the top of the Gardiner Hill, we saw great numbers of elk. I counted twenty-six bands, numbering hundreds in all. There were few bulls. We had a good time with one solitary bull, a great fellow with a fine set of antlers, which kept along in sight of us for some time. We saw one little band of old bulls together. One grand band of elk crossed our trail not 100yds. ahead of us, giving us the prettiest and closest view of elk I had in the Park. There were about seventy-five head in the bunch and they joined another band of perhaps twice that number in a hollow not far to the right of the trail. We could see little scattered bunches of elk all over the hills to the right of us, there seeming to be more over toward the Yellowstone than on the south side of the trail, though we saw many there also. We saw no other game but elk, except one band of blacktail deer, which we trailed for some time along the road at the foot of the Gardiner Hill, and at length saw them leisurely making off up the side of Mt. Everts. There were fifteen of the deer, I believe. We saw these within three miles of the Post.

TIERRA CALIENTE.

The run of the Gardiner Hill was an affair more laughable than serious. Hunt, the sojer man, went down first, and as the hill is a sort of corkscrew affair, Billy and I had several good views of him sliding on his back. Some of the pitches were pretty steep, and Billy and I ingloriously sat down on our *skis* and slid that way. I suppose we slid over a mile in that manner. Then we came to a warmer climate, the *tierra caliente* of the level of the Mammoth Hot Springs, and the going became soft, then slushy, then muddy. We put the *skis* over our shoulders, and began the laborious climb of the Post Hill. Hardly had we begun it when we came upon the ambulance and mule team which Capt. Anderson had kindly sent out to meet us. The 20-mile journey, our last *ski* trip in the Park, was over. We learned that the storm of the day before had been so severe that Capt. Anderson had not sent out the team at all, rightly believing that we could not travel on such a day. Gauging our speed of travel to a nicety, he made a two minutes' connection with the ambulance and our party on this day. Of such is the accuracy of the military judgment and philosophy, which in matters of this sort is based primarily on the theory that a fellow isn't a fool, and that every fellow knows how to take care of himself.

WOULD BE A SOLDIER.

Once more we met Capt. Anderson's hearty greeting, and once more I sank into the pleasant life at the Post, Capt. Anderson explaining that there wouldn't be a train out from Cinnabar till the next Saturday, and no stage after the stage of Wednesday to which he didn't intend to send any ambulance anyhow, and to which I could, if I preferred, walk and carry my war bag. I concluded to take his reiterated and cheerful advice that I would just as well be calm and keep on my raiment. I think he had an eye out for recruits, for I found it so fascinating at the Post that I came near enlisting for a sojer. I would yet, if I could be sure the trumpets would always continue to make my shoulder-blades creep and that Capt. Anderson would always continue in immediate command.

No. 14.

THE END AND SOME CONCLUSIONS.

A HARD TASK IN PROTECTION.

AS I WRITE the concluding paper of a series perhaps too long, it is August and not March, and the sweltering heat of the lowlands has taken the place of the cool breath of the mountains. There have been important changes in the situation since the time the material for this story was gathered, but the change has been all for the better and all in the way of benefit to the public and to the sportsman. There seems to be no reason now to change the belief that the FOIREST AND STREAM Expedition was "lucky" in every way, unless in the story the writer has failed altogether to give any true notion of the Park in winter and of the situation there as to the protection of the game. One might easily fail in this, for the subject is a large one and all its details are large. One deals here in immensities, and to write of immensities conveys no impression whatever unless the reader has some yardstick of immensity by which to measure.

On one point I am especially anxious to be clear, and that is the extreme difficulty of protecting the Park with the means provided by the Government. The task set by the authorities at Washington is altogether too large. Two troops of horse and one scout cannot protect the Park at any season. In the winter these two troops are not two troops. They are only so many

215

Bison in the Hayden Valley, 1894. Montana Historical Society Research Center, Photograph Archives, Haynes Foundation Collection

men as can travel on *skis*. The army regulations do not exact a knowledge of *ski* work. For $13 a month you can get many men who will act together, who will drill well, shoot well, fight well, be good soldiers under the regulations, but out of them all not all will be good mountaineers, adventurous *ski* runners, tireless climbers, fearless woodsmen and educated scouts. Some of the troopers will be near enough to all this to do work in the winter. The great majority will not. The authorities at Washington do not know this. Regular, formal—blind, that is almost to say in some respects—to them two troops of horse are two troops of horse, and should be sufficient. It is supposed that a trooper can ride fifty or sixty miles a day if necessary. In the Sioux campaign troopers often rode that far. Ergo, the authorities perhaps reason, troopers should ride that far in the Park on any day when necessary, and should be able to pick up a poacher in any corner of the Park.

Perhaps the great American public, which has long been robbed of the Park buffalo, of many of the treasures which it owned there, may unite in the above cheerful belief. Especially those who have ridden through the Park in comfortable stages may unite in the question, Why can not the Park be protected perfectly?

The authorities at Washington, the public at large, know not whereof they speak, or such questions would not be asked, and things would not be as they are. The authorities and the public do not know that there are two Parks to protect, and not one, and that the winter Park is fifty times as large as the summer Park, so that no trooper can cross it in a day nor in a month, nor in the entire winter. The authorities and the public should know, and I hope that even by the mite of these small writings they might be encouraged to begin to try to know, that the Park is not the Park, and that the two troops of cavalry are not two troops, for the greater part of the year and at the very time when protection is most imperative, as the news discovered by our party has conclusively shown.

Now all this time we read of the corruption of American politics, of the waste of public money, of the gigantic frauds by which this foolish and patient nation is successfully and successively robbed. We throw open the gates of our beautiful country and welcome in the outcasts of the Old World, creatures whom the Old World does not want and who cannot earn a living in that country. We welcome this low rabble, and make it equal to ourselves in the making and the enforcing of the laws of this land. We allow this rabble to lower the national American tone of respect for restraint and for law and order. We permit the growth of a carelessness for the public heritage of great game—even a carelessness and an ignorance as to so magnificent a possession as this great Park, which is to-day better understood and better valued by better class Europeans than by better class Americans. We permit the imported rabble to embroil us in riotous labor troubles—these men who could not earn a living in the Old World—and we are forced to spend millions of dollars to put down the troubles, even then in a deprecating way.[94] But meantime America has no money to spend for the America of the past and of the possible. There must be no "waste of the public funds" by which a half dozen, or two, or one additional scout shall be given the public to help guard one of the public's most priceless possessions. The public shall not even have its two troops of the guard actually two troops, or one-tenth of that, during the most important part of the year. No. We must not do that. We must go on in the good old way. Meantime America is not America. America is no more. We have opened the gates and we have been flooded by a debasing tide. We have bartered America, the once unrivalled and even now the land of wonders, and have sold her for the humiliating price of a few political votes. Under these broad truths, for which these columns are hardly the proper place, lie none the less the difficulties of game protection in this country, and many of the difficulties in properly protecting the Park and its remaining specimens of some of our vanishing game. Congress has made a great step for the safety of the Park, but it has not yet done all that is needful. It needs to realize the value of this great region and its game as any other country would realize.

Congress needs to set the mark for a change in sentiment, and to invite a sentiment American at heart, which shall keep America, or at least the rarer portions of America, free from further spoliation. No railroads in the Park, no more game killed in the Park—this is what an honest American Congressman should say. Saying that, he may vote to save a little money out of some well-known scheme, and devote it to the placing of six, or two, or even one additional mountain scout on the Park guard, which now has only one scout.

Congress has not 200 men on guard at the Park in winter. It has just one man. His name is Burgess, Park scout. This is the only man of whom Congress can officially ask duty such as the necessities of the service exact. This U. S. Army, of one man—one man upholding the safety and dignity of this whole great country in one of its richest treasure vaults—must cover a territory larger than the State of Connecticut, rougher than the White Mountains, deeper under snow than Labrador, colder in climate than Manitoba. If we are to have success, even under the efficient new law, the U. S. working army must be made larger than one man.

THANKS TO BOTH.

Fresh from the wild country up the Park, and fully impressed with the immense extent of it, its impenetrability, its savage inhospitality to the winter traveler, I could only say to Capt. Anderson that it seemed to me a wonder that the poacher Howell had been caught, and yet more a wonder that the guards of the Park, from commanding officer to private, were not discouraged at the task set before them—a task which by reason of fundamental lack in its conditions, could never be more than half done, since (at that time) the detection of crime, difficult as it was, could never be followed by proper punishment.

Up to that time, in common with the general public, I had been absolutely ignorant of the way the Park was protected or what its protection meant. If this story of the Park in winter has made some few others acquainted with these facts, then a great purpose of the FOREST AND STREAM enterprise has been gained.

Meantime, thanks, let me say, to Capt. Anderson and the FOREST AND STREAM, Congress has given the public since that time (in the month of May) a law which in one sense revolutionizes the whole situation at the Park, and makes the once impossible task now in a way fairly practical and certain. With the killing of a buffalo made a penitentiary offense, the attached penalty running as high as $1,000 or years in the penitentiary, or both, Capt. Anderson has something to stand upon. When the report of the next arrest of the Howell kind comes in he can feel unqualifiedly exultant and can know that the arrest means something.

Summing up on the facts, it is not likely that another poacher will soon go into the Park. Should he do so, and should he not resist arrest and so be brought in for trial, he will be retired from active public life for a while. The average bad man of the mountains, however, while he may have a disregard for local or State laws administered by his friends, has a superstitious fear of any United States law. He doesn't want to run against Uncle Sam, for he knows Uncle Sam's arms are long and his heart hard when it comes to going after a criminal. In March it was not impossible to go into the Park and kill some buffalo heads for sale without serious risk, and every hunter in Montana, Idaho and Wyoming knew it. Today, since the little FOREST AND STREAM expedition went in—whether or not because of it—it is a crime to do that same act, and every one of those hunters knows this, too, for news of this sort flies fast in the mountains in its own mysterious way. One or two of the more daring may go into the great winter country after some of the few remaining great animals which still remain there, but the pitchers of these will go too often to the well.

The day of poaching in the Park approaches its waning. The American public, let us hope, has begun in some measure to see to what great extent and of what priceless possessions it has in the past been robbed. Agitation has had its result. The change since the snows of winter were deepest in the Park has been a great one. Every lover of nature, of fair play, of decency, can only congratulate himself when he gazes on that picture and then on this. I imagine that Capt. Anderson has entered on this season's campaign with greater zest than ever before. The public has only to wish that he may enter on many and many another, for his equal in that post will not be found. FOREST AND STREAM, which hopes that it has been useful in securing a better law for him to work under, will hope also to see him some day given more men of the necessary sort to help him in the still exacting and difficult task of enforcing the law. Let us all hope that the Attorney-General will not delay the appointment of deputy marshals who shall also be competent scouts until the stock of buffalo is cut down still more or perhaps placed beyond the possibility of a survival. The Park law is excellent, and it may of itself deter poaching, but no law is altogether good which is not sustained by proper machinery of enforcement. Troops of cavalry do not constitute such machinery when they cease to be cavalry, but are dismounted for eight months of the year by snow.

The primary object of the FOREST AND STREAM expedition was to learn about the existing numbers of the big game in the Park. The conclusions as to that have been given from time to time earlier in these articles. I give them with all diffidence on my own part, but with confidence after all in their general accuracy, since they are in the main founded on the good judgment of experienced men such as Hofer and Woody, who were on the ground with me. Beyond this, we base the accuracy of our report on careful and conscientious work in the region covered, leaving nothing to guesswork when possible to do otherwise.

As by our earlier record of the antelope, I can summarize

by saying that we think there were about 400 antelope alive in the Park last winter, all on or near the Gardiner Flats.

Twenty-five Thousand Elk.

Judging by what we saw at Yancey's and near there, I should not think an estimate of 25,000 elk would be extreme, allowing that not all the elk have drifted to the northeast corner of the Park where we saw so many. If the elk are as scarce in the Pelican country as they are in Hayden Valley, and if the East Fork country really has most of them, then 25,000 would be a liberal estimate.

Not Over Two Hundred Buffalo.

I do not personally believe there are over 150 buffalo left alive in the Park. I will say 200, more out of deference to those who say, "There certainly must be more buffalo than you think," rather than for any reason I can see for such belief. I know the popular estimate was 500 head, but while that may be right, we could discover no reason for thinking it was right. We discovered many reasons for thinking it quite wrong. The Park was never so thoroughly traversed as it was this winter. It was covered very thoroughly in the main buffalo range, and partially on what might be called the alternate winter range of the buffalo. We had the reports of every officer, every soldier, every scout, every hunter and even the solitary poacher who had been in the Park, besides our own knowledge. I can make up no actual count even equalling 150 head. The winter range is so small that these men and ourselves would be more apt to see the same bunch twice than to pass by even a small bunch unseen. I add the 50 head only because of the latter possibility. I know Captain Anderson in his last report thought the buffalo far more numerous than this, but he made his report on data not so thorough as those of this winter, and I believe even his informants of last year advise him in accordance with our smaller figures of this year. He told me that without further reports he could not again report over 250 head alive. I do not think he will put it so high as that.

It was the chief accomplishment of our expedition to show how mistaken was the general idea as to the numbers of the Park buffalo, and how alarming the possibility of their absolute extinction. Against this easy work of revenge or of mercenary greed let us hope the authorities will take especial measures, at least for the coming winter.

OTHER GAME.

We have nothing to submit by way of figures as to other game. Mountain sheep were seen by others, and there seems to be a band or so. We saw none. We saw in all about twenty-five deer, all blacktail, and all near the Mammoth Hot Springs (two bands only). As to the bears we could not, of course, say. We saw one and the trail of another. We saw the trail of two mountain lions and of innumerable foxes. There seemed to be more foxes than coyotes, even. We saw a few lynx trails, and one trail of a wolverine. Some of the wild fowl I have already mentioned, but we saw no grouse or ptarmigan of consequence, two in all only, I believe. There were a few mountain jays—"camp robbers," some Clark's crows, and once in a while a raven. Kingfishers, bluebirds, water-ousels and wild ducks (mostly mallards) were wintering on the Gardiner below the Boiling River. My recollection is that we saw two eagles, but I have no note of more than one. The tracks of the pine marten, of the squirrel and of the "snowshoe rabbit" were common. The upper Park was very silent and bare of visible life, even in small animals.

ALL WERE KIND.

The officials of the Northern Pacific road were very kind to FOREST AND STREAM in every way. Capt. Anderson was so kind that it is useless to try to thank him properly, and Mr. Deane was very kind to let us into the hotels of the Park Association after they were closed, and Mr. Haynes was exceptionally generous and kind in allowing the use of his magnificent game pictures, the best ever made in the Park. Every one, it seemed, united in the effort to be courteous and helpful to us, and to all there as much as to the actual members of our party the thanks of the readers of this paper are due, if any be felt at all. The paper has already made acknowledgment of this un-squared account, to which acknowledgment we must add our personal one.

LAST DAYS AT THE PARK.

Billy and I put in our last days at the Park—or rather my last days, for he lives right at the edge of the Park—while I was waiting for the weekly train down from Cinnabar, in fishing for trout in the Gardiner and Yellowstone rivers. We got trout, too, though not any such very big ones, as it was too early. Then one morning the time came to go, and I said good-bye to Capt. Anderson and the pleasant gentlemen around him and started for Cinnabar, where finally I left Lieut. Lindsley and Billy. Billy was tougher and browner even than when he went in. Every man of the party was lean and hard as though trained fine. The reflection from the snow, even on the coldest days, had burned us all to copper-color. We were all in perfect health and great form. No possible regimen or system of exercise would put a man in as splendid shape as a month's trip through the mountains on the *skis*. The beneficial effects of that trip—the greatest one of my life and one not likely to be again taken by myself—endure to-day. And even now I can see the rushing flood of the noble Yellowstone, and can see the great white mountains and the geysers at the rising of the winter sun. I can almost feel the shadow of the forests at night, and hear the rushing of the mountain streams, unfettered even by the general shackles of the cold. The white plains, the black cañons, the dominant peaks, the brilliant lights of the varying sun, all make up a picture seemingly almost unreal, but bright, vivid, imposing and I hope enduring. It was a journey for a life-time.

Notes

These notes include further reading on people and events covered in the introduction. They also give explanations of difficult turns in the narrative, and clarifications of problems that developed when Hough could not gather the information he needed at times, because the data did not yet exist.

1. A fine source on Frederick Schwatka's 1887 attempt to "explore" the already thoroughly-explored park is *Yellowstone's Ski Pioneers* (Worland: High Plains Publishing, 1995), by Paul Schullery. It owes much to a seminal article by William L. Lang, "'At the Greatest Personal Peril to the Photographer': the Schwatka-Haynes Winter Expedition in Yellowstone, 1887," *Montana: The Magazine of Western History*, Winter 1983, 14-29. Schullery devotes much of a chapter to Schwatka's expedition, and stresses one important factor of which Hough may have been unaware: Schwatka was seriously ill. He suffered from a vaguely-diagnosed but quite serious stomach ailment. The expedition also served as an excellent living laboratory showing the superiority of skis over what we today call snowshoes, for covering long distances, and also of traveling lightly. The ailing Schwatka, mounted on webbed snowshoes, and his overburdened crew struggled for three days just getting from Fort Yellowstone to the Norris Geyser Basin. After spending a day recuperating, they straggled only another four miles south, and turned back. After another break to recuperate at Norris, which then had a hotel, Schwatka, still on webbed snowshoes, joined a group headed for the Grand Canyon of the Yellowstone, but gave out after a couple of miles, defeated by illness and exhaustion, and one other crucial factor: the weather. The winter of 1887 would go down as the most bitter and relentless that Western settlers had yet experienced, in their brief history in the high plains and the Rockies.

2. In the course of this story, we will meet several men who should be more famous than they are. Elwood "Uncle Billy" Hofer is the first. As Schullery explains, he "remains one of Yellowstone's ne-

glected early heroes. He seems to have come to the area about 1877, and for the next half century was an ardent defender of the park and one of its foremost travelers" (p. 49). He worked as a trapper, a concessioner, a guide, and had other jobs, too. We learn the most about Hofer from his own pen. A few weeks after Schwatka's attempt, still in the brutal winter of 1887, he set out on his own circuit of the park, on proper "snowshoes" this time—that is, on skis. The trip that resulted may have been most important for his careful record of every aspect of the place, "the first serious attempt to survey winter wildlife and conditions in the park....His detailed accounting of wildlife numbers and distribution, and his many observations of what winter was really like, were the first such report produced" (*Yellowstone's Ski Pioneers*, p. 50). He wrote up his ski journey through the park in a five-part series in *Forest and Stream*—a kind of dress rehearsal for his trip with Hough. The electronic publisher ProQuest has digitized the series, which started in the April 7, 1887 issue of *Forest and Stream*, and appeared weekly, to finish on May 5.

3. It is beyond the scope of mere endnotes to give biographies of such major figures as Haynes, for whom a book-length biography is overdue (we do have various collections of his photographs). For our purposes—that is, for more on Haynes' early trips to the wintertime park—see Schullery, *Yellowstone's Ski Pioneers*, 27-48; Lang, "'At the Greatest Personal Peril to the Photographer'"; Jeff Henry, *Snowshoes, Coaches, and Cross Country Skis: A Brief History of Yellowstone Winters* (Emigrant: Roche Jaune, 2011, 46-53); Richard Saunders, *Glimpses of Wonderland: The Haynes and Their Postcards of Yellowstone National Park* (Bozeman: Saunders, 1977); and Freeman Tilden, *Following the Frontier with F. Jay Haynes: Pioneer Photographer of the Old West* (New York: Knopf, 1964). Hough's *Forest and Stream* series is the best source on Haynes 1894 trip. Haynes himself did speak to a reporter from the (Anaconda) *Montana Standard* at the end of his trip ("In the National Park," April 2, 1894, p. 6), giving him a brief overview immediately after the fact. Haynes' bison count was even lower than the one Hough would produce: "We saw all the buffalo that now remain alive in the park," he told the reporter, "in my opinion about 100." He and his party had, by ski, covered 313 miles, a number he did not appear to regard as a mere estimate.

4. If it is beyond the scope of mere endnotes to give major biographies, it is also beyond their scope to run down all the doings of a

frontier rogue like Howell. Again, Hough's series is our best source on him. From other sources, we know that Howell was in trouble again later in the summer of 1894, when Superintendent Anderson had him arrested when he reentered the park. According to Howell, he was merely passing through, but Anderson had him charged for returning after having been formally ejected, and, under the new law Howell himself had brought into being when he was arrested for poaching the previous winter, he was sentenced to a short jail term and a fine. What is most interesting is the attitude of the some of the locals. The *Montana Standard* saw fit to publish a letter from Howell filled with scurrilous abuse of Anderson ("Howell's Side of It," August 3, 1894, p. 6), and later abused Anderson in its own words, calling him "a man who has been fitly characterized as the 'Czar of Wonderland' by reason of the high handed, despotic and autocratic manner in which he rules the great national pleasure ground" ("Ed Howell's Hard Luck," October 27, 1894, p. 7). We forget today that "Czar," in the 1890s, meant "degenerate tyrant." We have forgotten utterly that game laws were at first regarded, by rural folk accustomed to doing what they pleased with the local wildlife, as an arrogant imposition from the alien East. Poachers were often Robin Hood–style heroes. The introduction to this book asserts that what we call "environmentalism," as a political movement, was founded not by hippies, or by John Muir, but by hunters and anglers, at a much earlier date (The Boone and Crockett Club, for instance, dates from 1887). This claim may be surprising to some, but is familiar to historians. A classic statement of this view is by John F. Reiger, *American Sportsmen and the Origins of Conservation* (3rd ed., Corvallis: Oregon State University Press, 2001). See also James Trefethen and Peter Corbin, *An American Crusade for Wildlife* (New York: Winchester, 1975).

5. *Forest and Stream* announced the capture in its March 24 edition, on the front page, as the first item in the journal: "The news comes to us by telegraph from a staff correspondent now on the ground, and while for the present full details are lacking, the capture is unquestionably the most important that has ever been made in the National Park." The story immediately noted that the poacher would, in conformity with the law, go nearly unpunished, "a disgrace," it declared.

6. The "action" was the Lacey Act, discussed in the introduction. It was not law yet, as Hough was writing, but would become law soon.

7. Of all the U.S. Army superintendents, George S. Anderson is the best known today, because of his energy and activism, and the impact it had (like all the army superintendents, his actual title was Acting Superintendent—for three decades, the army presence in the park was supposed to be temporary). Anderson kept a diary, available today in the Yellowstone National Park Heritage and Research Center. He wrote up his own job description in the *Journal of the United States Cavalry Association* ("Work of the Cavalry in Protecting the Yellowstone National Park," March 1897, 6-10). He contributed a history of the park and of his own efforts against poaching, including his side of the Howell affair, to a Boone and Crockett Club book edited by Theodore Roosevelt and George Bird Grinnell ("Protection of the Yellowstone National Park," in *Hunting in Many Lands: The Book of the Boone and Crockett Club*, New York: Forest and Stream Publishing, 1895, 377-402). An early history of Anderson's superintendency by Ralph Pierson emphasized how thoroughly hated Anderson was by area residents who lived outside the park; Pierson quoted a news story that described the man as "a military despot," and it was a relatively temperate news story ("The Czar of Wonderland," *Westerner's Brand Book,* Denver Posse, 1955, 375-86). Pierson followed Howell's career through to its improbable conclusion: our last record of him was of a later superintendent hiring him as a scout to catch two stagecoach robbers (and Howell succeeded where the efforts of more honest men had failed). Anderson retired a brigadier general, a towering rank for a soldier of his or any era, and died in 1915. The most thorough biography of him, and the most touching, may be his obituary in *Forest and Stream* ("Death of General Anderson: His Work Largely Responsible for the Yellowstone Park of To-day," April 1915, 234-35). "His death," the obituary concluded, "leaves a vacancy that cannot be filled." The article was bylined "By G. B. G."—plainly George Bird Grinnell.

8. The Yellowstone Park Association, quietly underwritten by the Northern Pacific Railroad, operated the hotels and transportation inside the park. Aubrey Haines, in his classic history of the park, gave an outline of its operations during this era (*The Yellowstone Story: A History of Our First National Park,* rev. ed., Boulder: University Press of Colorado, 1996, Vol. 2, 41-53).

9. Until recently, Pete was a mystery, and a tantalizing one, since he must have been among the finest skiers of his generation. We do

not know much about him. Still, in 2013, the Yellowstone National Park Historian, Lee Whittlesey, found hard information that filled in some of the gaps. His full name was Pete Nelson, and the *Livingston* (Montana) *Herald* reported his departure in March, 1896 ("Exit Telephone Pete," March 26, 1896, p. 3). He was leaving for Sweden with his savings, $1,400, and, in an unexplained twist, was abandoning his wife and child. Whittlesey has also found references to him in the park archives dating from not long after the Yellowstone Park Association set up the telephone network, in 1886 (Whittlesey, Personal Communications, March 1, 2013, 15 March 2013). The most intriguing account of Nelson appeared in the *Livingston Enterprise* on February 19, 1887, during the same winter that defeated Schwatka and almost killed Haynes ("Park Letter: Thrilling Adventure of Telephone Superintendent Nelson at Gibbon River," p. 3). The *Enterprise* correspondent, G. L. Henderson, described him as "by far the most indefatigable and powerful snow-shoer that has ever climbed these mountain steeps." Henderson gave, at length, the story of a dilemma Nelson had recently faced. A massive avalanche had blocked his path near Norris Geyser Basin, and the only way through that Nelson could find was the cavern the Gibbon River had carved through the snow. He followed the cavern until it collapsed, and he was nearly trapped. Henderson reported the incident in the dramatic, sensational newspaper prose of this era—"by thought-directed energy he was able to force his way back from death unto life"—but such hazards were merely part of Nelson's job.

10. Felix Burgess is the next of our subjects who would have been famous if anyone had thought to publicize him. If a dime novelist had written up his life, he might be as well-known today as Kit Carson or Jim Bridger. As it is, he is partly lost to us. Haines included a thumbnail biography in *The Yellowstone Story*, Vol. 2, p. 445. The Western artist Frederic Remington rode with Burgess, Superintendent Anderson, and a train of cavalrymen during an 1893 trip through the park, the story of which he told in his book *Pony Tracks* (reprint, Norman: University of Oklahoma Press, 1961, 109-20). He drew a portrait of Burgess on horseback—"Nearly Forty-Five Years a Scout," the caption proclaimed—and paused briefly in the story of his trip to describe him:

> Burgess, the scout, was a fine little piece of a man, who had served the government with credit for over thirty years. He had breasted the high divide in a dozen places, had Apache bullets

whistle around and through him, and withal was modest about it. He was a quiet person, with his instinct of locality as well developed as an Indian's, and contented with life, since he only wanted one thing—a war. I think he travelled by scent, since it would have been simple enough to have gone over easier places; but Burgess despised ease, and where the fallen timber was thickest and the slopes 60°, there you would find Burgess and his tight little pony picking along. (111-12)

In the *Anaconda Standard* interview with F. Jay Haynes, after his return from his 1894 ski trip, Haynes included the interesting information that, when he caught Howell, Burgess was doing other duty. Emerson Hough's account of the capture, in chapter one of this book, made it look as if Anderson had sent Burgess explicitly to capture Howell. In fact, Burgess was escorting Haynes when he heard the fatal rifle shots.

11. We will meet quite a few soldiers in the pages to come. We know less about the officers than we would prefer, and little or nothing about enlisted men. We can read the bare service records of many in Francis B. Heitman's *Historical Register and Dictionary of the United States Army, from Its Organization, September 29, 1789, to March 2, 1903* (2 Vols., Washington: Government Printing Office, 1903). These massive volumes have been digitized by Google Books and other free digital libraries. For the broader outlines of the era when the U.S. Army protected the park, see Paul Schullery's chapter on the subject, "A Single Rock," in *Searching for Yellowstone: Ecology and Wonder in the Last Wilderness* (Helena: Montana Historical Society, 2004, 108-27), and his earlier "A Post of Honor" in *Mountain Time: Man Meets Wilderness in Yellowstone* (New York: Simon and Schuster, 1984, 170-82). For the army specifically during the winter, see Henry, *Snowshoes, Coaches, and Cross Country Skis*, 62-75. These are only a handful of the many secondary sources. The soldiers themselves—or at least their commanding officers—left a record in, among other places, the annual reports of the Superintendent to the Secretary of the Interior. These reports have been digitized by Google Books.

12. Howell's camp was on Astringent Creek, in the valley of Pelican Creek, due north of Yellowstone Lake but deep in the backcountry. He had entered the national park near the present Northeast Entrance, and since he named Specimen Ridge as his major obstacle, he

had apparently followed close to the path of the modern road, down Soda Butte Creek to the Lamar River—at night, surely, to avoid unwelcome military company—then at some point turning south and climbing Specimen Ridge, named for its petrified forest. If he followed, say, the Crystal Creek drainage, the climb up the ridge would have been 1400 feet, leading into dense and trackless forests. Altogether, the one-way trip was perhaps fifty miles, perhaps sixty, with nothing like a welcoming home to receive him. No wonder Hough felt a grudging admiration.

13. See below: Hough has good reason to suspect Sheard.

14. The introduction to this book gave only a brief outline of the segregation scheme, which had a tangled and astonishingly lengthy history. Richard A. Bartlett, in *Yellowstone: A Wilderness Besieged* (Tucson: University of Arizona Press, 1989, 309-16), followed it through its multiple deaths and resurrections.

15. William S. Brackett owned a ranch in Montana's Paradise Valley, the name for the Yellowstone River valley after the river exits the park and turns north. As Hough's description suggested, Brackett's Paradise Valley property, near the present town of Emigrant, was what rural folks call a "hobby ranch" (Brackett described it in one piece of his writing that people in the future may value, "Indian Remains on the Upper Yellowstone," *Annual Report of the Board of Regents of the Smithsonian Institution*, Washington: GPO, 1893, 577-81). Brackett wrote segregation-scheme propaganda for *The American Field: The Sportsman's Journal*. Hough mangled its name with a low-key irony typical of his style: the publication claimed to be *The Sportsman's Journal*, but was actually *The Miner's Friend*—the ally, that is, of heavy industry.

16. All three of these figures—the first two historical, the third fictional—raised violent rebellions, Bozzaris as part of the Greek revolt against rule by the Ottoman Empire, and L'Ouverture against French rule of Haiti. One-eyed Riley, added as comment and serving as another example of Hough's ironic style, was a character in a startlingly obscene old Irish folksong (family-friendly versions existed, too). His daughter having been seduced, Riley came to murder the seducer, who, however, got Riley's weapons away from him.

17. Earlier that year, *Forest and Stream* had published a letter from a correspondent it identified only as "a gentleman living in the vicinity of the National Park" ("Game Destruction in Montana," February 17, 1894, p. 140). The gentleman reported that " 'Not long ago Mr. Sheard, the Livingston (Montana) taxidermist, wrote a letter to a man who a year before had been the winter keeper at the hotel at the Grand Cañon in the National Park and whom Sheard supposed this year to be in the same position, telling him he had better get a bottle of strychnine and poison some of those cross and silver gray foxes at the cañon this winter. Their hides can be sent by mail.' " They would be sent to Sheard, that is, who would cure and sell them, and split the take. The *Forest and Stream* writer went on, with the dry wit typical of the journal, to observe that "Sheard is president of the society for the protection of game at Livingston and does it more damage than any man in the country."

18. The "perfesh" was the "profession"—they were all newspapermen, and note that Hough treated them more kindly than he did the taxidermists and merchants.

19. In the previous installment, Hough had allowed the segregation advocates to damn their own cause just by quoting their intemperate opinions. Here he assembled and quoted the most impressive opponents of the scheme he could find: Superintendent Anderson, a prominent Montana businessman (J. D. Losekamp), a prominent Montana engineer (P. M. Gallaher), a representative of the Northern Pacific Railway (Charles S. Fee), and Billy Hofer, perhaps the greatest expert on Yellowstone National Park at that time.

20. Despite Hough's reference to "white mountains that line the deep-sunken Yellowstone"—white with snow, of course—the proposed rail route he described would actually have followed the Black Canyon of the Yellowstone, along the northern edge of the park, and through some brutal terrain indeed. The second route, up the "Gardiner Hill" and over to the valley at Yancey's, was the route he would follow much later, at the end of his visit to the region. It approximated the route of the modern road from Mammoth Hot Springs to Tower Junction. We will hear more of it and Uncle John Yancey in the final chapters.

21. The New World district was the mining area in and around

Cooke City. It was in the news in the 1980s and 1990s when mine owners proposed major operations, despite the probability that mine waste would run down ultimately into the Yellowstone River. A series of buy-outs stopped the mining, although the area remains a picturesque mess, environmentally.

22. A feature of this era is the dizzying speed with which railroad companies were proposed, born, merged, killed, and reborn. The Chicago, Burlington and Quincy Railroad would, in 1894, build a rail line from Sheridan, Wyoming, to Huntley, Montana, just outside Billings. The actual work on the line was done by the Burlington and Missouri River Railroad, which had merged with the Chicago, Burlington and Quincy years earlier. People on the plains still called the line by its old informal shorthand, the "B and M." The telegram that Losekamp received while Hough was visiting Billings was an early announcement of the future line. Near the turn of the century, the company would build another line from a starting point near Billings south to Cody, Wyoming—as close as track would ever get to Cooke City, and the only rail service it would ever receive (David J. Wasden, *From Beaver to Oil: A Century in the Development of Wyoming's Big Horn Basin, Cheyenne*: Pioneer Printing and Stationery, 1973, p. 233-36).

23. Losekamp here put his finger on the reason the segregation scheme lived as long as it did. A railroad always meant a generous right-of-way. Bartlett records an incident in 1885 when a false rumor that the latest segregation bill had passed created what the *Livingston Enterprise* called a "stampede." In a single night, in midwinter, "almost every man at Gardiner and Mammoth Hot Springs" ran to secure claims on preselected acreage inside the park (p. 313).

24. The Clark's Fork of the Yellowstone should not be confused with the Clark Fork River, which runs far to the north, passing Missoula, Montana and flowing into the Columbia River near the Canadian border. When the Yellowstone River leaves the park, it runs north to Livingston, Montana, then turns east toward Billings and the high plains beyond. A series of rivers flow north to meet it, among them the Clark's Fork of the Yellowstone, which joins the Yellowstone River just west of Billings at Laurel, Montana. The Clark's Fork was unobstructed and remote enough that the Nez Perce tribe was able to either follow the river or stay close to it, to evade the U.S. Army during the 1877 Nez Perce War.

25. A Chinook wind is a warm, dry wind that blows downslope on the lee side of mountains that create a rain shadow. Meteorologists call it a foehn wind.

26. When he spoke of "the Blacktail," Hough was referring to Blacktail Deer Creek, Blacktail Deer Plateau, or both, which Hough would cross on the passage to and from Uncle John Yancey's, mentioned above.

27. The Forest Reserve Act became law in 1891, and by signing it President Benjamin Harrison created the Yellowstone Park Timberland Reserve along the south and east boundary of Yellowstone National Park (Harold K. Steen, *The Beginning of the National Forest System*, Washington: US Department of Agriculture, Forest Service, 1991, p. 24). Despite the name, the Reserve is often thought of as the first National Forest. With some boundary changes, it is now part of Wyoming's Shoshone and Bridger-Teton national forests.

28. Gallaher's map was unnecessarily complicated. He merely proposed running a spur line southward up the Clark's Fork, past Cooke City and into the Big Horn Basin, to end somewhere near the present town of Cody, Wyoming. Gallaher was correct to see the Big Horn Basin as a future center for agriculture. It is so today, the farmland watered by a reservoir on the Shoshone River, which Gallaher, below, called by its old name, the Stinking Water River. His proposed railroad line would have avoided Yellowstone National Park entirely.

29. As noted, the Northern Pacific Railroad quietly funded the Yellowstone Park Association hotels and transportation service. The funding was sometimes referred to as "secret," but if so, it was a poorly-kept secret. Building the park infrastructure had, as Haines noted, required "deficit financing" (*The Yellowstone Story*, Vol. 2, 44)—hence, Fee's choice of words, when he said that he and his company "stand behind" the hotels and stages.

30. At nearly 11,000 feet, Electric Peak, the tallest of a line of summits to the south, towered over the Yellowstone River valley and the railroad that ran beside the river.

31. The ambulance had entered the park and begun its climb toward Fort Yellowstone, through a broad expanse of sagebrush and

cactus that remains today the single best place to look for pronghorn antelope in Yellowstone National Park. As then, a moderately patient viewer is nearly guaranteed a look at the antelope in this area. They are much harder to find almost everywhere else in the park.

32. Today, the town is spelled "Gardiner," the river "Gardner." The river was named for Johnson Gardner, one of the area's first mountain men, and the original name was eventually restored to the river, but not the town. In 1894, both were spelled "Gardiner," a convention Hough followed throughout. See Lee Whittlesey, *Yellowstone Place Names* (Helena: Montana Historical Society, 2006, 112).

33. As with the antelope, the situation has not changed. The cliffs above the Gardner River, to the east of the road and river, are today the one place in the park where bighorn sheep show themselves more often than not. They also routinely turn up next to the road, "very fearless and tame" as Hough noted.

34. According to Heitman (Vol. 1, p. 444), Charles Moore Gandy joined the U.S. Army as an Assistant Surgeon in 1883, and was listed in 1901 as a Major and Surgeon. He turned up in a letter to the *Boston Medical and Surgical Journal*—forerunner to *The New England Journal of Medicine*—as a Lieutenant Colonel and chief surgeon at the United States Military Academy at West Point ("Physical Condition of West Point Cadets," August 15, 1907, p. 238). He retired a colonel and was laid to rest in his native New Jersey in 1937.

35. Captain Anderson's pets are still around today. Here, too, wildlife behavior has changed not at all. A platoon of elk is regularly visible in or near Fort Yellowstone.

36. According to the *Oxford English Dictionary*, the term "castor gloves" was in use around the turn of the 20th century to describe a type of soft glove made of goat-skin.

37. "Leggins" was one traditional name for chaps of the sort worn by cowboys, which cannot have been the intended meaning, because leather cowboy chaps were heavy and cumbersome. In this case, the word more likely referred to what we would call gaiters.

38. The maneuver Billy called "corduroying" is now almost always called "sidestepping."

39. "Galluses" were suspenders—fancy ones here, apparently.

40. Philip Danforth Armour, with his brother Herman, founded Armour and Company, which had become the world's largest food processor by the time of Hough's Yellowstone visit. His name survives most prominently today on packages of Armour Hot Dogs. Armour processed hogs in vast numbers, giving Hough a pun: he imagined literally cooking pork here because the segregation scheme, were it to succeed, would be an instance of Congressional pork-barrel corruption on a massive, Armour-sized scale.

41. The term *mal de raquette* was coined by the French-Canadian voyageurs, and translates into English, roughly, as "snowshoe sickness." It described injury to the feet and legs that occurred after walking long distances on snowshoes, especially when the shoes were carrying a load of snow—highly dangerous when a shoer walked one-way deep into the woods and suddenly found himself immobilized by pain. However, "*mal de raquette*" referred to "snowshoes" in today's meaning of that term. Neither Hough nor anyone else in the story at any time suffered *mal de raquette*, because they were using what we call skis, not snowshoes—another reason Hofer immediately steered Hough away from "web shoes" and onto skis, although Hough, as a beginner, did not notice. Nor did Hofer speak of his decision, which he would have regarded as too obvious a choice to bother mentioning. It did give us our first instance of Hofer possibly saving Hough's life.

42. "Whang leather" is a nearly-obsolete term for leather cut into straps. Its *Oxford English Dictionary* definition and timeline shows that it was in common use in the 1890s.

43. Mt. Washburn, near the Grand Canyon of the Yellowstone, is today one of the park's distinctive landmarks, easily spotted because of the fire lookout, communications structure, and warming hut on its summit. At 10,243 feet, it was one of several peaks that was at some point believed to be the highest in the park. Electric Peak was another. The true highest summit was Eagle Peak, 11,358 feet above sea level, but so far to the southeast that it was invisible to Hough.

44. Hofer and Hough's route is easy for us to follow, because in most places, when they were skiing hard for a distant objective, they followed the corridors which the modern Grand Loop Road follows today. Their first two days took them from Fort Yellowstone up a thousand feet and through the defile at the Golden Gate to Swan Lake Flats. They then headed almost due south to Norris Geyser Basin.

45. The reappearance of the Gardner River is potentially confusing. This river was indeed the same one Hough's ambulance followed when he rode from the town of Gardiner, at 5314 feet, to Fort Yellowstone. The river and Hough's party then diverged. Each took a long, curving course upward, the curves mirror images of each other, and Hough met the river again far above, at 7300 feet.

46. Today, the names of these two features are Brickyard Hill and Frying Pan Spring, the latter right next to the Grand Loop Road. See Whittlesey, *Yellowstone Place Names*, pp. 57 and 110.

47. The Norris Soldier Station was replaced three years after Hough's visit. This second structure burned in 1908 and was replaced again. The 1908 structure—near Norris Campground, and visible from the main road—is one of the older buildings in the park. Today, it is the Museum of the National Park Ranger.

48. The *Oxford English Dictionary* timeline shows "chirk" to be another nearly-obsolete term in common use in the 1890s. It meant lively or cheerful, a perfect description of the brazen and possibly sociopathic Ed Howell.

49. Hough's list of the thermal features they visited can be easily matched to the modern names. When compared to a map, they show that the two covered Norris Geyser Basin thoroughly. Their first stop, at what Hough called Great Growler Geyser, appears from its name and location to be the present-day Black Growler Steam Vent, and "Emerald pool" is surely the present Emerald Spring. All the other features can be matched precisely using Whittlesey's *Yellowstone Place Names*. "The Constant" is Constant Geyser (p. 73), "the Hurricane" is Hurricane Vent (p. 133), "Monarch Geyser" still goes by that name (p. 173), "Minute Man" is Minute Geyser (p. 172), "the Echina" is Echinus Geyser (p. 95), "New Crater" is Steamboat Geyser (p. 237), and "Congress Geyser" is Congress Pool (p. 73). Descriptions

like Hough's—Hofer actually deserved credit as coauthor—are valuable windows into the past in a part of Yellowstone that is as violently unstable as anyplace in this whole violently unstable part of the world. The seminal book on this subject is T. Scott Bryan's *The Geysers of Yellowstone* (4th ed., Boulder: University Press of Colorado, 2008). Bryan explains that one special feature of the water at Norris Geyser Basin is its unusually high levels of acid, specifically sulfuric acid. Among its other extremes, "Norris is also the hottest geyser basin in Yellowstone and one of the hottest in the world" (p. 262). As one could guess from Hough's description, Steamboat, when it is active, is the largest and tallest geyser in existence.

50. This at first bizarre reference is another example of the marvelous convergence of personalities and events that characterized Hough's trip. The previous year, 1893, the World's Columbian Exposition had erupted in Hough's home city of Chicago. One of its designers, Frederick Law Olmsted, included a "Wooded Island" specifically as a refuge from the madness, in the middle of one of his water features. A contemporary reporter explained, in a confused manner, that "He who is so disposed may wander over the bridge connecting, toward the south, with a smaller island, and there for a moment linger over the picturesque reproduction of an American hunter's camp," serving as "the headquarters of the Boone and Crockett club....The structure is built of rough logs, and within, over the rude fireplace, is the skull of a grizzly bear....The camp is under charge of Elwood Hofer, who, for the occasion, was relieved from his task of capturing animals in the Yellowstone, or National Park, for the Smithsonian Institution." So wrote Hubert Howe Bancroft, who, in his *The Book of the Fair* (Chicago: The Bancroft Company, 1893, 449-50), by making Billy sound like the city dogcatcher, reminded us to be grateful to Hough for so regularly getting his facts straight. One historian credited Theodore Roosevelt himself as having ordered up the Hunter's Cabin, although any one of a number of Boone and Crockett founders may have engaged Hofer. Billy could be seen there "Wearing fringed buckskins and sporting long hair and a wide-brimmed felt hat," and telling tales of the vanished frontier (Michael Steiner, "Parables of Stone and Steel," *American Studies* Spring 2001, 54-55). The sheer weirdness of the situation is striking. Elwood Hofer, perhaps the most skillful wilderness guide of his time, traveled east to the great western city of Chicago, in a railroad car surely. Once there, Hofer, a genuine, living mountain man, played a fake mountain man in a fake mountain

camp in the middle of the vast city, and none of the fairgoers had any idea that they were actually looking at the real thing.

51. When he referred to "Lady Evalina," Hough surely meant *Evelina, or the History of a Young Lady's Entrance into the World*, the 1778 sentimental favorite by Fanny Burney.

52. As noted in the introduction, spelling the more obscure proper nouns was a challenge for Hough. He occasionally had to spell by sound. "Blandon" Hill was, and is, Blanding Hill, named for an early park road foreman (Whittlesey, *Yellowstone Place Names*, p. 53-54).

53. Again, the approximate path Hough and Hofer took is easy to follow, because they were mostly in the corridor of the modern road. In this case, they were close to what locals sometimes call the "Norris cutoff," the middle link in the figure-8 of the Grand Loop Road, running from Norris to the Grand Canyon of the Yellowstone. When today's drivers reach Cascade Creek, traveling from Norris to the Grand Canyon, they know the Canyon is near.

54. Hough was quoting Virgil, no less. The original, from the *Aeneid*, was "facilis descensus Averni," the last word referring to a lake the Romans thought to be the opening of the underworld. So the phrase means, approximately, "The descent into evil [or ruin, or destruction] is easy."

55. Apparently a misspelling: James Dean was head of the Yellowstone Park Association at this time (Haines, *The Yellowstone Story* Vol. 2, p. 48).

56. Canyon Village today is made up mostly of structures that date from the Mission 66 project, a major push by the National Park Service to upgrade facilities during the 1950s and 1960s, and from more recent reconstruction and remodeling work. In 1894, the area was more primitive. The hotel described here was the second structure to do duty as a hotel, replacing an earlier temporary building. The 1894 hotel proved temporary, also. It was replaced in 1910-1911 by an elegant and enormous structure designed by Robert Reamer, the architect who also designed the Old Faithful Inn.

57. As noted, Hough had trouble with the name of the too-quiet

winter keeper: "Folsom" should have been Fossum. We know frustratingly little about him. He does turn up in park records as one of two workmen who added a wing to the superintendent's house in 1885 (Lee Whittlesey, Personal Communication, 20 November 2012). The *Livingston* (Montana) *Enterprise* mentioned him briefly in 1886, stating merely that he had worked in the park that summer and fall and intended to spend the winter in Wisconsin, which was perhaps his home state ("Local Layout," December 11, 1886, p. 3). Fossum appeared in the *Enterprise* again on August 20, 1898, when the "Personal Points" column described him as a "specimen dealer" at Mammoth Hot Springs (p. 6). He also made a dramatic appearance in Ernest Thompson Seton's *Wild Animals at Home* (Garden City: Doubleday, Page, 1922, 70-71). True, Seton was on the wrong side of the turn-of-the-20th-century "nature faker" affair—he was accused, that is, of producing sentimental fabrications when he wrote of animals—but the story he told sounded just like something Fossum would do. Seton had just been describing an encounter with an angry bull elk:

A friend of mine, John Fossum, once a soldier attached to Fort Yellowstone, had a similar adventure on a more heroic scale. While out on a camera hunt in early winter he descried afar a large bull Elk lying asleep in an open valley. At once Fossum made a plan. He saw that he could crawl up to the bull, snap him where he lay, then later secure a second picture as the creature ran for the timber. The first part of the programme was carried out admirably. Fossum got within fifty feet and still the Elk lay sleeping. Then the camera was opened out. But alas! that little pesky "click," that does so much mischief, awoke the bull, who at once sprang to his feet and ran not for the woods but for the *man*. Fossum with the most amazing nerve stood there quietly focussing his camera, till the bull was within ten feet, then pressed the button, threw the camera into the soft snow and ran for his life with the bull at his coat-tails. It would have been a short run but for the fact that they reached a deep snowdrift that would carry the man, and would not carry the Elk. Here Fossum escaped, while the bull snorted around, telling just what he meant to do to the man when he caught him; but he was not to be caught, and at last the bull went off grumbling and squealing.

Fossum recovered his camera, and the photograph, reproduced in Seton's book, came out perfectly. ·

58. A problem developed here with the numbering of the original series. Both the June 23 and June 30, 1894 installments in the series were labeled "No. 6." Given the way the *Forest and Stream* printers designed the entire series, this error could only have been a slip by the compositor, or an editor. Unfortunately, the error then continued through the rest of the series. In this book, to prevent confusion, we will change the number of each remaining chapter, from this point to the end. From here, in the original, each installment was one digit lower.

59. Hayden Valley is a distinctive, wide-open, rolling expanse of meadows bounded on one side by the Yellowstone River. For drivers traveling on the modern road from Fishing Bridge north to Canyon and encountering it for the first time, it does not look like a "valley," probably because it is so big. As modern visitors discover instantly, all that meadowland, dense with botanical nutrition, makes it a favorite place for wildlife. As Hough would show, it always was.

60. "Lookout Rock" is Lookout Point today (Whittlesey, *Yellowstone Place Names*, p. 158).

61. In the Catholic Church, when the Pope gives a decisive opinion meant to guide the rest of the church on some issue, he is speaking "ex cathedra."

62. The Oxford English Dictionary records "motte" as a U.S. regionalism, commonest in Texas, for a group of trees in otherwise open prairie.

63. Chicago had more than one statue of Christopher Columbus; Hough was probably referring to the one that was new when he was writing, an outsize bronze now in Arrigo Park, but produced originally for the same World's Columbian Exposition that brought Billy Hofer to Chicago. The state of Montana commissioned a silver statue of Justice and dispatched it to, yes, the World's Columbian Exposition. The model was the actress Ada Rehan.

64. A *frappé* dessert or drink is one served chilled or partly frozen.

65. That Larsen and Holte, who lived in the park, had never seen a bison is striking proof of how rare the animals were at that date. That

Hough could make this statement in a tone that suggested he was not at all surprised is more proof still.

66. In this installment, *Forest and Stream* ran a photograph of this cabin with the caption "LITTLE TROUT CREEK SHACK." However, Billy was correct, as historians working in the park have just recently concluded. The photograph of the place where the party spent that night was actually a photo of the upper Alum Creek soldiers' cabin (Lee Whittlesey, Personal Communication, 21 November 2012; see also Henry, *Snowshoes, Coaches, and Cross Country Skis*, p. 65).

67. Given the problem we have today—of overabundance— Hough's bison census looks like a scaremongering undercount. It was not. The number really was that low, and it continued to fall. According to Paul Schullery, it bottomed at between 25 and 50 by the end of that decade. Mary Meagher, long the National Park Service's Yellowstone bison expert, combed the old records and found that the low count was an astonishing 23 in 1902, although as always, the census takers missed a few animals (*The Bison of Yellowstone National Park*, The National Park Service Scientific Monograph Series Number One, 1973, 17, 21). Mary Ann Franke's *To Save the Wild Bison: Life on the Edge in Yellowstone* (Norman: University of Oklahoma Press, 2005) is an updating of Meagher's earlier work. The park's managers rounded up bison and treated them like domestic cattle, which looked to them like the only way to save the herd. See Schullery, *Yellowstone's Ski Pioneers*, 116-27, and James Pritchard, *Preserving Yellowstone's Natural Conditions* (Lincoln: University of Nebraska Press, 1999, 10-12). Both discuss this emergency intervention in the context of the old and unresolved question of how and when humans should make such aggressive moves, or whether such interventions should happen at all.

68. Here, finally, the party temporarily left the corridors of the modern roads, heading through what is today deep backcountry. They trended southwest along a route that would bisect the Lower Loop of today's Grand Loop Road, running diagonally across the bottom half of the figure-8 to emerge at the Lower Geyser Basin. They might have been off the modern roads, but they were close to the route the Nez Perce tribe followed when they crossed the park during their 1877 flight from the army—hence, the name for the valley and creek that the party followed. They were also close to one of the original stagecoach roads (see Haines, *The Yellowstone Story* Vol. 2, p. 46), al-

though given the snow, that hardly mattered, and poor Holte assumed Billy Hofer himself was lost.

69. The party had now returned to "civilization." Fountain Geyser, during this era, erupted so regularly and voluminously that it rivaled Old Faithful in popularity, and the Fountain Hotel stood nearby. The hotel is long gone. Old Faithful won the popularity contest when Fountain Geyser became irregular and, for a long time, dormant.

70. Private Matthews' remains finally turned up on June 9, 1895. For years to come, rumors would circulate that he had been shot to death by poachers, but his remains showed no sign of violence. He was buried in the army cemetery at Mammoth Hot Springs. His tombstone gave his name as "David J. Mathews," and added that he "Perished from exhaustion and exposure." Lee Whittlesey, *Death in Yellowstone* (Lanham: Roberts Rinehart, 1995, 75-76, 210).

71. "Prismatic Pool" is today Grand Prismatic Spring.

72. "Excelsior Geyser" is today Excelsior Geyser Crater. Early in the history of the park, it regularly erupted with a size and power unmatched anywhere else in Yellowstone, and the leading theory states that the eruptions were so violent that the geyser blew its own plumbing system apart. See Bryan, *The Geysers of Yellowstone*, p. 181-83.

73. For Hough to call the river the Madison was odd. Repeatedly, in the previous installment, Hough correctly called this river the Firehole, which comes together with the Gibbon to make the Madison River. He knew it was the Firehole River. However, early in park history, some watercourses that today have their own names were a "Fork" or extension of the larger river into which they drained. The Lamar River was at one time called the "East Fork of the Yellowstone," and Lava Creek the "East Gardiner River." The Firehole was once known as the "Upper Madison" or the "Madison Proper" while at the same time being called the Firehole, and the Gibbon was the "North Fork of the Madison."

74. Although it rarely intruded on the story of Hough's ski tour, it is worth noting that the nation was in the middle of the worst economic depression it had known to that date. As so often, the collapse occurred when a bubble burst, resulting in the Panic of 1893. Unreli-

able railroad financing and overbuilding by railroad companies were the major causes, although the effects spread far and wide. We might regard the segregation scheme is an example of such railroad overbuilding, in this case a plan to overbuild that never got started.

75. A bird common in the region, more often called the Clark's nutcracker today.

76. "Peat Fountain" was probably a typographic error. Hough surely meant Great Fountain, today the largest geyser in the Lower Geyser Basin (and not to be confused with Fountain Geyser, near the old hotel).

77. The discussion that follows is utterly surreal—until you know that "pedestrianism" was a popular 19th century sport. In its heyday, it owed its popularity in part to the high volume of betting that went on among the spectators. It survives today as the Olympic sport of racewalking. Picture the peculiar, rolling stride of the racewalker, and Hough's description makes perfect sense.

78. The modern road runs past Gibbon Falls. After the falls, for the northbound traveler, the road is either near or right next to the Gibbon River, all the way to the Norris Geyser Basin. Canyon Creek debouches into the Gibbon River below the falls, but also cuts a long canyon that, in places, makes convenient routes down to the level of the river above the falls (Billy appears to have been intentionally, and intelligently, avoiding the dangerous terrain around Gibbon Falls). One can only guess which way the group went in the dark, since Hough was, as he made clear, so bewildered. They were, however, about the rejoin the modern road corridor, or something close to it.

79. Beryl Spring still goes by that name. It is next to the Grand Loop Road and the Gibbon River, inside the canyon that the river has carved.

80. At the bottom of the Canyon Creek Hill, Hough mentioned a bridge. It carried the party to the west side of the Gibbon River. Upstream, however, the river veered to the west to take a long, looping course around the Norris Geyser Basin. To get to Norris, Hough had to cross a second bridge, always scary when the structure is a log

footbridge covered deeply with snow, and underlain by a winter's accumulation of ice.

81. Gibbon Meadows and Elk Park still go by those names. Both are expansive, open, nearly flat meadows in which, as the name "Elk Park" suggests, wildlife are normally available. Hough, as we will see, had not really begun to seriously count elk, and had some surprises in store.

82. Another way to explain Hough's situation would be to say that, looking east from Fort Yellowstone, a traveler was confronted by Mt. Everts, an utterly impassible ridgeline miles long. To reach Yancey's on the other side, Mt. Everts had to be outflanked, and the only practicable route on skis, in that era, was to go around the mountain to the south. Hough was again following, approximately, the future route of the Grand Loop Road, but without its benefits. Travelers who have driven through Yellowstone will remember, when leaving Mammoth and heading toward Tower Junction, being suddenly—and for those with a fear of heights, terrifyingly—shot out across the Gardner Canyon. The road is at that point crossing what locals call "the high bridge," nearly a thousand feet long and at least two hundred tall, depending on the water level in the river. Hofer and Hough did not have that bridge, or other conveniences related to the modern road. On the far side was a hard climb through dense forest, breaking up at last, beyond Lava Creek, into an open landscape of sagebrush and meadow alternating with ridgelines and patches of forest, giving Hofer a variety of possible routes.

83. Captain Anderson here solved the problem of the Gardner Canyon. The ambulance aided them in their struggle against gravity, in roughly the same place the high bridge provides that help today.

84. "Gardiner Falls" is an old name for Undine Falls on Lava Creek. The creek, as noted above, was once called the "East Gardiner River." See Whittlesey, *Yellowstone Place Names*, p. 257. We can now tell exactly where they were: on the future Grand Loop Road, and just about to pass out of the forest and into the open country beyond Lava Creek.

85. The Devil's Gut is today simply called the Cut: Whittlesey, *Yellowstone Place Names*, p. 80. It is a section of Blacktail Pla-

teau Drive, a one-way gravel road that veers south from the Mammoth-to-Tower Grand Loop, serving as a scenic tour for cars and a trail for mountain bikes in the summer, and a ski trail in the winter. Again, we can tell exactly where they were: the party was entering a narrow, twisting section of road that plunged down toward the valley that was their destination. Even today, when the road is maintained regularly and is only primitive to the extent that it lacks asphalt, the National Park Service ski maps, at the Cut, change the trail difficulty rating to "More Difficult."

86. Hough overestimated the drop. The high point in the Cut was 7570 feet, and Yancey's was 6270—almost exactly 1300 feet. The Cut and the drop below it do, however, give every apprentice skier the same impression they gave Hough.

87. Again, it is beyond the scope of mere endnotes to give biographies of major figures in the early history of Yellowstone National Park. On Uncle John Yancey, Haines, *The Yellowstone Story*, Vol. 2, 238-42, is a good place to start. It includes photographs and a number of contemporary accounts of both Yancey and his hotel.

88. As with John Fossum, we know less than we would like about Woody, whose first name, as the introduction notes, was Tazewell. Happily, he was friendly with Theodore Roosevelt, whose description of Woody meshed well with Hough's. In an article for *Century Illustrated Magazine*, Roosevelt described a rare occasion with him:
"My friend Tazewell Woody…was a very quiet man, and it was exceedingly difficult to get him to talk over any of his past experiences; but one day, when he was in high good humor with me for having made three consecutive straight shots at elk, he became quite communicative, and I was able to get him to tell me one story which I had long wished to hear from his lips, having already heard of it through one of the other participants of the fight. When he found that I already knew a good deal of it, old Woody told me the rest."
The future President of the United States thus succeeded, after long effort, in getting the story Hough missed, of the fight with the "1,000 Sioux" Yancey mentioned to Hough. Roosevelt said this event happened in the spring of 1875 "on the Yellowstone," and the core details matched Yancey's hint: Woody and two others had stood off a war party of Sioux, although—perhaps aware that such numbers were always wrong even when they came from the best

sources—Roosevelt did not even guess at the size of the war party ("In Cowboy-Land," *Century Illustrated Magazine*, June 1893, 282-83).

89. Again, the "Roaring Fork" was Hellroaring Creek. Both it and Cottonwood Creek emptied into the Yellowstone from the north. The general view Hough and the rest had, of the north bank of the Yellowstone, is visible from the modern road as the view opens northwest of the Hellroaring Creek Trail parking area, on the Mammoth-to-Tower segment of the Grand Loop. Although it is difficult to tell the exact spot to which Woody led them, the vantage from the modern road reveals the same stretch of country Hough described.

90. The "East Fork of the Yellowstone," again, was an old name for the Lamar River (Whittlesey, *Yellowstone Place Names*, p. 146). Junction Butte was named for the junction of the two rivers—not of the roads, as visitors sometimes believe. The name was much older than the roads (Whittlesey, p. 142).

91. To get to Junction Butte, the party had to cross the Yellowstone. They did so by the only way possible in that area, over the wooden toll bridge built by John H. "Yellowstone Jack" Baronette in 1871.

92. A "spike" is an immature male elk, so named for his undersize antlers.

93. Depending on their route, the group would have crossed Geode Creek between one and two miles after their exit from the "Devil's Gut." The creek flowed north to join the Yellowstone, invisible to them inside its canyon. From here to "the top of the Gardiner Hill," the landscape was almost all sagebrush and meadow, with wide-open views.

94. Recall that, after the Panic of 1893, the United States slipped into the deepest economic depression in its history to that date. Hough was writing in Chicago in the summer of 1894. One of the biggest strikes of the era, the Pullman Strike, began in the Chicago South Side community of Pullman, and spread from there to shut down much of the nation's transportation grid. The strike was happening while Hough wrote much of his series, with Chicago as ground zero.

SCOTT HERRING has a Ph.D. from the University of California, Davis, where he teaches writing. He went there after a long sojourn working in Yellowstone National Park.